Brain-Savvy HR

A neuroscience evidence base

First published by Head Heart + Brain 2014
157
41 Millharbour
London E14 9ND
United Kingdom

www.headheartbrain.com
info@hhab.co.uk

British Library Cataloguing in Publication Data

A CIP catalogue record for this book is available from the British library

ISBN 978 0 9929007 0 0

"Jan Hills provides a comprehensive and extremely readable account of neuroscience and its relevance to all of us who work in organisations. Packed full of insights, case studies and practical advice, this book is further strengthened by a solid foundation of scientific research. Not only is it a fascinating read, but it offers a collection of tools and tips which all HR professionals will be able to apply. A truly valuable contribution to this emerging topic for the HR profession."

Jerry Arnott
Director, Civil Service Learning

"In the 20 years I have known Jan she has always been at the forefront of thinking on how to pragmatically drive high performing teams and individuals; tapping into their own unique talents and insights. Her latest work in the area of neuroscience goes further than ever before in dissecting this personal code and is an invaluable resource for leaders in people strategy."

David Thomas
SVP Human Resources Asia, at Manulife Financial

"Anyone who has been keeping up with their personal development will have come across increasing references to neuroscience. It seems to stand in stark contrast to all the encouragement for HR to be business-savvy but, it seems when it comes to change, it's just as important. We know the nature of work is changing and we live in a time of perpetual unrest but to achieve and sustain change of the type we will see in the NHS, it will need us to do better – understand staff, engage them better and help them to feel fulfilled in the work they do. This is a book which will help HR professionals with that challenge."

Dean Royles
Chief Executive, NHS Employers

"I am always hoping to find more practical and tested HR practices to address the business issues and challenges; HR practice impacts people and people impact business results. A real understanding about people is essential especially as there is no 'perfection' in anybody. We must use a more rational understanding. We need tools to help to illustrate the most changeable, unclear, indirect and complex part of human beings. That is our mind. I am new to the neuroscience area and believe this book is pr viding an angle to look at the mind and its role in business."

Cindy Zhou
Sr. Director, Human Resources and Administration,
Oriental DreamWorks

"Brain-Savvy HR has helped me make effective change a reality, it has allowed me to support my client groups to think differently and more positively about issues they are facing.

It's the perfect book to keep at your desk and pick up when you are stuck. I particularly found the 'why we need to change' section useful when working with difficult customers.

It's a fascinating and incredibly useful read – a must for all HR professionals wanting to make a difference!"

Gemma Porter
Senior HR Professional, Civil Service

"Brain-Savvy HR shows us that we are generally failing to make changes that stick because we are not being brain-savvy in the design and implementation of our change initiatives. Written in clear and easy language, this book shows us how understanding more about how the brain functions and applying this in the design and implementation of initiatives, enhances the chances of success. We are given practical tools, supported by case studies, which really help bring things to life. I will not be approaching organisational development projects in the same way again."

David Onigbanjo
Senior HR Business Partner, Civil Service

"For too long we have pretended that managing organizations is simply a combination of grown-up rational analysis, combined with special experience and gut-feel. While that may have served us well enough for some time, it won't be enough for the future we are creating. Neuroscience continues to provide evidence to prove what does and doesn't work when it comes to humans working together effectively, and you need to learn the difference fast. Jan has done a great job of bringing together the various strands in a very usable way – pay attention!"

Alan Arnett
Leadership Development Explorer, Insurance Industry

"A timely book, one that I would expect will find its way onto the shelves of many HR practitioners and will be referred to again and again. Jan does an excellent job of linking neuroscience with practical applications. She is a true 'translator' of how the business world can benefit by paying attention to what the world of brain science is sharing with us."

Linda Ray
NeuroCapability founder and co-founder, NeuResource Group

"This book is easy and enjoyable to read either in one hit or dipping in and out of chapters. It provides an insightful and accessible introduction to the application of neuroscience in HR. I found it got me thinking about thinking in new ways, with the added benefit of scientific underpinning that will also help me to explain it to others."

Gillian Smith
Senior HR Leader, Civil Service

"This book is crucial for HR practitioners who work in environments that demand an evidence base. It moves the 'touchy feely' into hard wired science."

Deborah O'Dea
Chair HR for London

"In banking we are going through unprecedented change. An understanding of neuroscience has helped us find new and better solutions for the challenges we face today - this book provides plenty of practical insights across all the HR disciplines."

Maria Bentley
Global Head of HR, Wholesale Banking, Nomura

"If you have ever wondered whether there was a better, more effective way to approach your work, this book is for you! Through a compelling balance of scientific evidence and illustrative case studies, Brain-Savvy HR offers straightforward, insightful approaches that will help all of us be more successful and fulfilled at work."

Tricia Naddaff
President, Management Research Group

"This ground-breaking book is a valuable guide not just for HR, but for any business leader who wants to engage with their team and drive higher performance. Jan and her team have provided valuable brain-savvy insight to the development of HR programs in Uniqlo that are having real business impact as we expand rapidly across the globe. Jan demystifies the field of neuroscience. This book contains a wealth of case studies and materials that provide scientific evidence to show that different leadership practices do a make a difference and why."

Lynda Tyler
SVP HR and Group Officer, Fast Retailing

Thank you

The evidence from neuroscience shows that we are social animals: we need the support and cooperation of others to thrive. Never is this truer than when publishing a book. There are a huge number of people who have helped. Here I would like to say special thanks to a few of those without whose help this book would not have been written.

Firstly, heartfelt thanks to Lindsay Hanson and Sarah North who worked tirelessly on this project with me. Lindsay wrote the chapters on interviewing and development centres, and Sarah did all the proofreading and project management. But even more invaluable was the encouragement and support I received from them both.

Paul Matthews, author of Informal Learning at Work, generously shared his experience and contacts and made the publication process much easier. Jennifer Stevenson turned my reams of words into a coherent, engaging and readable book. The wonderful illustrations are the work of Bill Porter who also does our videos with his colleague Ed Sowerby.

No book on neuroscience in business can be written without acknowledging David Rock, who first brought the scientists and their work to the attention of the business world through the Neuro Leadership Institute. And of course I must also acknowledge the work of the neuroscientists who have brought us the insights that are transforming the way we lead businesses and manage change. Those who have been a particular inspiration to me include Matt Lieberman at UCLA, Dean Mobbs and Kevin Ochsner at Columbia and John Coates at Cambridge.

Thanks also to my study group, both in the UK and the US; our discussions on applying neuroscience to business helped to formulate many of the ideas in this book. As did our discussions at the Breakfast Club for HR Professionals.

Jamie Lawrence and his readers at HRZone.com enthusiastically engaged with my early articles on neuroscience for HR – it was their interest that convinced me to write this book.

And finally, thanks to our clients at Head Heart + Brain, who inspired me to find better ways to help them solve their business issues and in doing so encouraged me to apply the findings from neuroscience.

Contents

1   **Introduction p. 2**

     3   **Neuroscience for HR people**
           Why, what's coming up, and how to use this book

     7   **Brain basics**
           Understanding how the brain works

    15   **CORE principles**
           A brain-savvy model for relationships

2   **Neuroscience at work in HR p. 20**

    21   **Our study**
           What worked in the past won't work now

    25   **Our study**
           The background and numbers

    36   **Case studies**
           Organisations using neuroscience to solve business issues

3   **Leading purpose p. 50**

    51   **"Why are we doing this?"**
           Having a clear purpose and direction

    55   **"Where should I be focusing my attention?"**
           Choosing where your attention should be

    61   **"Empathy is the answer... or is it?"**
           Empathy and perspective, which you need when

    65   **"What's the truth about being creative?"**
           4 myths about creativity, and how it actually works

    69   **"Gut feeling: is it a useful guide in business?"**
           What is it and is it reliable

    76   **"Is there a science to making better decisions?"**
           Logic, emotions, and whether you've had lunch:
           the science of decision-making

82 **"Biased decisions? Not me"**
A bias check for your decisions

86 **"I'm just doing what I'm good at –
or am I stuck in a rut?"**
Understanding habits

90 **"So, I need to think about my thinking?"**
Introspection: the essential skill

94 **"Goals... how do I set them up right?"**
6 steps for success in setting up your goals

98 **"How do I get my HR initiative agreed?"**
The neuroscience of being influential

102 **"Is there a better way to have a difficult conversation?"**
The right way to have the conversations we dread

106 **"Is it really possible to make change happen easily?"**
5 discoveries that will save your change programme

4   Leading the function p. 112

113 **"We don't have in-groups – we just have the right
kind of people."**
Why our brains love to categorise, and how to limit the
damage of in-groups and out-groups

119 **"So, are male and female brains different?"**
Gender differences in the brain, and whether it matters

124 **"My 'feedback' is your 'criticism.' How can I get it right?"**
How brains process feedback: what does and doesn't work

129 **"I dream about performance management that works."**
Brain-savvy performance management

134 **"Are we missing out on free rewards?"**
Brain-savvy reward strategies

138 **"Thanks for coming in to meet us: please tell us about..."**
First-round interviews: how being brain-savvy can help

143 **"Welcome back: it's good to meet with you again..."**
Second-round interviews: avoiding bias in selection

146 **"Why are people so resistant to change?"**
The threat response and change – how to make it more
rewarding

149 **"Once upon a time there was an HR leader..."**
The neuro-power of stories

5 Leading talent, engagement and learning p. 156

157 **"Emotional Intelligence: our leaders aren't convinced."**
The persuasive science of EI

161 **"We're spending enough money – why isn't our training
and development working?"**
A different type of audit: make connections,
anticipate resistance and allow time for learning

166 **"Why do we put training into buckets?"**
Training for the role rather than core skills

168 **"Will our training produce the kind of leaders we want?"**
It's about the design: a quick fix won't change behaviour

173 **"Is the future of learning programmes virtual?"**
Beyond faceless cost-saving: the real advantages
of virtual learning

177 **"I keep telling them they should be using coaching..."**
Coaching vs telling: here's the evidence of what works

181 **"They just need to copy the role model?"**
It's not just about showing how, but understanding why

185 **"A nice hotel, plenty of coffee, role-play exercises...
what have we missed?"**
5 ways to make your Development Centre work

189 **"If talent is our number-one priority, why don't we have
a queue for our top jobs?"**
Change your talent culture and develop the pipeline

195   **"Not another staff survey..."**
      4 steps for creating effective engagement

199   **"Can we make work more fulfilling?"**
      Understanding the see-saw between task and people focus

202   **"How trusting should we be as an organisation?"**
      The science of trusting your people, and why it matters

6   Leading yourself p. 206

207   **"I know I'm smart..."**
      Talent mindset: what do you believe about your abilities?

211   **"I'm great! Why do I need self-awareness?"**
      Self-knowledge makes for better performance

216   **"Am I good enough?"**
      Self-esteem or self-compassion: how to develop a high-status mindset

221   **"How can my memory of the event be completely different to everyone else's?"**
      How memory works, and what you can do to get around its limitations

227   **"Would I pass the marshmallow test?"**
      The success factors of self-control

231   **"I set goals, but making progress is hard."**
      6 ways to keep going with your goals

235   **"How can I get out of this rut?"**
      How behaviours become habits, and how you can make new ones

240   **"I need to get creative. Easier said than done."**
      Brain-savvy techniques to boost creativity

245   **"'Aha!' I solved it!"**
      Insight: how to develop it

250   **"Only people who can't multi-task say it's a problem."**
      Multi-tasking is a myth: here's the evidence

254 **"What's all the hype about meditation?"**
The business benefits of mindfulness

258 **"I can't avoid stress in my job."**
Not all stress is bad for you

263 **"Life's tough: what's the key to thriving?"**
Mental toughness: you need it, and it's a skill you can learn

268 **"I'm lucky: I don't need much sleep"**
The evidence on how sleep affects your work

272 **"A 'power pose' will make me better at my job?"**
How your body affects your performance

276 **"Moving up the career ladder via the gym?"**
Physical fitness: it really does give you the edge

279 **"How can I cope better with setbacks?"**
Developing the power of resilience

284 **"What's that X-factor... the power of connection that some people have?"**
The neuroscience of presence, and how you can learn it

References p. 290

Further reading p. 338

Index p. 342

Brain-Savvy HR

A neuroscience evidence base

by Jan Hills

How to read this book

Our evidence base

Brain basics

1   Introduction

Why HR people need to know about neuroscience, the basics of how our brain works, and a quick-reference model to use in your daily decisions.

Neuroscience for HR people

Why, what's coming up, and how to use this book

If you've opened this book you must have a bit of interest in neuroscience. It may be no more than a thought that it's one of those trendy things that's caught the imagination of the media: there's always plenty of coverage, especially in the US, of the latest neuroscience research, from the impact of an approaching spider to why we are dishonest.

In fact, neuroscience is not so new: it was born as a specialist field of scientific study in the 1960s with the Neurosciences Study Program sponsored by Rockefeller University. And pretty quickly academic connections began to be made between neuroscience and psychology.

The first of these was the study of cognitive neuroscience, focused on cognitive functions such as perception, attention, and memory, which then developed into social neuroscience in the mid-2000s. Most of what we are concerned with is, strictly speaking, social or cognitive neuroscience, but we use the term neuroscience throughout for ease and brevity.

The academic and public profile of the discipline was further consolidated by the establishment of the NeuroLeadership Institute in 2008, which aims to *"encourage, generate and share neuroscience research that transforms how people think, develop and perform."*

But you'll also have spotted that this book is written for HR practitioners, so we're assuming you have an interest in understanding what neuroscience has to say about human behaviour, leadership and change, and how that might have an impact on organisations, and HR policy and practice.

Why neuroscience for HR?

Why do we think an understanding of neuroscience is essential for HR practitioners? That's an easy one to answer: because it tests management theory, and provides a sound evidence-base for HR practice.

What's more, in our work as HR and leadership consultants, and particularly in our work with leaders in organisations, we've found that explaining how the brain actually works has been very effective in persuading leaders to be less resistant, and more open to changing their own behaviour. Most leaders like the strength of evidence in science: it clicks with them.

The other reason we find the insights of neuroscience so useful is that they get leaders to think carefully about their own thinking processes, beliefs and experiences. Leaders recognise how their own brain reacts, and the research results make sense to them personally. This is a valuable tool in the HR armoury in creating the kind of insight and commitment that translates knowledge into action.

For ourselves, as HR professionals, neuroscience research explains the *why* of our policies. *Why* is it a good idea to include social rewards? *Why* is an engagement policy working with some people and not others? *Why* it is important to understand the role of emotions in making decisions on talent? *Why* may bias creep in to decisions without anyone noticing?

We call all this "Brain-savvy HR," as shorthand for HR practice that is informed by an understanding of how the human brain works.

And we wrote this book as an introduction to neuroscience for HR: showing how it explains why people act the way they do; how we – and the people we work with – *can* change; and the way key concepts for us, like engagement, reward and motivation, work in the brain. We wanted to share some of this important evidence, propose how it can inform HR work, and give you some answers to a few thorny questions.

What you'll find in the book and how to read it

No we don't mean to tell you how to read but how you might get the best from the book. We know you are busy and probably won't want to read it from cover to cover so this part is a guide for your reading.

The *Brain basics* section which follows is a brief description of basic brain functioning in layman's terms. It also describes a couple of key concepts and models that are referred to in the other chapters: you'll probably find it useful to read this section first.

Then we give you the results of some research we carried out in late 2013 to understand attitudes to neuroscience within HR, how widely accepted it is within the profession, and the results of its application.

Neuroscience at Work in HR presents some interesting findings, especially in relation to the level of understanding of the science. And you'll find case studies of how organisations are applying the findings of neuroscience in areas as diverse as change, leadership development and wellbeing. The research is a snapshot in time, and we hope that future research will show even more widespread infiltration of neuroscience principles into the profession.

Then we get into the meat of how neuroscience can help you in the work you do.

Leading purpose

This section takes its name from one of the major findings of *The Success Profile for HR Leaders* research we did in 2008, which revealed that one of the key attributes of a successful HR leader is having a *clear purpose* and a guiding sense of direction for the HR function within the business.

The chapters here unpack the process of creating a purpose for your HR team, explore how you make decisions, where you focus, and how you gain the insight and creativity you need to clearly take the function forward.

Some of the chapters in this section introduce the latest research on various key issues (such as creativity) and are followed up with practical applications in the following two sections. So in the section on *Leading yourself*, for example, you'll find out more about how to apply this research to becoming personally more creative.

Leading the function

This is all about applying the findings of neuroscience to policy and practice in HR. What's the science saying about reward and recognition, or implementing change, or helping the function work together?

Specialists can dip into a pick 'n' mix here: you may only be interested in the chapters on your particular areas of expertise, or HR business partners may find useful evidence throughout to support their approach and share with their business clients. This is also the section that will challenge your current thinking about policy and practice.

Leading talent, engagement and learning

Neuroscience is giving us lots of new insight on how to better engage, develop and build a talent culture. In reading these chapters you will challenge your thinking about current practice and learn how to create successful practice and design programmes and policy which improve learning and behaviour change.

Leading yourself

The final section is about you. How you can use an understanding of neuroscience to manage your own performance, your mindset and your skills. Different chapters may grab your interest – there are lots of findings to challenge or add to your understanding of personal performance.

And lastly... tell us what you think

Following the principles of neuroscience, and practising what we preach, we'd love to have your feedback. Lots of clients and organisations we've partnered with find it very useful to share their understanding of the work we've done with them, and tell us about their insights and how they've applied them in their work.

We're hoping to track the progress of HR in applying the principles of neuroscience, and create a community of practitioners who share their ideas, challenges and successes. The website we've set up will help you make connections with like-minded others. The site also has a number of additional resources that complement this book and delivers some of the ideas in video format, which can be useful for sharing with clients or your team. You'll find us at www.brain-savvyHR.com

Brain basics

Understanding how the brain works

Many of our assumptions about why humans developed a large brain, and particularly a large prefrontal cortex, rest on our abilities in logical, rational processing.

Basic Brain Structure

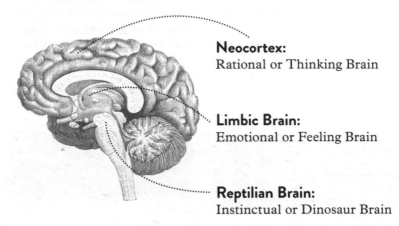

Neocortex:
Rational or Thinking Brain

Limbic Brain:
Emotional or Feeling Brain

Reptilian Brain:
Instinctual or Dinosaur Brain

But another theory is that we're shaped by our social interactions and suffer when our social bonds are threatened or broken. Our well-being depends on connections with others: this is a primary need in the brain. (In which case, we would say that Maslow got it wrong with his hierarchy of human needs:[1] physical needs followed by safety needs, followed by social needs... Social relationships would be as essential as food, water and shelter.)

Why did the brain develop like this?

As humans we would be unable to survive without social connection. A baby only survives because it can attract a carer who puts the baby's needs before their own. If humans are rejected from their group they cannot survive. This urge to connect is one of the reasons we have a big brain: because we've used our brain to connect within our tribe, and these connections motivate us to work together and develop rewarding social interactions.

And all this has an impact on the way we manage businesses.

Social pain

Research at UCLA by social neuroscientist Matt Lieberman and his wife Naomi Eisenberger came up with the rather surprising finding that the brain networks for physical pain are also used for social pain[2] (the "pain" of rejection or humiliation, for example). Whilst social pain may feel different, just as the pain of a stubbed toe feels different from stomach cramps, the networks processing it in the brain are the same.

People around the world, in many languages, use descriptions of physical pain to express social pain: "she broke my heart," "he hurt my feelings..." It turns out this is more than metaphorical: social pain *is* real pain. The connections are so close that the Lieberman / Eisenberger research also found, astonishingly, that social pain can be alleviated by taking conventional painkillers. If you're feeling cold-shouldered by your colleagues, or offended that you're not invited to the management off-site, it might actually help to take an aspirin.

Lieberman says, "The things that cause us to feel pain are things that are evolutionarily recognised as threats to our survival and the existence of social pain is a sign that evolution has treated social connection like a necessity, not a luxury."

The implication for our work in business is that we should pay much more attention to the impact of social rejection: issues like giving feedback in public, challenging social settings and the importance of teamwork.

Social rewards

It also means we're missing out on the power of social rewards. Connection to a social group is critically important for our emotional well-being; positive feedback about increased social reputation lights up reward pathways in the brain. Being treated fairly by others also increases activity in the ventral striatum and ventromedial prefrontal cortex, two key components of the brain's reward system.

A fundamental assumption in most organisations is that work is an economic exchange: time and skills are given in return for money. We assume that people are narrowly self-interested, focused on gaining benefits for themselves, and avoiding physical threats and doing things for others.

But this doesn't explain why so many people give their time and expertise freely: as volunteers and fundraisers, football coaches and school governors. Social reward is hard-wired into us, and it's a motivational end in itself; being connected makes us feel good. These mechanisms of social pain and reward are fundamental to how humans work.

Understanding other people

Another social skill our brain has developed is the ability to understand what another person is thinking, and their goals and motivations, in order to be able to predict, to some extent, other people's behaviour. In many ways we need to be able to read other people's minds – and we can.

We use these skills every day. For example, we make assumptions based on circumstances, gender and appearance, which enable us to cooperate. ("You're like me, you're not a threat to me, we can work together...") This ability is not part of our general ability to think and analyse. We use our prefrontal cortex network for analytical thinking, but a completely different part of the brain – the default network – is used for understanding other people.

Thinking about ourselves

This area of the brain also largely manages our thinking about ourselves. If you're thinking about your favourite sweater, a childhood birthday present, or reflecting on your personality ("Am I lazy, or am I having a relaxing Sunday?") you will be using this area of your brain.

It's also the area that enables you to be influenced by others. The more active the medial prefrontal region is when someone is trying to persuade you (for example to adopt a new policy, or hire a particular candidate), the more likely you'll be to do it.

Lieberman says that our minds are less like hermetically sealed vaults that separate each of us from one another, and more like "Trojan horses":[3] letting in the beliefs of other people without our realising the extent to which we're being influenced. It has the effect of ensuring that we have the same kind of beliefs and values as people around us, creating the social harmony we depend on.

This network for mind-reading goes quiet when we're busy with cognitive kinds of thinking like solving a maths problem or thinking about business strategy. And when we're engaged in the mind-reading type of thinking we quiet the cognitive circuitry.

As soon as the cognitive thinking or task is done the social network (the default or mentalizing system) is activated. These two work a bit like a see-saw: one is active (up), the other is quiet (down).

Thinking about other people when we're learning

The mentalizing system is active, like a reflex, whenever we're not engaged in a task or analytical thinking. And if we're primed to be thinking about the motivations of others, we will be more likely to notice and understand them.

And the more this network is activated when you are reading, hearing about an idea, or learning new things, the more likely you are to pass on the new information to other people. Learning with a view to helping other people activates this network. And it makes us more effective at learning than when we use our analytical brain. It seems we can't do both at the same time.

This has significant implications for us at work. Organisations tend to focus on systems and processes, and this pushes leaders to think rationally rather than socially. Over time this rational thinking becomes a habit – it's the way things are done – and less and less attention is paid to social connections. Leaders will be missing lots of social cues, and the information and opportunities which could provide relational solutions to problems. They end up focusing on analytical solutions: "we just need to run the numbers." Yet many of the toughest business challenges require social solutions (engagement, motivation, productivity to mention just three).

The Mentalizing System

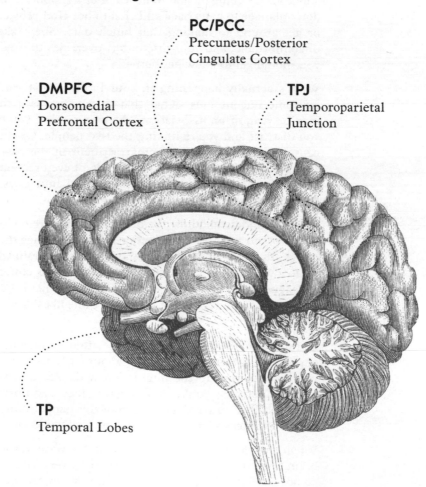

PC/PCC
Precuneus/Posterior
Cingulate Cortex

DMPFC
Dorsomedial
Prefrontal Cortex

TPJ
Temporoparietal
Junction

TP
Temporal Lobes

Interestingly, the degree to which your own medial prefrontal region has been active whilst reading this is indicative of how likely you are to discuss these ideas with other people.

Threat and reward

One of the fundamental ways in which our brain is "wired" is that we move away from threat and towards reward. And a "threat" doesn't have to be someone about to punch you, and a "reward" doesn't have to be a bonus. We could equally use the terms "avoid" and "approach" to distinguish the things that make us feel uncomfortable or comfortable. These reactions happen at an unconscious level, so we seldom put a label on why we act the way we do.

Imagine this scenario: there's a woman in your cross-function project team that you know you should build a relationship with. She's influential, and has a lot of insight into the politics of the organisation. It would make sense for you to understand more about what's going on and to have her as a supporter. But you just don't manage to hang back and chat to her after project meetings, or get around to making that lunch date. She makes you feel uncomfortable, and your discomfort overrides the logic that says you should get to know her better.

What's actually happening in your brain is that you're picking up some unconscious signal that this person is a threat. That may be real, or an association: she may remind you of someone you distrust and you're linking the two people. Or she may have caused you some kind of embarrassment in the past – perhaps she challenged you publicly and you don't even remember it now, but your subconscious does. The emotional, limbic system of your brain is activated: it perceives a threat and signals you to avoid her.

Once we understand how the brain works we are no longer at the mercy of our unconscious reactions: we can engage the prefrontal cortex, the rational, goal-setting system of the brain which allows us to override the avoid response. We'll have coffee with this colleague and realise that her off-putting manner is because she's ill-at-ease, and find that she's actually quite likeable as well as very useful.

Not surprisingly, the reward response often operates as the mirror-opposite of threat. You feel good about a situation or a person so you look forward to the interaction with pleasure: you're more willing to engage, you're more open to ideas, and probably more energetically creative. Again, most of this happens unconsciously, but it influences what you do and how well you do it.

When people learn about the threat / reward response in the brain, and apply it to their own situation, very often a light bulb comes on. Their insight enables them to formulate new strategies to overcome unconscious responses and do what will be best for the organisation, and their own career. Sometimes it's enough just to understand the science and why we've been responding in a particular way. At other times people may need tools or coaching to put together new strategies.

In-group and out-group

Another organising principle of the brain is to categorise; it's a shortcut that helps our brain to be more efficient.

The trouble is that we categorise people into in-group and out-group at work too. Our in-group is the people we see as similar to ourselves. Our out-group is the people who are "different." Once categorised, our brain filters all new information in accordance with the category, so it's hard to think of someone as friend if our initial judgement of them was foe.

This all happens in a nanosecond, out of conscious awareness, but for HR professionals it means that rituals like induction, team off-sites and sharing common goals are important for breaking down initial out-group judgements. This becomes even more important in teams that work remotely where there may be little opportunity for the personal encounters which can quickly break down initial judgements.

Our inefficient brain

Our brain is not as efficient as we might think. The executive functioning areas, those parts of the brain responsible for planning, goal attainment, rational thought and inhibiting impulses tire easily. The brain runs most activity in the energy-efficient older area of the brain, the basal ganglia, also known as the habit region.

Columbia social neuroscientist Kevin Ochsner (a colleague of Matt Lieberman), believes that 70% of what we do is governed by habit[4], and that includes how people do their jobs. It's a much more brain-efficient way of working but it can cause difficulties when change is necessary.

Many HR policies and cultures work against rather than with this habitual tendency, and implicitly assume our brain has infinite capacity. But as anyone would recognise, brains are quickly fatigued when we have to make a lot of decisions, and this can result in poor judgement.

Likewise, multi-tasking is a myth that leads to poor productivity and reduced cognitive functioning. For most efficient working we should plan for our creative or difficult tasks early in the day, and avoid routine tasks, like emails, in the morning.

Emotions matter

Many people in business still find emotions unacceptable in the workplace, and few leadership development programmes help leaders to understand and manage their own emotions, or the feelings of the people they work with. But work by the internationally recognised neuroscientist Antonio Damasio at USC has shown that all decisions have an emotional element[5]. Trying to maintain some kind of "stiff upper lip" at work is both damaging and unproductive.

Matt Lieberman has found that using simple language to "name" emotions *lowers* the arousal[6] of the limbic system, producing a quieter brain state which allows the prefrontal cortex to function more effectively. The implications of findings such as these for HR are profound: if people suppress their emotions in order to be "professional" they actually make it harder for themselves to function professionally, and create physical stress. We go into more detail on these findings in the individual chapters and also suggest ways to use your understanding of the brain in HR policy and practice as well as your own performance.

The Emotional Brain

Thalamus
Central relay station

Frontal Lobe
(Intellectual Brain)

Caudate Nucleus
Automatic Thought
transmission

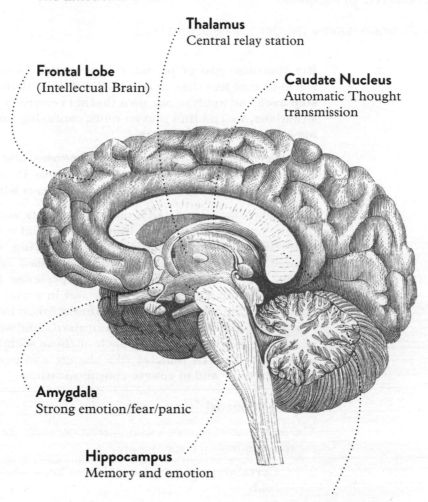

Amygdala
Strong emotion/fear/panic

Hippocampus
Memory and emotion

Anterior Cingulate Gyrus
Mood

CORE principles

A brain-savvy model for relationships

Relationships are of primary importance to us – in the workplace no less than at home. But if it's difficult for us to step back and analyse our own threat / reward responses to situations, we can find it even more confusing understanding other people's reactions.

And our ability to anticipate their responses, and take steps to mitigate them, is crucial to our success in negotiating with and influencing all the people we interact with at work.

We've developed our CORE model as a quick and easy way to help you understand and manage potential responses in yourself and in other people when influencing, suggesting change or building a relationship. It's based on research which has identified that people experience threat, or reward, in four key areas at work and in social situations generally. Understanding when a threat might be triggered (and how it could be avoided or minimised), and when a sense of reward can be created in each of these social elements is essential for HR policies like change and performance management – and of course communications.

The CORE model

The four areas of human social interaction where we experience the threat or reward responses are:

Certainty: our confidence that we know what the future holds[7]

Options: the extent to which we feel we have choices[8]

Reputation: our relative importance to others (our social ranking)[9]

Equity: our sense of fairness[10]

The four CORE elements activate either the "primary reward" or the "primary threat" circuitry of our brains. For example, a perceived threat to our sense of equity activates similar brain networks to a physical threat to ourselves. In the same way, a perceived increase to our reputation activates the same reward circuitry as receiving a monetary reward.

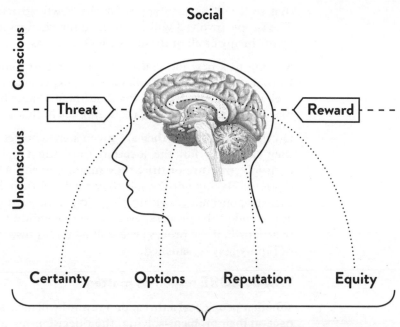

Social

Conscious / Unconscious

Threat ▷ ◁ Reward

Certainty Options Reputation Equity

The CORE elements operate at an unconscious level. Once triggered by a perceived **threat** or **reward** take the following steps:

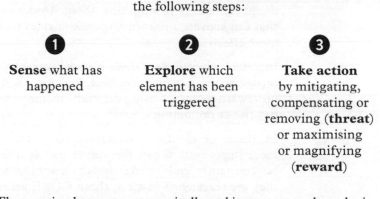

1 **Sense** what has happened

2 **Explore** which element has been triggered

3 **Take action** by mitigating, compensating or removing (**threat**) or maximising or magnifying (**reward**)

The reaction happens automatically and instantaneously and triggers our response before we've even had a chance to consider it rationally.

You'll find that threats are flagged up more often than rewards as we apply the CORE model. This is because our brains are wired to prioritise responding to threats because they're critical to our survival. At work that means we need to offer many more rewards than you might expect in order to create a feel-good response to a new initiative. And one threat can undo the benefits of a number of reward offerings.

Using the CORE model: an example

You're looking at restructuring a department which will mean that staff will have to apply for the newly structured positions. The people involved will experience the changes as threats or rewards in any or all of these four CORE areas.

Moving to a new job can create a threat to someone's sense of Certainty because they don't have any experience of that new role, they may not have worked for that line manager before, and they may not be as confident of their abilities in that area.

On the o er hand, if they are given some choices about the roles they can apply for, the location they might be working in, or their job structure or title, they might perceive a reward to their Options. Having got the job they may feel their Reputation and their responsibilities within the team have been enhanced. And at the end of the process, even if everyone didn't get a job in the restructure, if the process was robust and transparent their sense of Equity may be satisfied.

Why do CORE responses matter?

Whether people feel a threat or a reward will have a significant impact on their problem-solving, their decision-making, the amount of stress they experience, as well as collaboration and motivation. Knowing the drivers that cause a threat response enables us to design initiatives to minimise them. Understanding the drivers that can activate a reward response enables us to motivate people more effectively.

In a stable environment there is clearly great value in being able to recognise these many responses, for example using them to light up reward pathways using different methods to the conventional pay rise or promotion.

In times of change, understanding these responses is even more important. When the status quo is disrupted people will be constantly and unconsciously scanning for ways in which they are threatened in all of these CORE areas: they will be the subtext of every team meeting, the subject of every water-cooler conversation. Scanning for and analysing these perceived threats will divert resources from their prefrontal cortex: the part of their brain responsible for planning, decision-making and moderating behaviour. Performance and productivity will suffer as a result, decreasing morale and maximising disruption at a critical time.

If we can move a perceived threat from an unconscious to a conscious level it can be addressed. That may be as simple as a leader giving a categorical assurance of security or continuity, or devising alternative rewards that will compensate for threats.

Overcoming threats

Below are some of the typical threat triggers produced by a change scenario in each of the CORE areas, and the initiatives that may limit the threat or offer alternative rewards: invaluable tools for leaders driving change programmes.

Area where threat or response may be experienced	Common threat triggers	Actions to decrease threat / increase rewards
Certainty	Lack of information about the future plans and impending change: postponed staff meetings or monthly updates, only a few people "in the know" Unpredictable behaviour, especially by those in power: unexplained meetings and offsites, or visitors to the offices Job insecurity	Publicise agendas and timetables Tell people when they will know about the changes Create new routines Explain the strategy and new plans Break down large changes into chunks Help people see why the change is good for them personally
Options	Telling people what to do (the command and control model) Excluding people from shaping plans Dictating detailed processes Micro-managing	Give people choices Create flexible work patterns Develop high-level policy allowing for discretion and judgement Leaders set the overall direction, teams define the details Individuals design the detailed changes to their own role
Reputation	Giving detailed instructions, especially in public Leaving people out of activities and briefings Reducing the responsibility of a role Giving critical feedback	Ask for self-assessment of performance Give positive feedback, especially publicly Provide opportunities for learning and enhanced responsibility Ask for input and their expertise
Equity	Perceived favouritism Uneven workloads Unclear expectations Lack of transparency	Clearly explain reasons and context Make decision-making transparent Stick to agreed policies

For more detail on applying the CORE model to maximising your influence, read our chapter in the *Leading purpose* section, *"How do I get my HR initiative agreed?"*

Our
evidence
base

2 Neuroscience at work in HR

Our study of who's leading the way in the profession, and how neuroscience is solving business problems

Our study

What worked in the past won't work now

In late 2013, Head Heart + Brain commissioned a piece of research to help us understand what HR professionals know about neuroscience. We wanted to know how useful they think the findings are to HR, how they are applying the knowledge that they have, and the results they are getting.

The research took the form of an online survey, plus a number of in-depth interviews with senior HR professionals: Human Resource Directors, heads of leadership and talent, and those leading change in their company.

There were some surprising results in relation to the number of people using neuroscience in their work, and where the Early Adopters were to be found. Here's a summary of our findings, illustrated by quotes from the survey and our face-to-face interviews. And following you'll find the details of the numbers behind the survey, and case studies of neuroscience at work in HR.

New solutions needed

In our interviews, there were quite a few comments about where the HR function sees itself in the organisation, and a concern that the focus on process over the last ten years or so has led HR down a path that reduces its value to the business.

Many senior HR people expressed a concern that HR lacked skills in questioning, challenging and coaching the business. Of equal concern was the perception that many HR professionals don't see themselves as business problem-solvers, being focused on giving answers rather than exploring solutions.

Alongside this observation was an expressed concern that the issues organisations are facing, and particularly the challenges leaders need to overcome, call for a step-change in how HR helps the business, especially in the areas of leadership and the execution of strategy through people. Whilst many professionals recognised this need for change, there were frequent references to the difficulty of garnering support within the function, let alone across the whole business. Below, we summarise the business challenges our interview respondents described.

The application of neuroscience is not the only answer to these expressed concerns, which have been made for years. But there does seem to be an opportunity to reposition HR given the degree of change needed in the business and a recognition that what has helped in the past is not relevant today.

Next steps for HR

"How to explain business solutions to business-people in a way that helps them solve the problem. This is where HR needs to focus."

"In HR, we rely too heavily on trial-and-error methods to solve problems, rather than step back. We rush too quickly to action rather than really understand the issues."

The issues businesses are facing

The opening question for our interviewees was about the issues their business is facing.

Most spoke of the need to transform the business either because of competitive pressure or a change in the market: what had made the business successful to date was no longer relevant for the future.

This theme of the solutions of the past no longer working was particularly strong in financial services and related sectors like law and insurance. The solution for the issues of today was a focus on leadership. Interviewees commented on the demands being made on the leadership of the organisation; leaders could no longer rely on past experience, or tried-and-tested ways of doing business. This was changing the definition of what makes a "good leader".

The challenges that organisations face

"Currently our business is only improving at the same pace as the market. In the past it was easy to make money so people rarely questioned what they did. Now that doesn't provide the financial returns to the business. This is causing leaders to realise they can't do what they have always done. They are asking for help in how they make a change."

"Our leadership quality equals our business quality. We have to continually seek to improve both."

"In the past we have been a federation of businesses. Making the change to one organisation is much harder than anyone thought. It creates a threat to autonomy and reputation."

"Our business has been led by individuals who were allowed to get on with their part of the business. That won't work anymore. People need to pull together. We need to focus on the customer experience and that means collaborating across the business."

When HR was trying to help leaders make the shifts necessary, two themes emerged.

The first was a focus on helping the leadership team to work more collaboratively. These businesses had grown up either as strong independent business units that ran fairly autonomously, or the structure was being changed to achieve economies of scale. The future demands more interdependence, teamwork and collaboration. Leadership development was focused on a greater understanding of self and how the leader's style and behaviour affects everyone who works with them.

Past leadership development

"In the main we have not taught leaders about people."

"We have done massive amounts of training on behaviour but I question if we have pulled the right levers. You can't change behaviour without changing beliefs."

"Because we have in the past focused on task we have undervalued relationships and now it is hard to get out of the habit."

"It is hard to shift people who are used to just doing things themselves to become leaders who work through others."

"Previously we have amassed lots of data about individual leaders. They had lots of assessment but not much development to change."

The second major theme was the need to change the habits and competencies that had made the leader successful to date. In the main this was about a shift from the leader as technical expert to the leader as... a leader: someone who could inspire and take the business and the people forward with them.

Here the solution being put forward was largely the same: helping leaders to have more self-knowledge and be able to be flexible in their approach to people. In these businesses there was a recognition that this type of personal development had been missing from past programmes in the company and that much of what was needed was fairly basic self-awareness and understanding of relationships. The challenge for leadership development professionals was how to provide this to a cynical audience who in the main still believed it was "touchy-feely HR stuff."

Respondents also talked about the expectations of the next generation of talent in the workforce, who want different things from their career and from their leaders. This was driving a focus for a more connected, empathetic social leadership style.

New solutions

"We are trying to open up curiosity about self-awareness."

"Neuroscience raises awareness of self and collective awareness and can produce more durable outcomes."

"Understanding the science of relationships, how people think and their preferences, is the only way leaders can be successful."

"We need to transform how leaders change the business, based on our espoused values."

"The next generation wants more connection within the company and with leaders. If we don't provide this style of leadership they won't choose to work with us or companies like us."

"The next generation have different career expectations; being a partner (in a partnership structure) is not what many of them want. We must provide a different career path and our current partners need to engage in a dialogue about careers."

Given the business issues described, there was a lot of emphasis on change management. This is an area where neuroscience is being used either directly with business leaders, or to inform the approach HR is taking.

The other initiatives discussed were often about performance management. And this, in the main, stemmed from a recognition that the current approach was not working, or was not going to support the business strategy going forward.

For HR the challenge is to reskill; to be able to have a dialogue about solutions not process, to be willing to engage in a debate about what would work rather than come with a ready-made solution and to build confidence in creating an evidence-based approach that explains to business leaders why people driven solutions will work, not just what they should do.

Our study:

the background and numbers

It is not surprising that the majority of our respondents came from the UK but there was representation from every other region of the world including Australia and Asia.

Location of respondent %

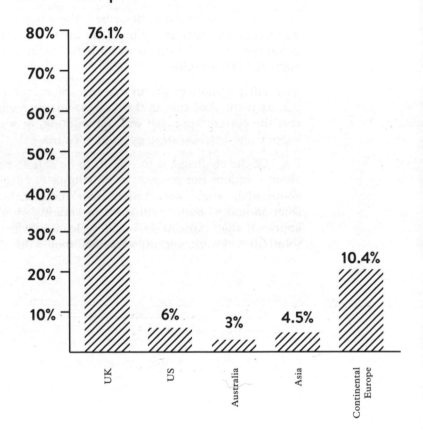

Industry of respondent %

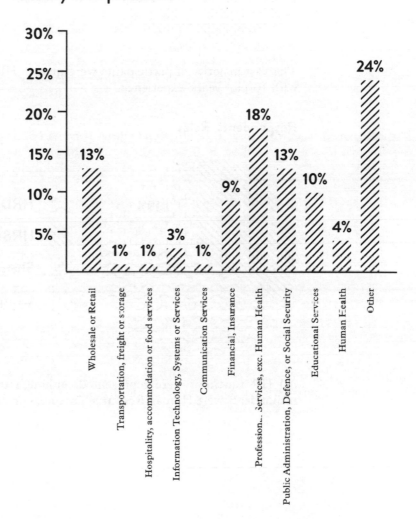

Most industries were represented in the survey and in the in-depth interviews.

Respondents: How many years' of experience?

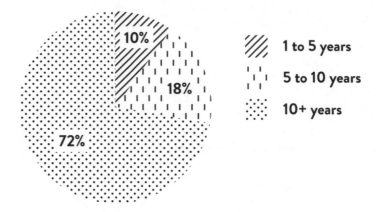

The vast majority of participants were mature HR professionals with 10-plus years' experience.

Respondents' Roles

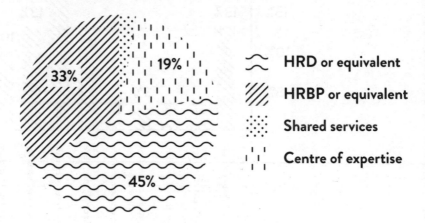

All HR functions were represented, although the majority of respondents were Human Resource Directors or equivalent.

What do HR practitioners know about neuroscience?

The answer is… a little. Sixty-four per cent of the HR people who took part in the research say they know nothing or very little about neuroscience and its relevance to HR. However 32% have some understanding and have applied this to their business.

Two-thirds of the people invited to take part in the survey or interviews said they knew too little about neuroscience or the implications for HR to be able to comment.

How do you describe your level of knowledge about neuroscience in the context of HR policy and practice

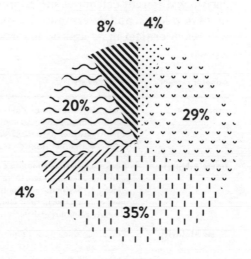

∨ ∨ ∨ **Little or nothing**

ı ı ı ı **I have read a bit**

//// **I have made a study of the current findings and know quite a bit**

∾ **I know quite a bit and have put my knowledge into practice**

\\\\ **I know a lot and have put my knowledge into practice**

:::: **I am an expert and have put my knowledge into practice extensively**

Diffusion of innovations

One way of looking at these results about where HR stands in relation to the application of neuroscience is through the lens of Everett Rogers' *Diffusion of Innovations*, a theory that explains how, why, and at what rate new ideas spread[11]. Rogers, a professor of communication studies, put forward the theory in his 1962 book of the same title. His theory proposes that diffusion is the process by which an innovation is communicated and adopted over time among a group, in this case the HR profession.

The innovation must be widely adopted in order to continue to be used and integrated into the way the group works. The theory classifies different categories of "adopters" by their rates of take-up of new ideas, and determines the speed at which an innovation will reach critical mass and be incorporated into how the group works.

Adopter category	Who they are
Innovators	These are the first individuals to take up a new idea. They're usually young, high social status and willing to take risks. Not surprisingly they have the closest contact to scientific sources and interact with other Innovators.
Early Adopters	The second-fastest adoption category, with the largest number of opinion leaders amongst them. Youthful, high social status, well-educated, they're more socially forward than Later Adopters but more conservative in their choices than Innovators. They tend to use early adoption to differentiate themselves.
Early Majority	This group waits until an innovation has been tested before they take up an idea. They have above-average social status and tend to have contact with Early Adopters. They're seldom opinion-leaders.
Late Majority	These are the sceptics: they'll take up an innovation after the average members of a group. They have below-average social status and are usually socially connected to people in their own group and Early Majority Adopters. They're rarely opinion-leaders.
Laggards	These are the last people to come on board with a new idea. They like tradition, and they don't respond well to change – often they're older and well-established or coming to the end of their careers. They have the lowest social status of all the groups. They may be socially isolated from their peers and show little or no opinion leadership.

Our results would indicate we have about 12% of Early Adopters amongst our respondents: people who know about and are actively applying neuroscience to HR policy and practice.

Analysing by region, Australia is an Early Adopter with all Australian respondents having applied neuroscience to their HR practice. The early-adopter industries are professional services and banking.

We found people who could be described as Early Adopters in change, leadership and learning and performance management.

There were also people applying findings within HR, especially in team-building across the function.

Our own experience largely supports these findings. Whilst we've worked with many mature HR professionals, the people who instantly see the application of neuroscience to HR, and who personally adopt the ideas in their own work, and apply them to their own performance, have tended to be younger professionals often just leaving a graduate-type programme and in their first HR role.

When does an innovation take off?

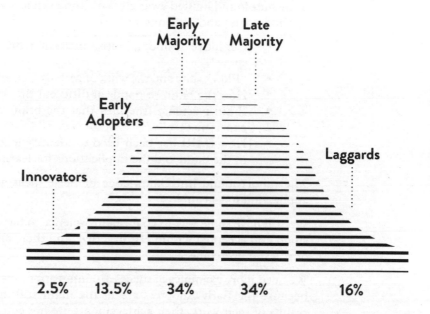

According to Rogers' theory the point at which an innovation reaches critical mass is usually around 18%, after which it is likely to become self-sustaining. His strategies to help an innovation reach this stage include adoption by highly respected individuals, and examples of its successful application.

We anticipate that the CIPD's recent endorsement of neuroscience[12] as part of HR's evidence base will prove to be a positive step towards critical mass. And we're confident that the case studies and examples of practical application you'll find in this book will also help to achieve critical mass.

Still a way to go

There is some confusion between neuroscience and Neuro Linguistic Programming (NLP), in the minds of some HR professionals.

NLP is the modelling of successful behaviour and the creation of tools which results from the model. Neuroscience is the understanding of how the brain and neurochemicals work. Both in the survey responses and our interviews a number of people talked about using NLP rather than neuroscience. We obviously still have a way to go in establishing the independent credentials of neuroscience, and we mustn't assume that everyone understands the distinctions.

The CIPD undertook a survey to measure the awareness and application of a number of new methodologies[13] and concepts in learning and development. Their 2012 report *From steady state to ready state* found limited awareness of, and even less application of methodologies and concepts such as:

- Cognitive thinking traps, including bias and "blind spots"
- "Flow" state and the work of Mihaly Csikszentmihalyi [14]
- How the brain responds at different times of life
- Brain plasticity (the idea that the brain changes with experience)
- How fMRI has been used to identify learning centres in the brain and the implications for learning design

The report found little knowledge of these ideas and even less application to learning.

We still have some way to go for neuroscience to be widely understood and accepted within HR practice, and there are a few more hurdles to overcome.

We need more examples of successful innovation. It's possible that because the Early Adopters are in the main still measuring the results of their work, their achievements are not getting visibility.

What's stopping neuroscience being applied more widely?

Particularly outside the UK, we spoke to HR leaders who really saw the potential for the application of neuroscience to solve business issues related to people. However, tools and training are needed to translate the results of neuroscience research into practical applications.

Using neuroscience in HR

"I have been interested for some time and have done bits of reading etc. The problem is many HR professionals are not interested in these issues and not mindful of how people behave given certain conditions. They are labelled differently i.e. if somebody shows emotion they are weak, if somebody says they are not happy about something they are the problem, not the manager or the organisation. You will need to have much more aware HR professionals and it would have to have a legal imperative."

"I think neuroscience helps explain what has often been a strong-ly-felt instinct in terms of approach to HR policy and practice. As I learn more, I can see how slight variations in approach could make for more effective HR practice."

"My personal experience has been very positive. We do not use it in the business but it strikes me that it provides an insight and context around change that we currently do not necessarily take account of. It also strikes me as useful in the context of helping individuals improve career planning in the context of internal change and the challenges that brings. In addition it could be that it would be useful in the arena of resilience and leadership."

How useful is neuroscience to HR?

We asked people how useful they felt neuroscience could be to the HR profession. A large number of respondents – 73% – said they believed it would be useful to apply the findings to HR policy and practice. These respondents included those who knew little about neuroscience.

Whilst this is a significant number of HR professionals who see neuroscience as potentially useful, there is still a group who are yet to be convinced. A third group are those who currently are not very interested. These broad groupings are consistent with how the theory of *Diffusion of Innovations* describes the adoption of ideas.

It was important for us to also understand the views of the people who were sceptical about how neuroscience might help them in their work. Most of them were concerned about proof of practical applications, and the difficulty of changing long-held views of people in their business:

Concerns about applying neuroscience to HR

"I am concerned that 'findings' in neuroscience undergo proper scrutiny and peer review before being published and touted to the HR community. I worry that sometimes new things are picked up and turned into the 'answer' to lots of things they were never designed for."

"It is hard to change old ways of working."

"I think knowing how a car works is not as important as being able to use it to its full potential, and safely – unless one is a mechanic. In a sense, HR people are the mechanics and should know about the application of neuroscience, but I think there's a danger that knowledge of neuroscience, with all its use, becomes the focus and the practical application is lost in the technical jargon and theory. This then becomes more important than the purpose of that knowledge."

Resistance to new ideas

In our own work, especially in leadership, we have found reluctance by a number of professionals to adopt new ideas even when they acknowledge that current approach, such as leadership programmes are failing to get results in terms of behavioural change.

Where people are actively using neuroscience in their programmes and are seeing positive results, the support for the approach, not surprisingly, is strong. But some of them are still having an uphill battle to get traction. A number of Early Adopters are concerned about other HR professionals, and the profession as a whole, being complacent or highly conservative about new ideas.

Some of these criticisms echo long-held concerns about the willingness of the HR profession to provide rigorous evidence supporting its initiatives, and the absence of any requirement for continuous development as a condition for maintaining membership of the CIPD.

Difficulties experienced by Early Adopters

"HR feels threatened by new ideas."

"I am a Psychologist with research experience in neuroscience between my first degree in Psychology and an MSc in Occupational Psychology. I am convinced of the utility of neuroscience in HR but sadly I have been obliged to leave HR per se as I was a lone voice and not able to convince my superiors... There are far too many people working in HR who still have the 'staff administration' attitude where it is merely rules and regulations and paperwork. They forget that they are dealing with human beings!"

"The science of HR is fundamental to the profession's credibility. HR has, in the main, lost its evidence base in favour of process."

"My background is Risk Management but I have recently (three years ago) transitioned into HR as Head of Learning & Development. I have found that some of the science applied in HR in general is pseudo-science, or is misinterpreted. I have found that among L&D professionals there is a lot stronger interest and debate about neuroscience and an understanding of how this can best be applied, but due to the limited understanding among general HR and senior management, it has been hard to apply the science and its implications. There is a tendency to go for established tools used widely in organisations, rather than a well-considered approach that would incorporate neuroscience (or behavioural science generally). Thus some of the tools implemented actually work against staff engagement, for example."

There is a call from many in our survey for more rigour in developing skills in HR:

More professional development and learning is needed within HR

"I am always surprised at how little HR people do to educate themselves."

"This will demand new skill-sets in HR and a change in the qualifications."

"Very few HR colleagues are curious about new ideas and developments. They are ok with their own ignorance. Some professionals in the centres of expertise are more curious. Business partners tend to be cautious about new ideas."

"At some point you learn some of the neuroscience but to really implement it you need a good sense of self and to change your own beliefs about what works."

But we believe the real issue is the need to build understanding and confidence in how science can be used to provide evidence for human behaviour and for changing behaviour at work:

More education is needed

"Until you have a really good grasp it is hard to talk about the benefits convincingly."

"It can be difficult when some of the team working on a project understand the neuroscience and are keen to apply it and the other half of the team wants to stick with the old stuff, even when they have not got good results from it."

"HR is still focused on process. Until they see their role as helping the business change and solve issues they will not fully see the benefits of or adopt this approach. Many never have business conversations; they are not curious. Business partners are still too 'statement oriented' and are not looking at how they solve new business problems."

"Our research (Hermann Whole Brain Thinking) suggests HR professionals' preference is not for science and research-based thinking. Adopting neuroscience and its implications will be a stretch for many HR people."

Ironically, what we are hearing from many in HR is a typical response to change. Sentiments expressed sound very like the archetypal threat response in the brain. Neuroscience offers better insights for addressing this resistance than traditional change management techniques.

Our interviewees, particularly outside the UK, saw the science as having the potential to make a significant change in the way HR solve business issues. A research participant from one of the companies applying neuroscience and getting good results told us:

> *"Over the next five years I see HR going two ways; those who are using neuroscience and getting valuable results that the business can understand, and those who are stuck in the old ways; working with outdated methods and their best guess."*

Case studies

Organisations using neuroscience to solve business issues

As part of our face-to-face interviews we asked people about the areas where they've applied neuroscience findings and how useful it has been in solving the business issues they're experiencing.

We also asked whether people were explicitly using the science (that is, teaching leaders about what the science is saying about self-awareness, motivating people and so on), or whether the science was "behind the curtain:" informing HR practice but not explicitly discussed.

For many it was too early to measure results, but anecdotal evidence seemed to suggest that the application of neuroscience ideas both through teaching leaders about the findings and using research to guide policy and design were positive.

We were able to draw together a number of case studies from our interviews, as well as our own work and work which was shared with us by other professionals applying neuroscience findings in business.

Where are people applying the science?

Of the 32% of people in the research who had applied the findings of neuroscience, the area where it had most commonly been applied was change. This is an area where neuroscience not only has robust evidence of the biological reactions to change but where, in our experience, results can be substantial.

Neuroscience and change

Two case studies illustrate how organisations have used their understanding of neuroscience to gain results across significant change programmes:

Case study 1: a bank using neuroscience in their change leadership

A bank, based in Australia, was undergoing significant change across most areas of the business and all the major functional areas.

Over a period of a year, Head Heart + Brain worked with their HR team to support the change programme to create a super-regional growth strategy in the business. Their issue was that the HR team as a whole had comparatively limited change-management skills, and many of the senior HR team were ambivalent about the change. Our challenge was to engage them all in the change, increase their commitment, and give them skills to manage themselves and their business clients through the change process.

After investigating the difficulties the HR team were experiencing and consulting the team on how they were used to managing strategy and change, we designed a three-pronged approach to their change programme.

The first stage was a change leadership programme for their top 200 HR people, based around a three-day workshop. The workshop encouraged these senior HR people to take responsibility for the change in themselves, their HR team and the business – integrating neuroscientific insights to help them understand what goes on for people during change, and how to manage their own levels of engagement.

The second stage involved working with their senior HR leaders to design change interventions based on our CORE model. This enabled them to diagnose, plan and monitor communications based on the potential threat or reward. All communications were written to maximise reward and minimise threat response. It sounds obvious, but they quickly realised that their habitual way of communicating created more threat than reward. Where it wasn't possible to eliminate a threat response, efforts were made to mitigate threat. So for example the threat of uncertainty about the outcomes of the proposed change was mitigated by training people in facilitating neuroscience-based change workshops, increasing their sense of options and increasing their positive reputation in the business.

The third stage gave the HR leadership the tools – the CORE model and our Leaders Change Charter – to engage their teams and business stakeholders in the organisational change. They took part in a two-day workshop learning how to use the tools in practice and how to pass on the skills to their teams, so that the HR leaders then led the next stage of the change process in the business as well as in the HR function.

Results were excellent: the client said *"What impressed me most about the work was the facilitation, interactive activities and reinforcement of concepts. Most importantly it provided us with tools and concepts we can apply to any change."* There was increased take-up of the responsibilities for change across the HR function, and the CORE model was widely used by business leaders in managing their own change efforts. During this turbulent time when there was also downsizing across the business, including HR, the results in HR's own staff engagement survey improved significantly.

The neuroscience

The neuroscientific principles deployed were understanding how the brain responds to change, and habit formation in relation to adopting the new ways of working.

Case study 2: legal change

This case study involved a legal firm who, decided to change the career path for lawyers across the firm. This was in response to economic, social and client demands and it was an adventurous new model for the business, based on value rather than seniority. The new career model changed how lawyers in the firm were trained and remunerated, and impacted on every HR process relating to all the lawyers in the firm, from newly-joined graduates to those making partner. The model would also need partners to be able to coach and manage lawyers to fulfil a mutual contract: the lawyers providing their dedication, motivation and skills, and the firm providing a rewarding career with excellent training and interesting client work.

The HR team told us that they began by educating themselves on the neuroscience of change and used this understanding to guide their change management and communication across the firm. Little was explicitly discussed with their internal clients so the application of neuroscience findings could be said to have been applied "behind the curtain." They applied their neuroscience understanding to:

- Complex change consultation; seeking to design the change and consultation processes in a way that mirrored the culture they hoped to create, and also raising awareness of their own biases.
- How people respond to change and in particular how they could use the understanding to predict the response of different people who would be affected by the change.
- Communications; making the shift from what the firm wanted to say to what the different populations needed to hear.
- They monitored threat and reward responses to stages of the change.

Despite this informal approach, neuroscience findings and their implications were woven throughout the change process. They planned communication based on CORE and wrote all communications to minimise threat.

Members of the change team also used CORE to debrief their own meetings and interactions with internal clients. They analysed where they might have inadvertently created a threat response and which actions elicited a reward response and used this learning to manage future interactions.

Some of the methods are still work in progress so results are only now being measured but anecdotal evidence is that this application of neuroscience "behind the curtain" has helped a challenging change programme.

The neuroscience
The main use was the neuroscience of how the brain responds to change, and particularly an understanding of the threat/ reward response. Change interventions were designed to minimise or mitigate threat and induce a reward response.

The other examples of applying neuroscience to change mainly used the SCARF model[15] either "behind the curtain" or explicitly in the content of change programmes.

Neuroscience in leadership and learning

Learning and leadership is another area where the application of neuroscience findings is being used. All the examples we came across, except one, involved including some content about the brain and how understanding the findings from neuroscience and its implications could give leaders insight to themselves or their team members. For example helping leaders understand the role of emotions in decision-making or how to create new ways of working by forming new behavioural habits. Most leadership programmes tended to take a modular approach with one or two modules covering insights into the brain. Examples of neuroscience application included:

- The use of the SCARF model for gaining insight into the leader's own reactions to threat and reward.
- Explaining the impact of threat and reward on influencing others.
- Using an understanding of neuroscience in stress and performance.
- Using SCARF to analyse team members' reactions and how a leader could flex their style.

The types of organisations applying the science to learning programmes ranged from a small software company through to global engineering and banking corporations. Whilst most interviewees reported great interest from leaders and participants, and said that the leaders and learners liked the evidence and scientific underpinnings of neuroscience, there was also recognition that to have a lasting impact tools were required to help people apply their insights to work based problems or behavioural change.

Case study 3: "embodied leadership"

There is evidence that every skill comes with a physiology, and learning both at the same time strengthens the ability to apply the skill and lead authentically.

A professional services firm designed a modular leadership programme over 18 months to develop its partners as leaders and to try to identify the leadership factors which would sustain the company in the long term.

Historically, the company had done little to develop its partners. The leadership programme they designed with a New Zealand-based consultancy firm used a mix of neuroscience and other methods to raise self-awareness, change behaviour and in and tap into what leadership meant to individuals.

The programme was designed around an action learning model and included two-day modules on different themes of leadership which included neuroscience, yoga and an emphasis on what is going on in the brain and body in different scenarios (for example, under stress, in a client meeting, during difficult conversations with the team or a colleague).

Between modules, participants worked together to apply new skills and learning in learning groups; using colleagues for challenge and support. An interesting feature was that challenge could only be posed in the form of questions, which had the effect of simultaneously building questioning skills and improving the application of the ideas in the programme. Partners could also learn meditation. And to the HRD's surprise they loved this aspect of the programme with many adopting the mindfulness meditation practice after the programme was complete.

The neuroscience used
The programme used the threat/reward response and the link between body and brain; an understanding of the impact on state of mind. The programme also covered mindfulness research and the findings that show mindfulness positively impacts stress and attention.

Case study 4: improving client interactions

This accountancy firm had observed that the analytical nature of their work led their people to unconsciously look for problems in everything, carrying a problem-orientation into conversations and relationships and generating a negative focus.

They introduced a programme to help partners understand the impact of their own emotions on client interactions, team energy and business success. The company wanted to improve the corporate culture, initially in the tax business and then across the organisation in order to improve its client relationships. As part of the programme partners looked at their own emotional profiles, these are called "core beliefs" in the model used, and the profiles of their colleagues and clients, and learned to analyse their profile and triggered behaviours and to flex their behaviour to improve relationships with others.

The personal insight into their emotional profile, including their core beliefs, and the impact of these on interactions was eye-opening for participants. Partners got better at "reading the emotions" of other people: engaging more personally with clients and their teams; asking how people *felt* rather than just what they wanted; overcoming their own self- created "narrative" about why a client didn't want a particular solution, and moving to asking for business and building meaningful relationships.

The programme also covered "labelling" and "faulty thinking" to help partners recognise and manage their emotional reactions and pause to engage their rational brain.

For example, partners were encouraged to ask for client feedback rather than allow a fear of what they might hear to put them into avoidance. Partners were challenged to understand that they were often operating from assumptions rather than true questioning and an understanding of their clients' needs. Appreciative enquiry techniques were also used alongside questioning techniques to guide the culture to more positive curiosity, with warmth and optimism.

The use of positive psychology focusing on the strengths of each partner helped to raise collective energy, improve levels of engagement and fostered collaboration by leveraging strengths rather than continuously criticising everyone's weaknesses. For example, positive psychology guru Martin Seligman[16] and appreciative inquiry expert David Cooperrider[17] were engaged to lead the firm's partner conference to engage clients in positive conversations. Tal Ben Shahar was engaged to teach positive principles including "re-framing" questions.[18]

The organisation is now using their understanding of the insights from the neuroscience of habit to encourage partners to form new behavioural patterns by practising new behaviours in client relationships for 30 days. Their work has led to an appreciable increase in the pipeline of new work.

The neuroscience used

The firm worked with the NeuroPower model developed by Peter Burow[19], drawing on the work of neuroscientist Matt Lieberman[20] and others. The science used included understanding the emotional brain and unconscious patterns of repetitive behaviour, the use of "labelling" to articulate and manage emotions, observation of "faulty thinking" to help individuals identify their own irrational self-talk, as well as positive psychology to direct mindset and energy.

Applying neuroscience to learning design

It was a bit of a surprise to find little evidence of the application of neuroscience in the design, structure and delivery of learning programmes, since our own work has focused a lot in this area. This involves using an understanding of learning and behavioural change "behind the scenes" to ensure learning programmes have the best chance of meeting goals and creating behavioural change.

How organisations are using neuroscience in leadership and learning

"Using neuroscience to back up coaching practice in management development programmes helps sell the idea based on strong evidence of how the brain works."

"Specifically in areas around rational and emotional thinking, logic and decision making where understanding and then applying a blend of both helps to round out how leaders make decisions."

"Starting to talk about what science is saying about the uselessness of multi-tasking is helping employees become more effective. We are also trying to push for more Emotional Intelligence training, but not a lot of support for that yet."

"Understanding leadership, followership and the dynamics of teams."

"We have used neuroscience findings in the content of our leadership programme but we have not designed the programme to maximise learning and behavioural change based on neuroscience. I think this is a mistake and something we need to look at as the next cohorts go through the programme."

Talent and diversity

An area where neuroscience is being used is in educating leaders about bias in decision-making. We were told about examples of this in talent assessment and also in diversity awareness training:

Case study 5: diversity programmes and talent assessment

This global bank introduced a training programme to educate their leaders about the science of bias.

Their workshop used actors to role-play recruitment and talent assessment scenarios in real time, so the participants could experience how the bias plays out, and discuss issues of fairness, their values, and the impact on the business.

The company reports that this has enabled their leaders to have a greater understanding of what is going on and be more reflective about decisions. The programme has also created a language within the business that allows leaders to challenge decisions at talent review meetings, for example questioning why so few women are included in the top talent categories or asking why their top talent only comes from a particular group or career background.

The neuroscience used
Bias in decision-making and responses to in-group/out-group and stereotyping.

Case study 6: gaining buy-in for talent strategy

Our next case study applied the findings from neuroscience to position a new approach to talent strategy in an organisation which had traditionally had difficulties sharing talent across the Group. The Group talent team knew that to meet the business strategy the Group needed to be more consistent in identifying talent, moving talented people to develop them and to persuade senior leaders to be more engaged and open to giving up their talented people for the good of the Group.

The team approached their stakeholder plan to gain buy-in by adopting the principles of threat and reward, the importance of social connection and CORE. This was done "behind the curtain" and informed their positioning of the talent strategy.

They also used an understanding of the brain to balance motivation and incentives with stakeholders. For example, they helped stakeholders understand their own areas of focus verses the needs of the Group as a whole. The team also used the principles of "nudge"[21] to help leaders see the long term results of their behaviour, how a shift might benefit them personally as well as their business and how they could begin to work differently.

Alongside these principles the team used powerful questions, education by visiting successful organisations and discussions with their senior stakeholders.

Once stakeholders had made behavioural commitments, social pressure and reward through recognition, was used to sustain what had been agreed.

This approach was a major shift for a department that had traditionally developed process and then sold in the steps leaders had to take.

The neuroscience used
The neuroscience principles used included understanding the importance of social threat and reward. Setting goals and reinforc-

ing new behaviour through social rewards as well as the CORE model.

Well-being programmes

Neuroscience is also being used in a variety of programmes related to stress management, well-being or "performance enhancement" (titles vary, according to the culture of the organisation):

Case study 7: partner well-being

An international accountancy firm introduced a partner well-being programme centred on cognitive behavioural therapy (CBT) to boost the resilience and health of their partners. The firm was aware that any time spent out of work by any of their 220 partners was costly to the firm because of their responsibility for client contact. From a commercial point of view, if a programme could reduce or prevent one person going off work due to stress or ill-health, the scheme would have paid for itself.

The programme covered a variety of aspects of physical and psychological well-being to help their leaders improve their fitness and nutrition, and identify, understand and prevent stress before it made them ill.

The feedback and employee engagement following a pilot scheme was so positive the organisation introduced a continuous programme to support all the firm's partners' health more proactively. They were initially invited to go on a two-day course examining how lifestyle, food, drink, exercise and attitudes can impact on health, behaviour and resilience. The scheme now offers longer one-to-one sessions, and a CBT-orientated health and well-being assessment has been incorporated into annual medical reviews. There is also an introductory course for new partners.

The organisation found that participants often had an intellectual understanding of stress and well-being, but they needed motivational techniques to help them make changes and overcome the gap between understanding and taking action.

The firm reports that the programme has improved commitment to the job and reduced presenteeism (partners coming to work not operating at their full potential). The programme helps them do their job better and makes sure they can perform at their optimum for the majority of the time. It has also enabled partners to spot where their colleagues may be under pressure and to be more supportive.

The neuroscience used

An understanding of brain based and bodily reactions to stress was used to give people the tools and behavioural strategies.

Neuroscience and performance management

Thirteen per cent of our respondents who were applying neuroscience were doing so in performance management, and said they were applying their understanding "quite a lot." Most of their usage would be described as "behind the curtain" - they were using their understanding from neuroscience but not explicitly describing that to the business.

One example was the HRD of a global engineering company who used her understanding of threat and reward in the brain to analyse why a new performance management process had been poorly received by the business. Her evaluation led her to redesign elements of the process to give greater autonomy and certainty, and to create more fairness in the process.

Case study 8: performance management

As part of a larger change programme, this firm redesigned their performance management process to reflect the culture they aspired to. They used neuroscience explicitly in two ways.

Firstly, they designed the whole process to reduce threat and maximise reward. Attention was focused on the communications, the language used around ratings and the performance conversation. The aim was to make the collection of feedback the responsibility of the employee rather than the boss, building in self-assessment and making the conversation two-way, giving more control and autonomy. The sequence of the performance conversation was also designed to minimise threat, beginning with a discussion on career and goals, and moving on through a joint assessment and allocation of rating.

Work was done to create a "growth mindset,"[22] applying the work of Carol Dweck. The culture of the firm had been markedly "fixed mindset:" smart people were hired and progressed through a number of milestones that proved their capability. The new business model meant the firm needed to recognise that while they might hire very smart people, a changing market and the different career paths open to employees required they adopt more of a growth mindset which would serve the firm and individual employees better in the long-term.

The performance management process and particularly the language used was growth-mindset oriented: ratings and feedback were described in terms of challenges and risks taken, and credit was given for effort. Goals were drafted by the employees and agreed by a performance coach, with longer-term career advice and sponsorship being provided by a senior manager.

The neuroscience used

Carol Dweck's mindset research is not strictly neuroscience although she has used fMRI scans to understand what is happening in the brain when people are asked about their attitude to learning. Her work provides a well-researched evidence base that was particularly useful in describing the shift in beliefs and culture the firm needed to help the change be successful. The science of threat and reward, and habit-formation was also used.

Application to the HR team

There was also interesting evidence of HR departments using neuroscience as they worked together as a team. One client we have worked with used the CORE model to help people to identify the triggers for threat, to describe their behaviour when threatened, and to share these insights with team members. The team then formed an agreement for how to avoid triggers and to support colleagues when they displayed signs of threat-induced behaviour.

Another example was an HR team who used the SCARF model to debrief meetings, based on triggers of threat and reward. Both examples created a neutral context for discussing potentially emotive events, and also helped people bring unconscious triggers to conscious awareness where they could rationally deal with the resulting behaviour.

What are the results?

We asked people what results they were getting using neuroscience. By far the biggest response was "it's too early to tell." But there are excellent examples in the case studies of organisations that are beginning to see measurable results.

From our interviews it is clear that no matter how insightful the findings may be for leaders and business-people, practical tools are essential to turn insight into new behaviour. One comment we heard repeatedly is that too often consultants are providing moments of insight but have little to follow up with in terms of practical tools. The biggest impact was made where practical tools were available. For example, leaders found an understanding of the importance of managing emotions in decision-making insightful, and accepted the brain research far more readily than theories like EI, but without the tools to monitor emotions and bias, the impact quickly dissipated.

Overall people reported that business leaders were open to the neuroscience, found it insightful and were more willing to accept the need for changing personal behaviour when the rationale was backed by science:

But as one research participant said:

"HR needs to change their own thinking and to practice the

application of the insights. And this takes effort!"

Views on neuroscience

"Giving leaders more insight into the science of relationships – how they and others perform – is the only way to improve leadership success."

"Senior leaders need to know the science behind the 'fairy dust' that HR sprinkles. If we don't describe *why* things like talent management are important to the business, it is intangible and we fail to get buy-in."

"Leaders are interested in the neuroscience because other explanations don't help them to get people engaged."

"Leaders in engineering like the science. They are looking for evidence on how to deal with 'people issues'."

"Neuroscience gives credibility to what HR does. It gives the power to demonstrate the *why* for leaders."

"Neuroscience has the potential to make the right arguments to sceptical managers."

3   Leading purpose

A clear sense of purpose is essential for success in HR. How neuroscience can help you develop the skills, insight and creativity to create a guiding sense of direction for the HR function within your organisation.

"Why are we doing this?"

Having a clear purpose and direction

You may have seen (along with 13 million other people) Simon Sinek's 2010 TED Talk. And although it's billed as being about leadership, and he talks about the Wright Brothers, Martin Luther King and the Apple Corporation, it's really about how to position messages. His premise is that great companies and leaders talk about *why* they're doing something,[23] not *what* they're doing.

He calls this the golden circle. Understanding why, and being able to explain the purpose of what you're doing, is, we have found, a success factor for the HR leaders we work with.

Simon Sinek's Golden Circle

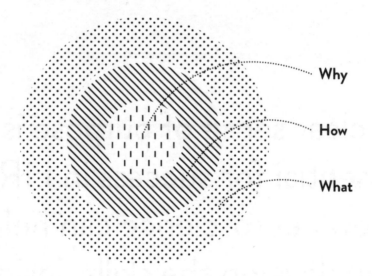

Why

How

What

Sinek's circle has *why* at the centre, *how* next and *what* at its outer edge, and illustrates the way most people and companies communicate their messages.

People tend to start at the outside by telling you *what* they do. In an HR presentation this might sound like:

> "We create a nine-box grid (*what*) by analysing our people and dividing them into nine boxes based on their potential and performance (*how*). This tells us how many high-performers with potential we have (*why*)."

But Sinek's insight is that the most successful companies and leaders talk first about the purpose or *why*.

This is because people don't buy *what* you do but *why* you do it. "Why" questions hook people in: we all like to understand the reasons for any initiative. *Why* creates a sense of purpose. People can more easily relate to *why* and apply it to how they see themselves. Sinek claims this is a result of how the brain is structured – and recent discoveries in neuroscience support this idea.

Why do we respond to "why?"

The brain can be thought of as having three major components, which correlate with the golden circle. The outer layer is the prefrontal cortex, responsible for rational thinking. The "what?"

The middle two sections make up the limbic brain which is responsible for feelings like trust and loyalty. It is also responsible for our feelings, all behaviour and major parts of decision-making. This is the area that drives people to act.

Neurological studies of decision-making are now showing this is not a rational logical process but an emotional one. And questions of "why?" speak to our emotions. If you talk about *why* you believe in your initiative you will attract those with similar beliefs. This is what makes people committed to an initiative, and passionate about it.

Matt Lieberman at UCLA has researched the role of mirror neurons[24] versus the role of the area of the brain known as the default system; this is also called adopting a Theory of Mind, or mentalizing.

This area of the brain is called the default system because we automatically default to thinking about ourselves when we are not doing a cognitive task. It largely overlaps with the areas activated when we're considering other people's actions, such as when we put ourselves in another person's shoes to understand them.

Essentially the brain has two systems for understanding other people: the default system, and mirror neurons. Current knowledge suggests mirror neurons are active when we perform goal-directed actions, and when we see someone else performing such actions. Lieberman's research looked at whether there are differences in how the two brain systems react when we see and think about the actions of other people.[25]

Which parts of the brain react to "what, how, why"?

A senior leader putting forward a plan for introducing sustainability within their organisation might structure their presentation by talking about:

> **What:** drawing-up and talking about the plan
> **How:** recycling bottles, paper and other consumables
> **Why:** to improve the environment

Lieberman's experiment aimed to understand if there are different brain regions involved when we're considering these three different types of questions.

What he found was that in order to understand "what," mirror neurons on the *right* side of the brain are active. Lieberman believes this adds the ability to "see" actions rather than just movement.

Understanding "how" activated the mirror neuron system in the *left* side of the brain.

Questions of "why?" were found to engage the default area of the brain. So, understanding motivation was the only part of the process which engaged the part of the brain which thinks about ourselves as well as other people.

This simple but fundamental understanding of the thinking process has huge implications for HR professionals: explain *why* you want to introduce a new initiative, to get people engaged and committed, before you get into the details of execution.

And the prospect of storytelling makes us pay attention...

In separate research we cover in detail in our chapter in *Leading the function* on the neuro-power of stories, Lieberman also found that the default system is activated when people hear information that they're going to relay to other people[26]. And the degree of activation indicated how likely the person was to pass on the information.

So, addressing upfront questions such as "Will Lisa be interested in this policy?" or "How will this impact my team's performance?" helps to prime people to think about your message and how it will impact others. This makes it much more likely they will pass on your purpose.

These issues wouldn't be so problematic if we could engage all our brain processes at the same time. But as we explore in our chapter on self-control in *Leading yourself*, some of them compete with each other. When the "we-thinking" default regions of the brain are active, the cognitive, analytical regions switch off – and vice versa.

Our activity-focused, goal-oriented mirror neurons seem to perform quite robustly with some additional cognitive load, but the default system doesn't. What this tells us is that it takes effort, focus and concentration to understand other people's motivation and why something is important; it's not an easy process.

Leaders who spend a lot of time in rational, cognitive thinking – assessing information, weighing up alternative strategies – may be out of the habit of noticing the information their default system is sending in. We all know senior people who just don't seem to tune in to personal issues, and who make little effort to understand themselves or others.

Neuroscience research implies that if you want those leaders, or anyone else, to engage with your purpose, you need to do some work explaining not just *what* and *how* but *why*.

What would you be saying if you were describing your purpose in terms of *why* it's important to the company? How would it be different to the way you talk about it now? Obviously each company's *why* is different, but what makes this new proposal central to your organisation's work?

"Where should I be focusing my attention?"

Choosing where your attention should be

If your home is like mine, you might be hearing the pumping of the water in the central heating, the low hum of traffic outside, and the clatter of bedsprings as a teenager finally gets out of bed.

What I was doing by asking you what you were hearing was prompting your brain to take control and draw your attention to sounds. That is what happens when an event jumps out of the background enough to be perceived consciously, rather than just being part of your auditory surroundings. Your attention is focused.

How does attention work?

Attention is not one brain process.[27] Recent research in neuroscience shows that we focus in many ways, for different purposes, drawing on different neural pathways – some of which work together, while others tend to compete.

The sudden loud noise that makes you jump activates the simplest type of paying-attention: the startle reflex. A chain of neurons from your ears to your spine activates the fear response in a tenth of a second – increasing your heart rate, hunching your shoulders and making you cast around to see if whatever you heard is a threat. This reflex requires almost no brain power and has been observed in all animals.

Top-down and bottom-up attention

A more complex type of attention happens when you hear your name called across a room. This stimulus-directed attention is controlled by pathways through the temporoparietal and inferior frontal cortex regions, mostly in the right hemisphere – areas that process raw, sensory input, but don't concern themselves with what you should make of that sound. Neuroscientists call this a "bottom-up" response.

When you consciously "pay attention" to something – listening to your favourite song, or the CEO's speech about his views on the HR function – a separate "top-down" pathway activates. Here, the signals are conveyed through a dorsal pathway in your cortex: the part of the brain that does more complex processing, which lets you actively focus on what you are hearing and tune out sights and sounds that are not immediately important.

When it attends in this way your brain works like a set of noise-suppressing headphones, with the bottom-up pathways acting as a switch, ready to interrupt if something more urgent needs to capture your attention.

How is this relevant to HR?

When we work with HR teams one of the areas we investigate is where their attention is.

Few people and organisations seem to consider the importance of this, or the implications of their attention on their effectiveness.

HR functions are familiar with setting priorities, and focusing on initiatives in a planned way. But they may not be aware of where they are giving attention, especially in the day-to-day choices they make.

Broadly, there are three areas where your attention may be, and they represent different ways of looking at your role and the role of the HR function, its relationship with its clients and hence its performance.

Where individuals in HR and ultimately the whole HR function place their attention makes a difference. To focus attention requires awareness, discipline and an understanding of the distractions that will draw attention.

When working with HR functions we ask them to consider their areas of attention on a three-point model: Self, Other and Context. Categorising attention in this way sheds light on skills and consequences for HR effectiveness. It helps them to understand where their attention is, the implications of that attention and what is missed because of it.

Paying attention to yourself

Self-knowledge covers a number of areas.

First is understanding your own perspective on issues, goals and initiatives. Many people take little time to understand what they think, or more importantly what they feel, about the business and the HR agenda.

Second is getting in touch with your own inner voice. Professionals who can do this can draw on more resources to make better decisions.

Hearing your inner voice means paying attention to internal physiological signals. These signals are monitored by the insula, which is behind the frontal lobes of the brain.

Attention given to any part of the body increases the insula's sensitivity to that part. Tune in to your heartbeat, and the insula activates more neurons in that circuitry. How well people can sense their heartbeats is a way of measuring their self-awareness.[28]

We cover in some detail the neuroscience in our chapter *"Gut feeling: Is it a useful guide in business?"* Briefly, they are signals from the insula and the amygdala[29] with the help of the vagus nerve which create what neuroscientist Antonio Damasio calls *somatic markers*. These markers create a feeling that something is right or wrong. You'll recognise it as a piece of information that doesn't seem to fit, or a manager's opinion that troubles you, or a decision you feel uncomfortable with.

Somatic markers simplify decision-making by guiding your attention toward better options. They are based on tapping into historic memories, experience and patterns so they may not be correct, but they are an invaluable signal to check more carefully.

Consider, for example, the implications of interviews carried out by Cambridge neuroscientist John Coates with traders[30] at an investment bank. The most successful traders were neither the ones who relied entirely on analytics nor the ones who just went with their gut feelings. They focused their attention on a full range of information, feelings and data, which they used to refine their decisions.

When they suffered losses, they acknowledged their anxiety, became more cautious, and took fewer risks. The least successful traders tended to ignore their anxiety and kept going with their trading strategy. Because they did not pay attention to internal signals, they were misled.

The equivalent in HR would be to pursue the disciplinary case and ignore your gut feeling that the investigation lacked all the data. Or to continue to run the new leadership programme when your gut feeling was in favour of it, despite the fact that the participant feedback was poor.

Social control

"Social control" is the term for putting your attention where you want it and keeping it there when other issues arise.

This focus is one aspect of the brain's executive functions, located in the prefrontal cortex. It's often referred to as "willpower." We've covered control in more detail in our chapter on self-control in the *Leading yourself* section.

Social control keeps you and the HR function on track with your goals, despite distractions and setbacks. The same neural circuitry also manages emotions: people who have strong social control stay calm in a crisis, manage their emotions, and recover from a setback quickly.

The power of willpower

Reams of research points to the performance benefits of willpower or social control. Some of the most convincing data comes from a longitudinal study tracking 1,037 children[31] born during a single year in the 1970s in the New Zealand city of Dunedin.

For several years the children were given a number of tests on social control, including the famous "marshmallow test," where children were offered the choice of eating one marshmallow right away or getting two if they managed to wait 15 minutes.

In the original experiment[32] conducted in the 1960s by Walter Mischel, roughly a third of children immediately ate the marshmallow, another third waited but ate it before the full 15 minutes were up, and a third managed to hold out to gain the reward of the second marshmallow.

Years later, when the children were followed up, those who had exhibited the control to wait and resisted the temptation of the marshmallow were significantly healthier and more successful financially. Analysis showed that a child's level of self-control was a more powerful predictor of life success than IQ, social class, or family circumstance.

How we focus holds the key to exercising willpower, Mischel says. Three types of control are at play when you practice social control: the ability to resist desire; the ability to resist distraction so that you don't return to the desired object; and the ability to concentrate on the future goal and imagine how good you will feel when you achieve it.

Mischel maintains that the techniques he observed the children using in his original study can be successfully taught. This is one of the skills HR professionals can develop.

Paying attention to others

The word "attention" means "to reach toward" in Latin. This is a good definition of what successful professionals do. They can adopt the perspective of others: put themselves in other people's shoes, either cognitively by taking their perspective, or empathetically by actually experiencing how others feel.

HR people who can shift their attention to others can find common ground, their opinions carry weight, and their colleagues and clients want to work with them. They emerge as natural leaders regardless of the organisational level they hold.

Perspective-taking or *cognitive empathy* helps you to explain policy or practice in ways that are meaningful to the other person – a skill essential to being influential.

Having curiosity is important here. You also need to develop a high level of awareness of your own point of view so that you're not pushed off-centre by other people's arguments but can weigh them against your knowledge and the business goals.

The brain systems that allow you to think about yourself and to understand your feelings are the same as those that enable you to understand other people and which enable you to choose to direct your attention that way.

Tania Singer, at Leipzig's Max Planck Institute for Human Cognitive and Brain Sciences, says we need to understand our own feelings in order to understand the feelings of others.[33]

Using empathy and perspective

We cover in greater detail the differences between empathy and perspective-taking in the chapter *"Empathy is the answer... or is it?"*

Empathy is activated from older parts of the brain beneath the cortex that allow us to experience feelings quickly. These areas of the brain arouse the same emotional states in you as others are experiencing.

Accessing your capacity for emotional empathy depends on combining two kinds of attention: a deliberate focus on your own body signals, and an open awareness of the other person's face, voice, and other external signs of emotion.

These are all important skills for effective mentoring, managing clients, and being able to read group dynamics.

Paying attention to context

Giving attention to social context lets us act with skill in any situation. It helps you to follow social norms, interpret culture, and behave in ways that put others at ease. Brain circuitry that converges on the anterior hippocampus reads social context and leads you intuitively to act differently with, for example, your family compared with your team or your CEO.

In conjunction with the prefrontal cortex, this area controls the impulse to do something inappropriate. Neuroscientist Richard Davidson hypothesises that people who are most alert to social situations exhibit stronger activity[34] and more connections between the hippocampus and the prefrontal cortex than those who find it harder to get it right. With this type of attention you are better able to work in different national cultures because you are alert to subtle differences in expectation and behaviours. This skill also equips you to be a better facilitator and coach.

Activating networking

The same circuits may be at play when we map social networks in a group – a skill that lets you navigate the relationships in those networks well.

People who excel at organisational influence can not only sense the flow of personal connections but can also name the opinion leaders, and so pay attention to persuading those who will in turn persuade others.

Exploitation vs exploration

Whether you're paying attention to what needs to be achieved now, or to what needs to be achieved in the future, activates different parts of your brain.

Brain scans of seasoned business decision-makers[35] showed the specific circuits involved as they pursued or switched between thinking about current strategy versus thinking about new strategy.

Not surprisingly, exploitation (implementing strategy initiatives) requires concentration on the job at hand, whereas exploration, (thinking up the next strategy or a new product) demands open awareness to recognise new possibilities.

Exploitation is accompanied by activity in the brain's circuitry for anticipation and reward, which suggests it feels good to be on familiar ground.

When we switch to exploration, we have to make a deliberate cognitive effort to disengage from that familiar routine. The brain will experience discomfort, and even pain, which means you may find yourself avoiding this type of attention.

This is more difficult if you are lacking sleep, you're stressed, or are mentally overloaded. To sustain the outward focus that leads to innovation and new ways of working, you need some uninterrupted time to reflect and refresh your focus.

Attention and performance

The link between attention and performance is hidden most of the time. Yet attention is the basis of the most essential professional skills – personal, relational and organisational.

Attention forms habits; we pay attention only to the client or only to context. Our habits can make us more or less effective, and the volume of data we're dealing with in our daily jobs, or the brain is processing, leaves too little time to reflect on what is really important. The best HR professionals adopt skilful attention, so that they can direct their attention where it's needed when it's needed.

"Empathy is the answer... or is it?"

Empathy and perspective, which you need when

In his book *Give and Take* Adam Grant tells a story[36] of two friends who built a successful company together. After some time it was apparent one of them was giving less energy and focus to the business whilst still taking a salary and all his other perks. His business partner felt the inequity of the situation, but felt unable to challenge his partner, not least because of the close bond the two men had built whilst creating the company.

In effect, he was a victim of his own empathy. Only after stepping back and taking a more intellectual view was he able to see that his partner preferred starting a business to running it.

An essential "soft" skill

Empathy has a mixed reputation in business. Often valued by HR and fans of emotional intelligence, many leaders are somewhat uneasy about it, seeing it as one of the dreaded "soft" skills.

Soft skills are often seen as optional or expendable and to date it has been hard for HR to explain why they are important; neuroscience is beginning to help here. Empathy is far from "soft." It enables you to form deep relationships, influence and engage.

Studies by neurologist Antonio Damasio in his book *Descartes' Error: Emotion, Reason, and the Human Brain* showed that people with damage to the brain areas associated with empathy[37] had difficulties in forming and maintaining relationships, even though their reasoning and learning abilities remained intact.

What is empathy?

Empathy is usually defined as the emotional understanding of another person, and it enables crucial insights into their thoughts and feelings. We all feel empathy at some time; maybe at work it's most obvious with a friend or colleague with whom you have a shared experience, like working on a tough project, or designing a new initiative.

Empathy is activated from older parts of the brain beneath the cortex – the amygdala, the hypothalamus, the hippocampus and the orbitofrontal cortex – that allow us to experience feelings quickly. These areas of the brain arouse the same emotional states in you as others are experiencing. Your brain patterns match up with your client's or your colleague's: literally, "I feel your pain."

The benefits of empathy

People who can deeply understand how others are feeling create an emotional connection which in turn makes them more persuasive, and better able to make decisions that impact others and to gain their trust. People who tend to find it difficult to be empathetic are often seen as cold and unfeeling, and may underestimate the impact of their decisions on others.

Empathy can be focused on different aspects; being empathetic about either outcomes (the project failed for unusual reasons), or intention (the person wanted to achieve the right outcome but was distracted by a competing goal). Interaction with others hones these skills in a way that sitting in the corner office will never achieve.

When empathy is unhelpful

But getting completely absorbed in a staff member's situation will make it hard to help them – just as the businessman was unable to address the issues with his partner while he was identifying so closely with him as a friend who had gone through the trials of a start-up with him.

For example, being overly empathetic when a team member is stuck dealing with a difficult customer may keep you stuck in the same situation, whereas a wider perspective might help you to see alternative ways of improving the customer relationship.

And it should hardly be a surprise to learn that empathy may be less helpful in situations such as wage or union negotiations. Business academic Adam Galinsky has found that in negotiations those who were empathetic ended up with worse deals[38] than those with a more detached perspective.

The benefits of perspective

Perspective-taking or *cognitive empathy* enables you to understand how someone else understands the problem, situation or issue. This is the classic "putting yourself in someone else's shoes" and means that you see their point of view rather than feel their emotions. Perspective-taking enables you to explain policy or practice in ways that are meaningful to the other person, a skill that's essential to getting the best performance from your team, and engaging clients.

It appears that different perspectives activate different brain regions. The ability to reason about another's mind, as opposed to feeling what they're feeling, shows a shift from frontal to posterior brain regions and from bilateral to unilateral left inferior parietal. So from a biological point of view emotional empathy and cognitive empathy are activating different brain regions.

In Galinsky's study, the ability to take a perspective of what the other person maybe experiencing resulted in an increased ability to discover hidden agreements,[39] and to use them to make a better deal. For example, understanding that the union has to go back with some wins but not the whole deal they were asking for.

Can we learn empathy and perspective taking?

Research conducted with doctors by Helen Riess, at Boston's Massachusetts General Hospital, suggests that empathy can be learned.[40]

To help doctors perform mindfully by monitoring themselves, her programme taught participants to focus using deep breathing and to cultivate a detachment – to watch an interaction from the ceiling, as it were, rather than being lost in their own thoughts and feelings.

"Suspending your own involvement to observe what's going on gives you a mindful awareness of the interaction without being completely reactive, you can see if your own physiology is charged up or balanced. You can notice what's transpiring in the situation," says Reiss.

Doctors were taught to notice if they were feeling irritated, for instance, and that it might be a signal that the patient was bothered too. These are similar skills to those needed by HR professionals when dealing with clients, or facilitating and coaching.

Riess believes that *acting* as if you are empathic can build the ability to become better at it.

If you act in a caring way – looking people in the eye and paying attention to their expressions, even when you don't particularly want to – you may start to feel more engaged. It's an idea that's supported by Harvard research where Amy Cuddy has found that putting yourself physically into a state can generate changes[41] in hormone levels consistent with that adopted state.

The right response for your culture

Different organisational cultures will be more attuned to either empathy or perspective-taking. This means having the skills that match the culture, empathetic or perspective-taking, may be important to success. For example being empathetic in a culture that values perspective-taking may lead to criticism of being "soft."

The important question is really which skill-set is more appropriate in any given situation. Having empathy when you need to sack a staff member for gross misconduct may not serve you well, whereas being able to understand another's feelings when presenting a change could be highly effective.

Perspective-taking can be extremely useful when planning for difficult conversations, or when it's essential to influence someone else.

So the real skill is to hone both your empathy and perspective-taking and to know which is appropriate in any given situation.

"What's the truth about being creative?"

4 myths about creativity, and how it actually works

> *"Think left and think right and think low and think high.*
> *Oh, the thinks you can think up if only you try!"*
> **Dr. Seuss, Oh, the Thinks You Can Think!**

Creativity is frequently touted as the solution to all our problems.

What to do with an unmotivated employee? Get creative! Want to make your job more interesting? Get creative! How to implement the CEO's budget cuts? Get creative! Want to solve world hunger? Get creative!

But for such a highly-valued talent there are a surprising number of myths. Let's start by dispelling some of the most pervasive.

Myth 1: you have to be a genius to be creative

The myth is you have to be like Einstein, Da Vinci or John Lennon... But everyone has creative ability. If you just keep a record, you'll see that you have creative ideas and insights all the time. The difference is often taking action on your ideas, rather than just generating the idea itself.

Myth 2: it helps if you're mad

Van Gogh, Virginia Wolfe... there are so many films about creative geniuses teetering on the brink of insanity (pianist David Helfgott in *Shine*, Nobel prize-winning economist John Nash in *A Beautiful Mind*) it's easy to assume a causal link. But none of these highly creative people did their best work in the throes of mental illness.

Myth 3: creatives are born, not made

In 2008 psychologist and author Robert Epstein published the results of a study which demonstrated that people can indeed enhance their ability to solve problems creatively, by developing four core competencies:[42] capturing new ideas; engaging in challenging tasks; broadening knowledge; and interacting with stimulating people and places.

Seventy-four business people who participated in his creativity training focused on these four areas were monitored and the application of the ideas measured. Epstein found that the rate of new idea generation increased by 55%, brought in more than $600,000 in new revenue, and saved about $3.5 million through innovative cost reductions.

Myth 4: right-brained people are more creative

This is probably the best-known of all the creativity myths, based on the 1960s left/right brain research by Roger Sperry and Michael Gazzaniga.

The myth attached to their findings is that "right-brained" people are more creative, while "left-brained" people are more analytical and logical. These two types are said to be the result of one half of the brain being more active than the other.

Forty years later, researchers have examined the fMRI (*functional magnetic resonance imaging*) scans of over 1,000 people[43] and have not found patterns where the whole left-brain network is more active in some people, or the whole right-brain network is more active in other people.

This most recent research does not contradict the idea that some of the brain's functions are biased towards the left or right side. For example, the left-hand side of the brain is indeed more engaged in language processing (in right-handed people), and the right-hand side of the brain is more involved in attention. But it does discredit the idea that there are distinct personalities based on a dominance of one side of the brain or the other.

So, what is creativity?

What does being creative involve, and can we train ourselves to be better at it?

"Creativity is the production of something both novel and useful,"[44] according to neuropsychologist, Rex Jung.

What happens when we're being creative?

What happens in our brain during the creative process is a question that's preoccupying a number of researchers. It appears that creativity takes place in several stages and calls on different parts of our brain according to the stage in the process and what we're trying to solve or create. And many of the brain regions work together but some work against each other at some stages of the process.

Cognitive psychologist Scott Barry Kaufman has identified the main brain areas which are important at different stages of the creative process:[45]

1   Understanding the problem

If you want to really understand a subject or a problem (for example, if you're listening to a lecture, your boss's introduction to a meeting, or a description of a breakdown in customer service), you will be using the "attentional control network."

This neural network is activated when you need to put demands on working memory and cut out other signals that might distract you. It facilitates efficient and reliable communication between the lateral (outer) regions of the prefrontal cortex and areas toward the back (posterior) of the parietal lobe.

2   Imagining how people will act

When you're thinking about how you, or other people, might *solve* the problem or could react to a potential solution, you'll be using the "imagination network." It's often referred to as the default network, and its role in understanding ourselves and other people is covered in a number of places throughout this book.

This network helps you imagine how an exercise might work in a leadership programme, or how employees might respond to the way a communication is worded. The imagination network is deep inside the prefrontal cortex and temporal lobe in the medial regions and communicates with various outer and inner regions of the parietal cortex.

3   Allocating brain resources

One of the features of creativity is an ability to let go of focused attention and relax, this it seems allows the brain to make new connections. We have talked more about this in the chapter on *Insight*.

To ensure the most helpful parts of the brain are recruited to solve your problem the "salience network"[46] monitors both external events and the internal stream of consciousness, and flexibly passes work to the most appropriate area. This network consists of the dorsal anterior cingulate cortices and the anterior insular, and is important for switching between the attentional control and imagination networks. The networks work with each other, but sometimes this cooperation can impede the creative process, if, for example, the attentional control network is too focused.

How can we enhance creativity?

A recent review provides a "first approximation" about how creativity maps on to the human brain.[47]

The advice that emerges is that you have to loosen your inhibitions and allow your mind to roam and make new connections. Then avoid your "inner critic." And reduce activation of the network which controls your thinking, and increase activation of the imagination and attentional flexibility networks.

One way of doing this is to relax and let your mind wander, or better still put the problem on the "back burner" and go for a walk, do some exercise or something else absorbing, and let your brain mull over the problem unconsciously. Then be on the lookout for the solution popping into your mind.

Understanding the different aspects of creativity can help you manage your creative tasks more effectively and help you to think about how you use your brain to best effect. You can find out how to have more creative ideas in the *Leading yourself* section.

"Gut feeling: is it a useful guide in business?"

What is it and is it reliable

> *"Never ignore a gut feeling, but never believe that it's enough."*
>
> **Robert Heller**

Much has been written on the subject of intuition. And a lot of it focuses on whether it's reliable, with many stories of how gut feeling has pointed the way to the solutions for important issues.

But what's the science of gut feeling? Does it exist, and is it reliable?

Most economic and business theories have been based on the assumption that decisions are made logically and rationally. From this also stemmed a number of decision-making theories and tools to help business people make the best decisions. These mainly involved taking rational steps to achieve a decision.

But until recently economics and business theory have not looked at the influence of the body on business decision-making.

Are our decisions always conscious and rational?

In the west we have inherited a culture dominated by the Cartesian dualism a mind-body split. And humans' core competence and distinguishing skill is rational thought, according to Plato. But conscious choice is being shown to have very limited capability in decision-making, and rational choice plays a very small and often weak role.

Studying the effects of behaviour on economics,[48] Kahneman and Tversky showed in the 1970s that economics is not a function of "Rational Man" making rational decisions, but rather that our minds affect our business decisions – in fact, all our decisions – in ways we are unaware of. (Kahneman won a Nobel Prize based on their work in 2002.)

Neuroscientist John Coates has taken this thinking a step further and shown the impact that our body can have on our thinking[49] and decision making.

How does this work?

Consider Andy Murray returning a tennis serve. The ball is moving too fast for him to work out rationally where to position himself and whether to take it on the backhand or the forehand.

His reaction happens in fractions of a second – his *body* does the thinking before his conscious mind can catch up.

This is similar to the speed at which some business decisions have to be made: there isn't always time for thorough analysis and research. Well-known investors such as George Soros admit to being guided, in part, by physiological responses. Soros reports that he used the onset of acute back pain as a signal that there was something wrong with his portfolio.

The notion of "gut feeling" implies that even in the most complex mental tasks – conducting union negotiations, for example – our body can give us guidance. But knowing when to follow that guidance and when to ignore it is not a simple matter. Here's where knowledge and experience come into play.

Making decisions with your body

The body evolved over centuries to respond to risks: is that a sabre-toothed tiger lurking in the forest? Business risk carries a similar threat – not to life, but nonetheless a significant risk to social reputation, certainty and choices, as we have described in *"Brain basics."*

Our bodily reaction is telling us more than we consciously know. As physical animals we have had to marshal the fuel needed for our muscles. So every thought we think comes freighted with physiological implications and triggers subtle shifts in breathing, metabolism, blood pressure, sweating and hormone levels.

The changes taking place in our body as we contemplate a decision, especially a decision we see as a risk, feed back to our brain, altering our thoughts. This unifies body and brain at a time when it's crucial that they co-operate seamlessly on the task at hand.

What this tells us is that we do not regard information dispassionately: we react to it physically. Sorry Plato, Descartes and all you rational-economists: there is no disembodied thought.

The wandering nerve

Central to this mind-body coordination is the vagus nerve. Vagus means "wandering" in Latin: it is a nerve rooted in the cerebellum and the brainstem, and multiple branches extending all the way to the lowest parts of your digestive system: approximately nine metres of it in all, touching most of your major organs along the way. Because much of the nerve is in the human trunk and we experience the feelings in this region, we've come to refer to these signals as "gut reactions."

The human vagus nerve system has an estimated 500 million

neurons[50] – about five times as many as there are in the brain of a rat. It's so complex it has been called our second brain.[51] And most of the "traffic" in this nervous system is sending sensory information about the state of our body's organs "upstream" to our brains. Eighty to ninety per cent of the nerve fibres are dedicated to communicating to the brain.

So when people say "trust your gut" they're really saying "trust your vagus nerve which connects your gut to your brain." Visceral feelings are literally emotional signals transferred up to the brain along this highway.

Messages also travel downstream from the conscious mind through the vagus nerve: directing organs to create an inner calm and "rest-and-digest" during times of safety, or to prepare the body for "fight-or-flight" in times of threat. So if you find it hard to eat your lunchtime sandwich before a crucial meeting, that's your vagus nerve at work.

The vagus nerve system governs how you respond to pressure and how you recover from it, revving you up or slowing you down depending on signals from your environment.

Unfortunately, the effect of the vagus nerve's response in arousing you for an important event ("danger!") can be to make you feel intimidated or insecure. Not helpful before an important meeting.

Gut feeling and different kinds of decisions

These signals from body to the brain (and back again) rarely register on our conscious awareness. So what evidence is there that they actually have an effect on our decision-making?

A number of scientists from different disciplines have studied conscious and unconscious decision-making. Kahneman has called them fast and slow decisions:[52] fast decisions being intuitive gut decisions, slow decisions being taken rationally, step-by-step.

A useful study summarising the link between body signals and decision-making[53] has labelled the two types of brain processing as automatic and controlled. An automatic decision is involuntary, effortless, happening in parallel with other steps and usually isn't open to introspection. Afterwards you find it hard to say how you reached that conclusion.

Controlled decision-making is voluntary: you decide to make that decision; it takes some effort and proceeds one step at a time. It's a process that is largely open to introspection: we can explain how we came to that decision.

Making good decisions... but we don't know why

Most of our thinking is automatic,[54] or fast in Kahneman's term.

For example, in one experiment people were asked to predict where a cross would appear on a computer screen. There was logic to the pattern, but it was so complex the participants were unable to work it out consciously. Despite this, they got better at predicting where the cross would appear. They weren't able to explain how they did this: they were learning the rule pre-consciously.

Much of our processing of information is similar to this – it takes place below the surface. When you *know* the compensation data is wrong, or a manager's rating of talent is over-egged, you are accessing pre-conscious information.

Can I learn to develop gut feeling?

Contrary to popular myth, intuition is a skill that can be developed.[55] And part of our understanding of how this works arose out of a dispute between Daniel Kahneman and Gary Klein, a researcher of naturalistic decision-making.

Kahneman doubted intuition was real but Klein supported it. In discussing their different viewpoints it became clear that a significant issue was the different types of people they were studying.

Klein studies the way experts make decisions, based on their deep knowledge built up over years: a fire-fighter who knows how to tackle a particular type of fire, or a nurse sensing a baby is unwell before symptoms are apparent. Kahneman worked with social scientists, political forecasters and stock-pickers: subjects whose predictions were often no more accurate than chance.

Both came to agree that the essence of intuition is recognising patterns: it's the brain's natural method of predicting. When we develop an expertise we are better able to see the pattern.

Given this, they decided intuition can be relied on if two conditions are met. People need to have deep expertise, and they must work in an environment that is predictable enough to produce patterns. "Intuition needs stable regularities in the environment," says Kahneman.

Our bodies do the data-tagging

Once expertise has been developed it's our body that alerts us to pre-conscious decision patterns. As we discuss in the following chapter on decisions, emotional tags, or markers the brain attaches to data,[56] allow us to sift through it and decide what is meaningful and what's not. Emotions allow us to filter the vast amount of data our brains take in all the time.

The scientists who developed this theory of emotional tagging argue that rationality does not help us without these emotional markers.[57] They believe that good judgement requires us to be able to listen carefully to signals from our body. The brain affects the body, but the body also affects the brain. When we're hungry or thirsty our thoughts change and we become more focused on these physical needs. But this is also a two-way process.

For example: you're feeling depressed and low, but for the sake of appearances you put a smile on your face, stand up straight and walk purposefully. These physical changes send signals to your brain and your mental state actually changes to a happier one.

Changes like this can be upward, or downward. Fear can be a self-perpetuating cycle: you're fearful, your heart rate increases, your breathing changes and you start to sweat – and all these changes increase your sense of threat. Psychologist William James described this as far back as 1884: "Everyone knows how panic is increased by flight",[58] he wrote.

Fast and efficient decisions

So, emotion does not make us move, but the movement does create emotion.

This may seem counter-intuitive, but it makes sense in survival terms. We need to *move* to survive, rather than sit and analyse how we feel. So when the brain wants to send a fast response it uses electrical signals rather than slower-moving chemicals in the blood.

Gut feelings economise on limited resources to direct our decisions pre-consciously, steering us away from potentially dangerous options.

Unconscious learning

Damasio and Bechara, the researchers of emotional tagging, tested this with a gambling game in which the cards were stacked. Two decks of cards yielded low immediate rewards but choosing them over time maximised total winnings. The other two decks had higher cards but were more risky.

Players did not know which decks were the most profitable but their pre-conscious quickly picked up the patterns[59] and they began to avoid playing the risky decks before they could consciously say why. This learning was signalled by their bodies through a sweat reaction which could be measured in the electrical conductivity of their skin. A spike in sweating "told" them to stay away from the risky decks.

Your body can know more than your brain

Our body and the pre-conscious regions of our brain are highly attuned to threat and reward. The trick is to learn to listen to them rather than our conscious brains, which have only a tenuous hold on such messages from our physical body.

For example, it's been shown that patients with severe brain damage[60] which meant that the two sides of their brains were unable to communicate effectively, when asked via only one side of the brain to wave their hand, or giggle, "made up" stories to explain why they were doing such things.

In other research, it was found that people frequently trick themselves into thinking they understand the true reasons for their actions[61] when their commentary was actually nonsensical in explaining them. Scientists speculate that one of the main jobs of our conscious brain is to keep our life tied together, so it makes sense to our self-concept.

Is gut reaction reliable?

Similar "story telling" has been identified when traders responded to a questionnaire[62] on their stress levels and trading losses. The traders' hormone samples clearly showed their stress levels and the risks they had perceived, but their written answers did not correlate with their physical reactions. The traders responded that they didn't feel stressed by heavy trading losses, but the researcher concluded that their hormones had a firmer grasp on risk than their prefrontal cortex.

Gut reactions, it turns out, may have a *higher* rate of accuracy[63] in their ability to predict outcomes than the most carefully-laid, "scientific" plans. In his book *Gut Feelings: The Intelligence of the Unconscious*, Gerd Gigerenzer, director of Berlin's Max Planck Institute for Human Development, says a gut reaction can be so accurate because it makes great use of the capacities of the body and brain that were designed in order to help survival.

"Gut feelings are based on simple rules of thumb," says Gigerenzer: "what we psychologists' term 'heuristics.' These take advantage of certain capacities of the brain that have come down to us through time, experience and evolution."

The brain has also evolved to sort through the vast amount of information that comes from experience. This ability to sort fast enables us to find the quickest and most efficient route to a decision, based on a set of pre-conscious data. "This streamlined simplicity," says Gigerenzer," is evolution's way of adapting to uncertainty."

Can I train myself?

The key question is whether we can train ourselves to notice these pre-conscious signals. The evidence is promising.

Several scientists have shown that heartbeat awareness is linked to body sensitivity.[64] In tests, people are asked to time their heartbeat, or to check if their heartbeat is synchronised with a repetitive tone. Those who are able to monitor their heartbeat accurately are also shown to be better at noticing and tuning in to gut reactions.

So when you're making decisions, especially if you're under stress, it's worth getting a second opinion, or doing a check for bias, or tuning in to your gut feeling. Our body seems to provide a very effective early warning system, and all of these may be more reliable than rational analysis.

"Is there a science to making better decisions?"

Logic, emotions, and whether you've had lunch:
the science of decision-making

> *"The whole purpose of places like Starbucks is for people with no decision-making ability whatsoever to make six decisions just to buy one cup of coffee."*
> **Joe Fox in You've Got Mail**

Skinny soya, double shot, no-foam, espresso... Decisions, we make them all the time. And as with habitual decisions, often we don't realise we've been making any kind of choice at all.

But when you're aware that you need to make a decision, maybe an important one, how much do you know about the process you're about to go through, and what might trip you up?

What *is* a good decision?

Economists who study decision-making would define a good decision along the lines of: "the better your decision the more it aligns with what people *should* do if they made optimal choices."

Economists look at decisions as rational choices. For example, one well-known experiment which neuro-economists refer to gave a group of people $20 each, and asked them to bet on the toss of a coin.[65] They are told they can place $1 bets on 20 tosses of a coin (there's nothing tricky about the coin – it's chosen at random). Each losing bet will cost them just their $1 stake, while each winning bet will earn them $2.50. What would you do?

If you were going to bet at all, from a rational, cool-headed perspective you should bet every time, because the amount you can win is higher than the amount you are likely to lose.

Or do we need to make *happy* decisions?

But what about more complex decisions, where each option has pros and cons that cannot be easily quantified and compared? Buying a house: do you buy a small house in a really desirable area, or a larger house close to work but on a noisy road? Changing jobs: do you go for the exciting opportunity with the high-risk start-up where you could really make your mark, or stay with a large organisation that offers structure and certainty? Or deciding which leadership development supplier to use: do you go for the most cost-effective, or the one with the new and interesting approach and great references.

Some people like to list all the factors on a spreadsheet to try and bring some clarity to the process, but there isn't a calculable answer to these types of decisions – even if sometimes we try to act as though there is.

Neuro-economist Baba Shiv says we have to use a different definition: "A good decision is one in which the decision-maker is happy with the decision[66] and will stay committed to it." All the indicators may be pointing towards appointing one leadership development supplier, but how happy are you going to be working with them?

Overlooking the critical factor

If this is beginning to sound like "just stick a figure in the air," keep reading for some science findings that might enlighten your decision process. However this is also where the science of decision-making begins to clash with entrenched business beliefs.

Most business-people – yes, I mean HR people – spend time constructing neat, logical rationales for their decisions, be they the next pay round or the company's diversity policy.

What we tend to miss is the role of emotions. I challenge you: how many of your plans to get the management committee to agree a policy takes into account their emotional state? And how often do you take into account your own emotions when you need to make a decision?

Emotions make the call

Think of a situation where you've had a strong proposal with facts, reason, and logic on your side. You thought there was absolutely no way the person with budget approval could say no to your perfectly constructed argument. To do so would be impossible, you think, because there is no other logical solution.

And then the decision-maker digs in their heels and comes up with a totally illogical alternative. You are completely floored and spend the rest of the day ranting to your colleagues about this irrational individual and feeling thoroughly frustrated.

This is typical of what most HR functions do when they sit down to plan their strategy, or to think about getting buy-in to a policy, or selling any other recommendation they want to get adopted.

Oh, and it's what we nearly always do as individuals, when we want to get our boss or a client to agree a proposal. We go in armed with the facts, and attempt to use logic to persuade them.

Whether consciously or unconsciously, we believe that with enough data and reasonable argument to explain the proposal, we can construct a solution that is simply irrefutable and our stakeholder will agree.

But you're probably not going to get the answer you want, at least not the first time – because according to the latest findings in neuroscience, decision-making isn't logical, it's emotional.

How are emotions involved?

Emotions have a role as mental shortcuts that help us resolve inconsistencies and conflicts, and commit to a decision. And it's been found that the areas for decision-making and emotions are physically linked in the brain.[67]

Neuroscientist Antonio Damasio has studied people with damage in the limbic area, which manages emotions. These patients were unable to experience emotions: they could say how they *would* feel if they saw a car crash or a child hurt, but they would speak quite impassively about an upsetting event or family trauma. And they couldn't make decisions. They could describe logically what the process should be, but found it very difficult to make even simple commitments, such as deciding the date of their next appointment or which restaurant they would go to.

This suggests emotions are very important for choosing. In fact even in what we believe are logical decisions, the very point of choice is arguably *always* based on emotion.

We talk about decisions that "feel right." Damasio's view is that emotions provide a tag that helps us in the process of choice,[68] marking factors as good, bad or indifferent.

Damasio's finding has enormous implications for decision-making in business. Building a purely logical case for a change in policy or business direction means leaving out the key component in decision-making: the real factors that are driving the stakeholder to come to a decision. In the brain there is interplay between deliberate, analytical processes and the more primitive, visceral paths to a decision.

The physical processes

Decision-making networks and emotional centres are physically linked in the brain. Networks in the limbic system are devoted to processing emotions, while corresponding regions in the cortex integrate emotional information with what we know about the world.

Emotions are expressed through body sensations or a state of mind which provides cues to decisions that we want to make. This is totally independent of our ability to analyse data.

Damasio doesn't believe that emotion and feeling work in opposition to reasoning, but that they provide essential support to the reasoning process.

Author and therapist David Jetson claims that the unconscious brain is far more dominant in decision-making than we might previously have believed.[69] "Research shows that our conscious mind – our thoughts and memories – are involved in only one to nine per cent of every decision," he says. "The rest is unconscious."

Emotional vs rational decisions

We're trained to regard emotions as irrational impulses that are likely to lead us astray. The people in popular culture who are seen as being the most "intelligent" and logical are those who exert the greatest control over their emotions – or who seem to feel no emotions at all. Think Doctor Spock.

"The belief in the academic field is that emotions are essential to decision-making,[70] otherwise you'll end up making bad decisions," says neuro-economist Shiv.

"But I can show the opposite as well," he says: "Brain-damaged patients can make better decisions than normal individuals." Shiv calls these results "frinky," a word his son concocted to mean counterintuitive and funky.

For example, brain-damaged patients who feel no fear did better on the coin-tossing experiment described above. Shiv says this is because they did not experience the effects of what's known as Prospect Theory in behavioural economics. Developed by Nobel prize-winning psychologist Daniel Kahneman, and the late Amos Tversky, Prospect Theory proposes that we are risk averse,[71] finding the pain of loss to be much greater than the pleasure of equivalent gain.

This is what Shiv's experiment found. The healthy participants passed up opportunities to place a bet, and as fear mounted with each coin toss were less and less likely to take the gamble. They earned an average of only $22.80. By contrast, brain-damaged patients who felt no loss aversion earned[72] an average of $25.70.

Emotions: help or hindrance?

So what is going on? Are emotions a help or a hindrance to good decision-making? There's no simple answer: it depends.

Kahneman proposes in *Thinking Fast and Slow* that we all have two ways of thinking.[73] System 1 is a fast, instinctive and emotional brain, specialised in identifying and recognising danger as well as rewards such as food, sex or social connection. System 2 is a slower, more deliberative and more logical brain process that uses data and analysis.

Kahneman says that because the more cautious and analytical System 2 is lazy and tires easily we often accept the quick-and-dirty assessments of the intuitive, largely unconscious System 1.[74] "Although System 2 believes itself to be where the action is, the automatic System 1 is often where decisions are made," he says.

Kahneman's analysis suggests we should be taking account of emotions, and also taking time to check with our logical brain.

The power of hormones

How you feel affects how you decide, and how you feel is affected by the mix of hormones in your body. Neuroscientist and former Wall Street trader John Coates found that the risk appetite of traders was influenced by the hormones testosterone and cortisol. They took more risks when testosterone was high but became risk averse when cortisol peaked.

Baba Shiv says the time to make tough choices is in the morning when our hormones are most likely to favour decision-making:[75] serotonin is at a natural high, calming our brain and making us less fearful about risk. Later in the day, as serotonin starts to decline we find it more difficult to be decisive.

Hunger and tiredness

Check whether you're feeling hungry or thirsty; research has found that people who had eaten a satisfying meal took less risk[76] to achieve financial gain than before they had eaten.

And a study at Duke University was the first to show that sleep deprivation can change the way the brain assesses economic value,[77] and that this happens independent of the effects of memory and attention.

The study demonstrated that sleep deprivation increases sensitivity to positive rewards while diminishing sensitivity to negative consequences. "Even if someone makes very sound, risky financial decisions after a normal night of sleep, there is no guarantee that this same person will not expose you to untoward risk if sleep deprived," says co-author Michael Chee.

Getting a good night's sleep is going to put you in a better state to make important decisions. So make sure you go to bed early before making that big spending decision.

Give yourself time

It's also useful to take *time* to reflect on a decision. The saying "sleep on it" is backed up by neuroscience research.[78] Neuroscientist David Creswell has found that people who had to make a decision based on many competing factors made better decisions (judged by experts) when they had reflection time. Even a few minutes helps. So in a meeting give yourself or your stakeholder time before the decision-point, and make the suggestion: "Shall we take a break for coffee now, and come back to this when we've had a chance to consider it?"

Your decision-making checklist:

- Check for any unconscious bias, such as loss aversion, when you're making an important choice. (You can read more about this in *"Biased decisions? Not me"*).
- When you need someone else to make a decision, build in an emotional as well as a logical argument. Consider what their emotional starting point will be on the issue, and how you can shift their emotional thinking.
- When you're making a decision, check your mood and the time of day and try to make important decisions in the morning, or when you've eaten and are physically comfortable.
- Finally, give yourself time to reflect on data, especially if it's complex. Ideally, sleep on major decisions.

The neuroscience is challenging traditional views about business decisions. You can use this knowledge to improve your choices and how you make proposals to stakeholders.

"Biased decisions? Not me."

A bias check for your decisions

Many people (and I include myself in this) can be *collectors* of knowledge rather than users. We see this on our training programmes: people will say "Oh yes, I know that model (or concept)" – and then you see them switch off.

My response is: "Have you used it in your work? What were the results?" There's usually a silence.

So, you may know about decision bias, and assume you're familiar with the concept, but the aim of this chapter is to help you *apply* decision bias analysis to the everyday issues in your work.

You may have followed our advice in the previous chapter on making decisions, and made what you feel is a good decision, but partiality has a way of creeping in. As an HR professional you evaluate people, products and services on a regular basis, but how confident are you that you're unbiased in all your judgements and decisions? Biases happen completely unconsciously – they operate as a kind of intuition, a "just knowing." Because of this it can be useful before you put a decision into action to check it for decision bias: rather like running a spell-check on a document before you send it.

What is decision bias?

The study of decision bias has evolved in behavioural economics, the combination of economics and psychology which looks at understanding how humans make decisions in reality rather than, as traditional economic theory would assume, completely rationally.

Behavioural economics also considers how circumstances influence decisions and create irrationality.

Research by psychologist Daniel Kahneman has described two human thought systems:[79] a fast track powered by instinct and emotion, and a slower system dependent on logic and careful consideration.

Often when you are making decisions your quick-thinking intuitive system jumps to conclusions or takes shortcuts that your rational thinking doesn't question. That can lead to bias. Whilst these intuitive decisions can be very helpful as we describe in the chapter on *Gut feeling*, they need to be checked rationally.

Lots of different types of bias have been identified but here are a few that can have a significant impact in HR.

1 Anchoring or setting a "first reference point"

The tendency to use reference points can lead us astray.[80]

For example, if a candidate asks for £100,000 salary which is way above what you planned to pay, and then comes down to £80,000, which is still above your budget, this feels less of an issue than if they had asked for £80,000 in the first place.

The initial offer influences your thinking throughout the process of coming to an agreement. The mind keeps referring back to that initial number.

This doesn't mean that making an over-generous offer is the right course of action, though in reality that's often what is done (think of car price negotiations, or house sales). There is evidence in salary negotiations[81] that when the initial anchor figure is set high, the final amount agreed will also be higher. This is a reason why *you* should open negotiations rather than waiting for the employee to tell you their number, because then you can set the anchor.

2 Favouring the status quo

It's extraordinarily easy to look more positively on options that perpetuate your existing approach. This includes resistance to technology solutions, and new processes and ways of working. It also plays out in areas like talent and recruitment. People are more comfortable with hiring or promoting people who will "fit in" than taking people with new and different experience which may help achieve business goals.

This type of bias often crops up in two common scenarios: when we're invested in the current approach (see the IKEA Effect below), and when there is some kind of loss associated with a change.

We see this in our work applying neuroscience to leadership development. An HR leader is well aware that their current approach has not changed behaviour, and they believe the evidence that a science-based approach will work. But to change direction would require a move away from what's well-known and familiar, and this is more difficult than staying with what they know. It's easier to stick with the same leadership provider that you used last year; the CEO knows them and you won't have to explain the reason for the change.

3 Finding confirming evidence

People naturally seek out information that supports our existing view, rather than evidence that's going to prove us wrong.

In HR terms this might be assuming someone on the talent list is there for life and dismissing data that contradicts the assessment. Or favouring the first results of an employee relations investigation and finding it hard to accept new information. Or when it is hard to take on board data that doesn't fit with your existing views on what creates success in business. For example, think about the findings in Adam Grant's book *Give and Take: A Revolutionary Approach to Success* which suggests helping others is the root to success at work.[82] This is counterintuitive. Surely selfish people succeed?

People are very skilled at maintaining a sense of certainty and this means favouring data that fits with what you already know. Our brain is wired to do this and so you work hard at explaining why your existing view of the world is right. This bias requires you to really challenge your assumptions and to keep an open mind and if you find yourself resisting new information, asking why.

4 Loss aversion

We are not equally attracted to gains as we are averse to losses. The term loss aversion, coined by Amos Tversky and Daniel Kahneman,[83] refers to our strong preference for avoiding loss compared with our wish to achieve gains.

This explains why, when you have invested time, costs or emotional commitment in something – or someone – you find it difficult to make decisions that would bring it to an end. That's why we're so often prepared to be tolerant of poor performance: we're counting the costs of the investment in the individual, rather than assessing the potential gains from replacing them.

5 Endowment

This is the extra value you attribute to an idea or project because it's yours, or you're identified with it. Your ownership creates an inflated sense of the value. Think of a place on the management committee or the leadership programme. A version of this is the IKEA Effect:[84] you've invested effort in putting together that self-assembly furniture. You feel as though you've "built it." In HR terms this might be your performance management process, the new service centre or the leadership programme you designed.

Endowment creates an inflated sense of value. A lot of commitment and company resources went into setting up the new service centre. The fact that it's now losing the company money having it in that location is difficult to recognise in the face of that original commitment.

A word about intuition

Intuition is not technically a decision bias: it's the way many biases get created, and therefore it's important to understand how it works.

There's evidence that intuition is the brain putting together knowledge and experience in new ways:[85] almost like neurons taking a jump to create a new pathway and hence new knowledge or insight. Experienced HR professionals can use intuition to add real value.

But just as intuition became an acceptable way to make decisions in business, science is now pointing to its drawbacks. Because the brain likes certainty, intuitive feelings make you feel good – you know the answer to the recruitment issue or the reward problem. It creates a reward in the brain.

Neuroscientist Robert Burton suggests this certainty bias fools us into placing too much store on intuition.[86] "We need to verify intuition with data," he says.

For example, when I worked in the city we had a top-rated strategist at the bank who advised investment managers where to place their funds. They hung on his every word! He confessed to me that all his ideas were intuitive and he then went to find the data to back them up. This is what Burton is advising.

HR professionals often "know" intuitively that a policy isn't working, or that a leader has favourites, or an employee is not really performing. Sometimes your reputation is enough for the business leadership to pay attention to your view. However, if you follow the science, this is a dangerous approach. And for me it also points to a lack of rigour. Your intuition may be right but what's the supporting data?

So how do you use these ideas?

You may find that forewarned is forearmed and knowing about these biases keeps you alert to checking for them. But you can also test your decision on an issue against the potential pitfalls above. It's always useful to ask someone to challenge your thinking to ensure you've identified and addressed any preconceived ideas. A similar approach, for important issues, is to ask colleagues to take the role of key stakeholders and ask challenging questions from their perspective.

Finally, be aware that we all make biased decisions and they are not always bad. The IKEA Effect works in the company's favour: it creates commitment to tough projects and bonds people to a common purpose.

"I'm just doing what I'm good at – or am I stuck in a rut?"

Understanding habits

"We are what we repeatedly do. Excellence then, is not an act, but a habit."

Aristotle

We often talk about habits. We say we've developed a bad habit. Or a good one. But what *is* a habit? And when does a behaviour shift from being a repeated action to a habit?

When you first decide to do something new – maybe setting up a new way of working with your team, or challenging your CEO about their behaviour, or taking steps to achieve a goal – you are taking an action. It's intentional, rational and goal-directed.

Habits are characterised by automatic behaviour: you don't have to think about doing that action every time. Our intuitive assumption is that actions become habits when we repeat them. But is that actually how the brain works?

Habits are more than repeated actions

One metaphor used to describe a habit is of a neural pathway that has been strengthened through repeated use. You could picture it as a footpath that has been used so often it is now a deep furrow in the ground. The depth of this well-walked rut makes it difficult to get off the pathway – to break the habit.

It appears likely that the habit synapses in the brain are strong and more likely to connect up. This footpath metaphor makes intuitive sense; the more you do something the more likely it is to become a habit. But that is not the whole story.

In terms of brain functioning, actions and habits are very different. They use different parts of the brain which respond and work in different ways. Understanding how and why they are different can be helpful in changing your habits, and helping others to change theirs too.

Habits and actions work differently

Think about a habit of yours. It can be a good one: something that you believe helps you. Or it can be a bad one: something you wish you didn't do.

Like the habit of taking a biscuit in a meeting, for example. You see the plate of biscuits and you automatically take one and eat it. You don't consciously think: "Do I want a biscuit? Shall I take a biscuit?"

Now, if you're hungry, that's fine. But what happens if you're not hungry? You see the biscuit, you *still* take it!

We all do this kind of thing. We go into automatic mode and this is what prevents us from changing or interrupting a habit to achieve a new goal. For example: you travel to and from work the same way every day. One day, you need to take a different route home in order to buy some milk. But as you walk through the front door you realise you've automatically taken your usual route and missed the shops.

This is a feature of habitual behaviour. Actions are more goal-directed: you would need to consciously take steps to avoid the biscuits because you're not hungry.

How are habits formed?

In a seminal piece of research at the University of Cambridge in the mid-1980s, Tony Dickinson proposed that rats that pressed a lever for a reward a 100 times could be said to be performing an action; as they continued to press the lever the rats developed an ingrained habit:[87] they pressed the lever even when they did not get a reward.

At some point, pressing the lever became a habit. There is no clear research to indicate at which point the change from action to habit occurs: it could have been 490 lever presses or six days.

You will be able to identify habits of your own that seem to have been formed very quickly, and others that have been much harder to embed.

Habits are energy-efficient...

This change from goal-directed action to habit happens in different brain systems, and more recent research suggests this requires more than repetition.

The action system is dynamic and responsive to changing circumstances. For example, you can change how you contribute at the management meeting when the agenda takes an unexpected turn. Or you can choose a piece of fruit instead of the biscuit.

However, this takes a bit of effort and can be tiring to maintain. The prefrontal cortex which is largely responsible for intentional actions gets fatigued and then the habit system wins out.

Part of the brain's design is to be energy efficient, and this means it pushes behaviours that are energy-hungry, like actions, towards more energy-efficient parts of the brain, where habits reside. The habit system is slower to gear up, but once it's running it can be hard to redirect.

Habits can be helpful

Habits are inflexible and don't adapt to changing situations. *Intentions* and *goals* might change, but habits will stay the same unless you intervene.

Habits are most useful when you need to trigger behaviour quickly, automatically and with little effort. So they keep you alive, they allow you to learn complex skills, and do many parts of your job for you – and they do all of these things whilst you're learning even more habits.

Neuroscientist Kevin Ochsner says as much as 70% of what we do is habit,[88] and that includes most of our job.

Actions and habits can be in conflict

Habits aren't just a natural extension of actions that have become "a bit more so." These two systems, action and habit can compete. And when there's a conflict, habit usually wins. This is why it's hard to take action to create new habits, or replace old habits.

We need both actions and habits in our life and work. And neuroscience has begun to uncover the separate brain mechanisms that control these two processes.

Researchers from the University of Sydney have conducted experiments that show two neural "loops" in the brain that code for actions and habits,[89] and have demonstrated how these loops either compete or coordinate to determine behaviour, depending on whether the intention and the habit agree or not.

Dopamine, the reward chemical in the brain, appears to play an important role, and current research is exploring how these two circuits actually work together and resolve situations where there is competing behaviour.

Triggering change: glucose or mindset?

In fact, damage to one system can result in behaviour being totally controlled by the other. According to the Australian researchers, the brain can compensate by making all behaviour habitual, or all behaviour intentional.

Studies led by Roy Baumeister in the US have shown that we can shift the balance between the two systems through willpower. The evidence suggests that glucose levels may determine the amount of willpower you have to resist habitual behaviour:[90] the lower your glucose level, the more likely you are to act from habit. It's a controversial idea, and not everyone agrees that glucose is responsible for our willpower or lack of it.

Carol Dweck, a leading researcher on success whose work we refer to in relation to setting goals and talent mindset, has suggested that it isn't glucose levels that determine our willpower but our mindset.[91] In other words, if you believe that glucose will help your willpower, then it probably will!

You're in control

If this is true, then willpower is not about what you *do*, but how you *think* about a situation[92] – which potentially gives you more control. If you're confident in your ability to resist temptation then you probably will.

In fact, several studies including Baumeister's work have produced results that support this idea, demonstrating that a good mood creates stronger willpower. So your mindset and your plan are crucial. To put this into action, have a look at our section on *Leading yourself* where we describe how to put together a brain-savvy plan to create new habits.

"So, I need to think about my thinking?"

Introspection: the essential skill

Have you ever had one of those mornings when you bite everyone's head off, send a batch of stinging emails and generally get awarded Grump of the Day?

Then at lunchtime you go for a walk and begin to think about why you have been reacting like that all morning.

The ability to introspect – to think about our thinking– has become something of a holy grail for business leaders. And with good reason: it's important in all sorts of leadership activities. Our ability to reflect on our beliefs and moods, and understand our assumptions, is essential for checking our decision-making and our actions in most areas of business life.

And recent research at University College London (UCL) has begun to show that this ability to think about thinking is rooted in our brain, and that we may be able to improve our ability to do it.[93]

How do you measure thinking about thinking?

Stephen Fleming's experiment at UCL asked people to engage in a visual decision-making task, in which the goal was to choose the brightest patch in a series of images. Some people are naturally better at this type of task than others, so the computer was programmed to give harder trials to the more skilled participants so that everyone's performance was roughly the same.

Participants were then asked to rate how confident they were in the decisions they'd made in the task. Matching their confidence rating with the accuracy of their decision-making gave a measure of their ability to introspect. That is, to think about their thinking. The researchers then used functional magnetic resonance imaging (fMRI) to relate this ability to the structure of the participant's brain.

They found two things:

- Introspective ability correlated with a greater volume of grey matter. That is, more neuron cells in the anterior prefrontal cortex, which is the area of the brain at the top of the information processing hierarchy. This area is thought to be involved in linking information about performance and confidence.
- People who were better at introspection also had more white matter or nerve connections in the same area.

We love patterns

One of the important uses of introspection is to check intuition. Neuroscientist Robert Burton says the brain is designed to recognise patterns.[94] They help us deal with ambiguity and indecision, and create feelings of certainty so we feel less anxious.

However, this "certainty bias," as Burton calls it, can be dangerous if it stops people considering something fully. Intuition, gut feelings and hunches, he says, are neither right nor wrong – but they are tentative ideas that must then be submitted to testing.

One way he suggests we do this is to think about thinking. We need to introspectively review ideas and the level of confidence we have in them. By doing this we can begin to learn and recognise when our feelings of certainty and conviction are involuntary mental sensations, rather than logical conclusions.

How can we develop this skill of thinking about thinking?

1   Practice mindfulness

Mindfulness is being in the moment, and observing your experience moment-by-moment in a non-judgemental way.

Studies have shown that even short periods of mindfulness practice provide significant health benefits,[95] increased attention and problem-solving ability, reduced stress and greater emotional control.

It's believed this happens because practising mindfulness thickens a specific set of neural circuits related to switching attention. Mindfulness increases the brain's ability to decide where to focus and when to switch attention.

It's possible that this enables people to recognise an unconscious sense of threat and to be able to intervene in the mental downward spiral that can be the result. This in turn increases self-regulation of emotions and the ability to control automatic reactions.

2   Learn about the brain

NeuroLeadership consultant David Rock believes that learning how our brain works also creates new abilities to think about thinking.[96] He suggests this is because:

- We notice more about how our brain is reacting because we know more about mental experience.
- We have language for mental experience, so are able to make choices within a fraction of a second about whether or not to follow a train of thought. For example, you may notice a rising threat response and be able to consciously decide whether to take action or relax

before the threat response activates emotions and takes over cognitive capacity. This increases self-regulation.

- By understanding the brain, we are practising switching attention, by swapping between "thinking about thinking" and being "in" an experience. Making active decisions to switch mental states builds the switching circuitry in the brain.

Rock maintains that people who study the brain over a long period of time should be getting similar benefits as those who practice mindfulness.

3 Adopt self-regulation strategies

In a long-term study now known as the "Marshmallow Test," Harvard psychologist Walter Mischel has shown the close link be tween self-regulation and personal productivity[97] – and ultimately success in life.

In this now-famous experiment, children were tested for their ability to wait for a treat: the marshmallow. The most "successful" children had strategies for distracting themselves from their yearning for the treat. Years later, following up with the participants, Mischel found that the children who were able to resist outperformed their peers on several scores including academic results, income and social success.

Like the marshmallow children, if people understand their own thoughts and feelings (if they are good at introspection), they will also be better able to direct attention away from whatever is immediately attracting them and remain focused on their longer-term goals.

Training leaders in thinking

Thinking about thinking is quickly becoming one of the key skills in business. While science can't yet say for sure that people can be trained directly in introspection, there is evidence that mindfulness and self-regulation techniques develop this ability. And being aware of your tendency to notice your own thinking, or how quickly you are distracted by external stimuli, is certainly a helpful starting point.

Leadership development needs to be including this type of awareness and skill building in the curriculum. It's encouraging to see that some companies are beginning to introduce mindfulness training, persuaded by the multiple benefits it can give their leaders. In some corporate cultures this may be seen as a little "weird," but then so was talk of "culture" itself 30 years ago – and now it is an essential component for any business strategy.

In the meantime we can train people and leaders to:

- check their assumptions – especially if they're tired, or have had a lot of meetings
- remember that we are subject to false-consensus effect: we tend to believe others believe what we do
- be aware that by focusing on strategy or analytical data they may be missing important social information such as how people feel about a change
- practice understanding others' point of view. We can build tools (and the requirement for this) into leadership development programmes.

"Goals... how do I set them up right?"

6 steps for success in setting up your goals

Success means different things to different people. And in HR there has been endless debate about what it means for the profession, and even our role within organisations. In our view there's far too much internal discussion about this amongst HR professionals.

So we thought that, instead of adding to the debate about definitions of success, it would be more useful to show you the science of how you can achieve your own success by looking at how to reach your goals.

There's lots of powerful evidence on this, so we're covering the big picture: how to set yourself up for success. And in our section on *Leading yourself* you'll find out more about how to stay focused as you pursue those goals in *"I set goals, but making progress is hard."*

1   Get the right mindset

Our own research indicates that your mindset is a major factor in success. And our findings are substantiated by the work of Stanford psychologist Carol Dweck, who has also found that personal beliefs make all the difference.[98]

People who have a growth mindset (those people who believe that talent and success is based on hard work and learning), do better in modern business than people with a fixed mindset (who believe you're born with a level of intelligence, or a talent, that determines your success).

Carol Dweck's research suggests that if you structure your goals to get better at what you want to do, you're likely to be more successful. If you're feeling low or de-motivated, check that you're not taking on a fixed mindset about your goal ("I can't do this...") when you could be noticing areas where you *can* get better, or you've made advances.

2   Don't try to do too much at once

David Rock says you can only really work on one or two goals at once.[99] And we'd say avoid setting two goals in the same area. That means don't try dieting and giving up smoking at the same time: it's going to be too difficult.

Generally it's best to focus on one goal and master that, rather than fail at everything you're aiming for. We advise people on our programmes to make a list of what they want to do and then pick one goal to work on.

Picking a goal that has a "rub-off" effect is also a good idea. For example, if one of your goals is to make more contribution in management meetings, and you also have a goal to improve your facilitation skills, you *can* practice both at the same time. Facilitating the flow and objectives of the meeting while making an effective contribution by holding a mirror up to what is going on with the management team.

3   Be clear on your hierarchy

There's quite a lot of useful research about the hierarchy of goals. And the clearer you are about each stage of the hierarchy, the better your chances of success.

Most goals fit into a wider purpose that gives you your long-term motivation to continue to pursue your goal. The hierarchy looks like this: your goal (*what* you're aiming for), *how* you will achieve it, and *why* (the purpose of your effort).

This might be a simple example in your personal life. Goal: clean healthy teeth. How: use a toothbrush and toothpaste every day. Why: taking care of your body.

A work example might be... Goal: provide predictive data for strategy decisions. How: set up a database and dashboard report. Why: the HR function adds value to the business strategy when the board makes use of the data.

There is also evidence that the *how* and the *why* are processed by different parts of the brain.[100]

Using fMRI (functional magnetic resonance imaging), UCLA researchers found that when actions are performed there was activity in pre-motor areas that are associated with the execution of actions in higher-order visual areas. What all this indicates is that visualising your actions is important.

"Identifying why actions are performed is done by areas of the brain associated with representing and reasoning about mental states," say the researchers. They believe this is evidence that different systems must be activated, as they each have a different purpose in the overall goal achievement. So linking them is important to maintain momentum. This means you would do well to visualise yourself achieving your goals as well as experiencing how you will *feel* when you have achieved them.

In our work it's not unusual to see people with goals but no steps that describe how they will move towards them. Or people who are learning a new behaviour or skill, but with no clear reason why they're doing it and certainly no feelings about how important it is to them. Not only are these types of efforts likely to fail, but the fallout can be a negative memory that reduces success in achieving future goals.

4 What *will* you do?

Focus on what you *will* do, not on what you *won't* do.

Typically goals replace one habit with another. By all means plan on how you will replace the old habit with a new one (your goal). But be careful not to focus only on the old habits themselves. Research on thought suppression ("Don't think about white bears!") has shown that trying to avoid a thought makes it even more active in your mind,[101] with your brain effectively deepening the neural pathway.

For example, if you're trying to contribute more in management meetings, make a plan along the lines of: "If I'm going to contribute then I will prepare my contribution based on the agenda, collect data, and give myself time to mentally rehearse before the meeting."

By preparing ahead of time your habit of being silent will get worn away until it disappears completely.

5 Be specific

This is about being brain-savvy. We have areas in our brain that are dedicated to achieving goals consciously, such as the prefrontal cortex, and areas which will work on the goal without your conscious awareness.

To create new behavioral habits you have to get these areas of the brain working together. The more specific you are, the less likely there is to be confusion.

Research on changing behaviour has shown that people need to have a vision of the future to resist impulsive behaviour[102] based on past habits. German scientists have established that vividly imagining the future results activates the hippocampus (the part of the brain responsible for imagining the future, and memory), and the anterior cingulated cortex (the ACC, is involved in reward-based decision-making).

Vividly imagining resulted in a greater ability to delay immediate rewards and reduce impulsive choices, helping to maintain new behaviour.

Achieving goals means creating new ways of working and this will only happen if you can overcome your automatic habit system by activating the planning and goal-directed prefrontal cortex. Where you have a clear, specific goal you can activate both the higher cortical brain and the limbic regions, to embed new habits with planning, priming and reinforcing.

6   Balance optimism with realism

We need to be realistic as well as optimistic.

It's true that the biggest predictor of success in achieving a goal is whether you have a belief that you can do it.

But at the same time you also need to be realistic about which things will be difficult for you, and plan around them. Don't underestimate the challenges. Most goals require time, planning, effort, and persistence. Optimism is important, but studies show that thinking things will come to you easily and effortlessly increases the chance of failure.

A study at New York University showed that those who thought it would be hard to lose weight proved to be more successful[103] and lost nearly 11kg more compared with both the control group and those who thought it would be easy. The participants who thought the target was easily achievable actually gained weight.

So you need a balance between believing in your ability and being unrealistic.

Believing in success is also essential for creating and sustaining motivation.[104] Other research has shown that having a clear self-image of the future helps you to stay on track towards your goal.

Establishing the right mindset, and setting up your goals clearly, will increase your chances of success. Then you'll be ready for our *"six steps for keeping going with your goals"* which you will find in *Leading yourself.*

"How do I get my HR initiative agreed?"

The neuroscience of being influential

> *"The goal of a presentation to your boss is not to get him to think you're smart, but to get him to think he's smart to support your idea."*
>
> @tom_peters

If tweets are the new quotes, this one from business guru Tom Peters seems to perfectly encapsulate how an understanding of the brain can help you to get your HR initiative agreed.

When you're trying to exert influence, there are three things you need to take into account:

- how you need to be in yourself
- what you know about the thoughts and feelings of your key stakeholders
- the culture or commercial environment

Understanding neuroscience can help with the first two. We've created the CORE model using the science of how the brain works to help you understand yourself and your stakeholders better. And we'll give you an example of how you can apply it to your work.

Surviving in a social setting

Neuroscience sheds new light on how people react in social situations[105] which can help you to form better relationships and be more effective at influencing other people. For example: the brain is highly evolved to work in a social environment. If that social environment appears to be threatening in any way, the brain switches into survival mode.

What counts as a threat?[106] If the environment doesn't provide the social support our brain needs: like being included in a group, knowing what's happening, feeling a connection with others, sensing trust and congruence between values and behaviours (the list goes on...)

Without the social support we need, older parts of our brain – the ones that govern fight or flight – are activated. And that takes resources away from the newer parts of the brain which help lateral thinking, connection-making, creativity, and the regulation of emotions.

This happens because, from an evolutionary perspective,[107] we didn't need those parts of the brain to protect ourselves in a threatening environment. There's no time for analysis when you're running away from a sabre-toothed tiger.

But in modern business, survival-brain mode impacts on our ability to engage with others and perform well at work. If we can get better at understanding this reaction in ourselves and our colleagues, we can build more productive relationships and be more influential.

The CORE model

CORE is a quick and easy way to remember the key principles of the neuroscience of relationships:

Certainty:	our confidence that we know what the future holds
Options:	the extent to which we feel we have choices
Reputation:	our relative importance to others (our social ranking)
Equity:	our sense of fairness

The four CORE elements activate either the "primary reward" or the "primary threat" circuitry of our brains. For example, a perceived threat to one's sense of equity ("my boss has favourites;" "some people get more information than others"...) activates similar brain networks to finding a stranger in Reception waving a knife.

Likewise, a perceived increase to your reputation ("They used a quote from me in the annual report!") activates the same reward circuitry in the brain as getting a pay rise. Your reaction is completely automatic and happens in a nanosecond, driving behaviour before you've even had a chance to consider your response rationally.

Using CORE in practice

The model can be applied in three main ways:

1. To understand your feelings about a relationship – useful for difficult relationships, or when you're concerned about a new initiative.
2. To understand a stakeholder better.
3. To plan how to position an idea when you need to gain agreement.

When we first meet someone we unconsciously categorise them as friend or foe. Foe is the default setting: it's safer to assume someone is a threat until we receive signals that reassure us.

Our brains are constantly scanning for threat or reward signals. In the 21st century workplace that can mean we react to things strongly and quickly, before we've had a chance to let our rational brains assess the situation. That means you may perceive a new team member as a threat, or be alarmed by changes to your role, or interpret a frown on your boss's face as dissatisfaction with your work.

How CORE works: an example

Imagine you're giving a presentation to your boss to agree a new project.

> 1. To manage their sense of Certainty it's important to include in your presentation how this initiative links to existing business knowledge or activity, reducing the threat of the unknown.
> 2. Give him or her some Options, so they don't feel corralled in one direction but feel they have control over the decision.
> 3. Create a sense of reward to their Reputation by showing how the idea will enhance their standing within the organisation. Avoid any suggestion that current work methods they're associated with are not working.
> 4. Finally, position your idea Equitably, making sure the way it's implemented will be fair to the stakeholder and their team.

Whether the person you're presenting to perceives a threat or a reward will have a significant impact on their problem-solving, decision-making, stress-management, collaboration and motivation. It's going to make the difference between whether they say yes or no.

Sometimes it's not within your power for you to create a reward for your key decision-makers. But it's still important to think about the specific person you're trying to influence: which of the CORE elements are most important to them in this situation, and what might trigger their sense of threat? How might they find this initiative rewarding for themselves? (Consider: what's in it for them)

Using CORE in practice

Here's a situation many HR professionals will recognise. You believe you have the solution to a long-standing problem within the organisation. Or you've got a creative idea for developing more engagement. But the person you need to persuade has batted the suggestion away once. They've asked for more evidence, and you feel apprehensive about going back to them.

1 Reducing threat

Look at your proposal from all angles, and use CORE to analyse what might be a threat to your stakeholder:

> **Certainty:** are you giving them information about how

this solution will impact on their work or their role? Have you painted a clear picture of the outcome?

Options: do they have some control over how the solution will be rolled out, or communicated?

Reputation: could they suffer any fallout by adopting this solution?

Equity: is there any way your proposal might be seen as inequitable or unfair? For example, does it result in more work for some teams, or reduce their access to resources?

2   Creating reward

You can also build in opportunities to create a sense of reward. These might not always be obvious to you, so this can be a useful analysis to run through:

Certainty: can you make links to existing activity or information which will explain how the solution will work? In what ways can you make it more tangible?

Options: what kind of choices can you offer to give your stakeholder a greater sense of control?

Reputation: how might this idea be seen positively by the rest of the organisation? Could it enhance the reputation of the stakeholder and their team?

Equity: how can you ensure the proposal is fairly implemented and has an equitable outcome?

Are you getting an idea of how CORE works? Once you begin to think about relationships through the lens of how the brain works, and you consider threat and reward responses, you can adjust your approach and you'll be amazed how much easier it is to be influential.

"Is there a better way to have a difficult conversation?"

The right way to have the conversations we dread

"Ah, Chris – could we have a quick word? You might want to shut the door. I always hate these chats. Worst part of the job... Especially when you've been a key member of the team.... We go back a long way, don't we? I wanted to talk to you about your goals... you know, how are you doing?... How do you think it's going? Bit tough?... Well, I'm glad we had this chance to talk."

We've all had them, most of us hate them, some of us will do anything to avoid them, and some of us manage to fudge the message so badly the other person doesn't even realise it *was* a difficult conversation at all.

Many, many HR professionals tell us they've spent what little budget they have on training for difficult conversations. No matter what the business climate it's the one thing their managers are willing to attend, and no-one ever complains about the budget spend.

But for all that, it's all made little difference. It's still the task that managers dread; they make a mess of them, and avoid them whenever they can.

We think we know why.

Don't ignore the emotions

The training wasn't tackling the right issue.

Most "difficult conversations" training starts with the process: the steps to follow and the evidence to collect. Then people role-play delivering the message, getting it word perfect.

Almost none of the training deals with emotions, and especially not the emotions of the person delivering the message. But in our experience that's what makes the difference. Telling someone you have worked with for years they are no longer doing a good job, or they are losing their job, hurts. It hurts them, and our empathy for them means we feel the same pain.

Managers seldom say, "I don't mind those conversations, I just need to get the evidence right first."

They say, "I hate it – there's no easy way to deliver that kind of message." Or, "I get really anxious beforehand, and I worry that it makes me seem cold." Or, "I dread someone getting really upset."

Of the three key elements in a difficult conversation, the steps and the evidence, or "the context" is only the first of them. By far the most important factor is how the manager feels. Yes, that's right: *their* emotions are even more important than those of the person sitting opposite them.

Why? Because the manager is the one delivering the difficult message and if their brain is overwhelmed because they are stressed, they won't be clear or able to tap into how the other person is feeling and will come over as muddled, cold or abrupt and unable to connect with their colleague. And all of that means the outcome is unlikely to be right.

So, the three elements:

1   The context

Yes, of course collect the evidence you need. Check that it's right: robust, and free from bias.

Know when and where you'll have the conversation and what the desired outcome is. Then once all that is clear, put it aside: concentrate on the people involved.

2   The other person

Managers need to consider how the employee is going to feel: imagine where they are on the subject and how they will react.

Most managers will assume this kind of empathy requires them to feel the same feelings as the employee. This is known as "*emotional empathy,*"[108] meaning an instantaneous body-to-body connection with the other person's feelings. It involves tuning in to another person's emotions and requires the ability to read facial, vocal and other nonverbal signs of how another person feels, moment by moment.

Research shows this type of empathy depends on our tuning in to our *own* body's emotional signals,[109] which automatically mirror the other person's feelings.

Psychiatrist Daniel Siegel calls the brain areas that create this type of empathy the "we" circuitry[110]. This is the mentalizing system which helps us think about others' motivations, goals and feelings.

Not that kind of empathy

In our view this is *not* the kind of empathy to activate when a manager is planning or engaged in a difficult conversation.

This is what sets off the panic alarm. Feeling the feelings of the other person triggers a classic threat response: "Don't want to go *there*!" Which puts a manager into avoidance mode, or calls for a lot of mental energy to override it in their limbic brain.

Redirecting that energy takes resources away from their prefrontal cortex. Which is why even the best-organised person can end up having a muddled conversation, with evidence being forgotten and a generally chaotic result.

The *right* kind of empathy

Instead, what's more helpful is for the manager to take on the other person's *perspective*. They need to engage their curiosity, rather than their emotions, with the other person's reality.

This has been called "cognitive empathy," or perspective-taking,[111] and is what we typically describe as being able to see the world through other people's eyes, or "putting yourself in someone else's shoes."

Cognitive empathy is mind-to-mind, rather than body-to-body, and gives us a mental sense of how another person's *thinking* works.

This way of thinking about another person's perspective gives an understanding of their view – it can tell us how best to communicate with that person: what matters most to them, their models of the world, and even what words to use – or avoid – when talking with them. Using similar expressions and words builds rapport and avoids misunderstandings.

And that pays off in many ways, including reducing a manager's uncertainty about how the conversation will go: a major factor in why everyone tends to avoid difficult conversations.

Managers who have developed their cognitive empathy will also be better able to pick up the norms and ground rules of the office culture, and anticipate how the wider team will react to the outcome of the conversation – always a consideration for managers.

And there is another type of empathy which can usefully be deployed for a difficult conversation.

"Empathic concern" taps into the brain's circuitry for parental love,[112] and helps people get in touch with their feelings of compassion, and express their care for the other person. Best deployed once the difficult discussion is complete and the next steps have been agreed: this is when the manager lets their team member know that they'll support them.

3   The manager

The other person the manager needs to focus on is, of course, themselves. We've covered some of the ways in which the right kind of empathetic preparation can help people manage their threat response (find out more about this in *Brain basics* in the Introduction).

As a starting point they need to understand, and possibly challenge, their own mindset. Managers with a fixed mindset, who basically believe "someone can either do it, or they can't,"[113] are never going to find it worthwhile conducting a difficult performance appraisal. "What's the point – they'll never change."

They may also need help in challenging the common business belief that a good manager will keep emotion out of this process. Encourage an understanding of how suppressing their emotions is likely to make things worse rather that better.

Teaching reappraisal skills is also invaluable. We find that many managers, with a little practice, can reappraise for themselves why the conversation needs to happen and why it needs to go well. The insights from empathy preparation can help.

Firing a poor performer may seem cruel, but leaving them to lose more confidence as they struggle on in a role that's not suited to them is even harsher. Making members of the team redundant is hard, but letting the whole business flounder puts more people in jeopardy.

And lastly, coach your managers in tapping into the mental and physical state that's going to work best for them in the conversation, and help them to be able to monitor this state in the moment.

You're not going to be able to introduce an instant yogic understanding for executives who are not used to being attuned to their body and the effects of stress. But very simple exercises like power poses or relaxing the shoulders can be instantly helpful, and many managers go on to use them in everyday situations and not just the conversations they've been dreading the most.

"Is it really possible to make change happen easily?"

5 discoveries that will save your change programme

Every client we talk to is struggling with a major change project, and most have pretty low expectations of what they can achieve.

What's really worrying is when you hear HR people talking about change as being largely an issue of process and project governance, and believing there's little they can do on the people side. At most there might be a passing nod to communications about the change programme.

This is ignoring the new understanding about how people actually think and operate in change situations. Creating a burning platform will not overcome a biological response to change. Whereas facilitation, engagement and letting go of "having all the answers" just might.

So here's the recent research from neuroscience that could inspire you to take a different view about what works. Our five recommendations:

1   Make sure people share beliefs

This idea comes from author and business advisor Simon Sinek, but it's based on an understanding of brain structure and how we make decisions.

People need to understand *why* a change is important to them personally. In Sinek's phase, they need to believe what you believe.[114] Much of change management is focused on *what* must happen. What do people need to do differently? What are the measures? What governance is in place?

But for change to actually work you need to focus on *why*. Why is this change important? Why is the change important to me personally?

And that doesn't mean just doing a good sell. You need to facilitate understanding so that people create the belief for themselves. Why? Because research indicates people will only be motivated to stick with a change when they create a clear vision of the outcome for themselves.

Scientists in Germany have found that people are more able to resist the temptations to go back to old ways of working or behaving, and more likely to stick to their goal, if they have a clear picture of what the future will be like[115] once the change has happened. This activates the hippocampus, the part of our brain responsible for memory and for imagining the future, and *also* the anterior cingulated cortex (the ACC), which is involved in reward-based decision-making.

Passionate believers attract more believers

Scientists have used computer modelling to measure when a minority belief becomes the prevailing belief[116] in three different types of social networks:

> A small company or business unit where each person is connected to every other person.

> A large company where everyone has roughly the same number of connections.

> Opinion leaders connected to a small number of individuals, who each have a large number of connections.

Each model had a mass of people who held a traditional belief, but were open to listening to other ideas. A "true believers" minority who were unshakable in their belief proved to be able to convince others to change their views, in all three types of networks.

The threshold was 10%. Once 10% of a group holds an unshakable belief that an idea is right, it will be taken up by the majority. Below 10% nothing will change.

This research has significant implications for HR professionals leading change:

Are we measuring the number of people who are on board with the change?

Do they really believe in the idea?

Are the majority of our people open to listening?

How do we ensure our "true believers" are sharing their views?

Are we keeping up the effort until we've passed that critical 10% mark?

2   Change the language

How the change is talked about makes a significant difference to the ease of making the change.

In a paper that attracted a lot of media attention Ruud Custers and Henk Aarts showed that the pursuit of goals often happens out of conscious awareness and can be affected by outside influences, such as the language used.

People are warmer and friendlier when they're holding a hot cup of coffee,[117] They're tougher in a negotiation when they're sitting on a hard chair. And don't neglect the impact of a word of praise. The study showed that the use of positive cue words resulted in harder work and more persistence to solve a problem than neutral words given to a control group.

No-one ever left home to follow a leader who said "I have a plan." It's "I have a *dream*" that gets people motivated.

Are you threatening or encouraging your people to change? How inspiring have you made the future?

3   Increase people's tolerance for change

Some people seem to handle change better than others, and one

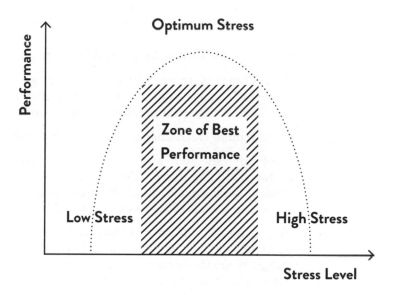

theory suggests this is related to the degree of arousal they experience.

In a neuroscience context, arousal is determined by the level of the chemical catecholamine. Everyone needs a degree of arousal to get off the sofa and take action. Too little arousal results in lethargy. Too much creates stress, which affects our memory, our ability to focus and creates feelings of panic.

Different people need different amounts of arousal to achieve optimum performance, and it may be that the base level of arousal of people who generally welcome change is *lower* than those who find change difficult.

Their lower arousal enables them to have a greater tolerance of the stimulus created in the brain when change occurs. Whereas people who already have a high natural state of arousal are "pushed over the edge" by the prospect of the uncertainty that change creates.

And someone's response will also vary under different circumstances. So an employee who is moving house, whose parent is ill, or whose teenager is leaving home may be less tolerant of change in their workplace.

The solution is not to recruit a team of low-arousal sofa-sitters, but to think about what is going on for individuals. Instead of labeling people as difficult if they react strongly to change, it makes more sense to work to reduce their arousal.[118]

Using a CORE analysis, consider how the change is impacting on their Certainty ("How is my job going to change?"), their Options ("Will I have the choice of a new role?"), their Reputation ("Will the skills I have still be valued?"), and their sense of Equity ("Is *everyone* being asked to reapply for their job?").

4   If you want to be successful, keep going!

It takes longer than you expect. Prepare to go into battle to fight for enough budget allocation to run a change programme for much longer than your organisation has planned for.

If you want to create change, you need to change habits.

Our brain responds to and encourages us to create patterns: regular ways of doing things. These routines are run by the energy-efficient basal ganglia, and habits save us brain-processing time. It can take a while to hard-wire some habits.

Trying to replace them with *new* habits will take longer because we literally have an emotional attachment to the old way of doing things. When the brain is told it needs to change, it's the equivalent of telling the brain something is *wrong*: the emotional centre, the amygdala, is activated, triggering the classic flight-or-fight response.

Whilst the prefrontal cortex can override this primitive brain response – so the team leader doesn't *actually* stamp and shout when you ask them to block out time for management training – changing habits does take a lot of brain energy, and soon becomes fatigued.

We can speed up the process if we make learning easier for people. And the evidence shows this will happen if they're engaged, personally motivated and have clear goals they believe in.

And the new behaviour needs to be "rewarded" to be embedded. Reward happens when one of the CORE elements is positively impacted, which might result from training people in new skills, boosting their reputation, or increasing certainty by telling them when you will communicate the next stage of the change programme.

No one knows exactly how long it takes to embed new behavioural habits but it's longer than when the ink has dried on the communications. Clues are people are no longer struggling in their new roles and are automatically behaving in new ways. They will also have probably stopped moaning about "the old days" and started to be engaged and positive about the company again.

5   Recognise the threat to your leaders

As we've said, our brain is wired to notice a sense of threat or reward.

A familiar change management process may not be producing the results that are needed, but for a leader it's going to tick all the old boxes. Whereas asking them to adopt a brain-savvy approach is mostly a threat for them; it's a change for them, and for their role in change.

So an important role for HR is to help leaders understand their own response to change and overcome the sense of threat which may make them resistant to these ideas. We created the Change Charter as a shorthand for what works.

HR can help leaders to:

Understand their reaction to the change

Identify where they are stuck or resistant

Facilitate insight into why the change is good for them personally

Encourage leaders to set their own behavioural change goals

Follow up to embed new behaviour through celebrating success

4 Leading the function

From interviews to reward: how the findings and insights of neuroscience can transform the effectiveness of your daily policies and practice in HR. Some of these chapters are about how you run your HR function to make it more effective. Others focus on what neuroscience is telling us about what works in how you design HR practices like reward and performance management.

"We don't have in-groups – we just have the right kind of people."

Why our brains love to categorise, and how to limit the damage of in-groups and out-groups

You know how this scenario goes. You're in a leg, working as part of the three-legged stool model familiar to HR, of business partners, shared services and centres of expertise. The structure has been in place a while but fundamental issues have yet to be resolved. The main gripes are about who does what, who has access to clients, and how hard the different parts of the function are working. Resulting in the usual arguments about reward and resources.

If you don't experience these issues, great! Unfortunately, we see them all too often, and the solution is usually to write reams of process documents to clarify who does what. They rarely make much difference.

Each of the three groups within the HR function comes with its own work styles, skills, expectations and status. So we immediately have at least three potential in-groups, and people can all too easily end up identifying with their group at the expense of the wider function. Once someone is categorised as "business partner," expectations are attached to them that determine how they behave and how others perceive their actions.

Understanding the brain and how it responds to such structures could prevent the downside of identifying too much with your colleagues in the same group and lacking connection with people in other parts of the function.

The in-group

In-groups feel fine if you're part of them. In fact, if you're part of the in-group you'll probably deny that the out-group is suffering any kind of disadvantages. Or if there are any disadvantages they're of their own making: "Shared services are too process-focused and don't understand the needs of the business unit;" "Business partners want everything customised and don't understand the cost of processing one-off requests…"

There has been lots of psychological research on the impact of in-groups, most of it relating to gender, racial and stereotype bias. Neuroscience is now beginning to break down the sequence of processes[119] in the brain that create this kind of bias, and the impact they can have on decision-making, social connection and the performance of groups that need to work together – as in HR.

Neuroscience is also pointing to what can be changed and managed, and what can't.

How our brain creates an in-group

One of the ways our brain manages the vast amounts of data it needs to process every day is by putting things into categories. As Gordon Allport, one of the founders of modern psychology, said: "The human mind must think with the aid of categories."[120] This categorisation in turn influences the way we judge things. And when it comes to people and groups, that can be an issue.

Every recruiter is familiar with the idea that we categorise the new people we meet within seconds of first encountering them. In fact, it takes just 200milliseconds to categorise a new face by sex and race. And after that we organise them into other groups or categories.

The amygdala is giving a completely unconscious quick-and-dirty assessment of whether the new person is a threat.

Building categories

The top level of categorisation is in-group or out-group. In-group is friend rather than foe, usually "like me" rather than "different from me." We store broad representations for our different categories,[121] says David Amodio of New York University.

That first categorisation affects our subsequent processing.[122] We will spend longer looking at the faces of people in our in-group. It will affect how we interpret their bodily movements and how much empathy we have for them in a painful situation.

Once we have categorised, we link to other stored information about that category: how similar they are to us, what characterises them, whether these characteristics are positive or negative. These stored characteristic and category links are built up over time, through socialisation and culture. They create the expectations we have of people – they're the lens we see them through.

Why do we create in-groups?

It may be helpful to think of this in evolutionary terms. We need other people for survival. Being excluded from the group threatens life and wellbeing. So people need to be able to work well in face-to-face situations and make connections with other people who may be able to help them, or who will protect them from threat by other people who are dissimilar.

This promotes a tendency to look for similarities within our in-group and to exclude anyone who is dissimilar. We have friends we met at school or university, we tend to lunch with other shared services employees, and most of us know relatively few people outside our social or racial group.

Viewed this way, the core social motivation of categorisation is sharing social understanding, getting along in the group and controlling socially different behaviour, which all serves to build trust within the group.[123]

So, categorising people into groups can be useful for our long-term safety, but it can also have consequences.

Understanding people

A study by the University of Missouri has shown that the effect of in-group identification becomes even more intense when people are threatened.[124] People turn to their in-group when they feel at risk of some type of harm. The threat could be anything from negative feedback to redundancies to competition for budget or even the sense that the boss favours one part of the three-legged stool over other parts of the function.

The researchers asked participants to complete a perceptual decision-making task while being monitored in a functional magnetic resonance imaging (fMRI) scanner. During the task they were exposed to the judgements about them from both in-group and out-group members; some positive others negative.

This research showed that being part of the in-group makes you feel good and you will be more able to understand the perspective of your in-group colleagues[125] and find it difficult to put yourself into the shoes of people in another group.

The implication is that we are less receptive to feedback from people not in our group, and find it difficult to adopt their perspective.

Blue eyes, brown eyes:
how quickly we can create group identity

One of the most famous exercises showing in-group/out-group bias was carried out in a classroom by Iowa primary school teacher, Jane Elliott.

On the day after Martin Luther King was assassinated in 1968 Elliott decided to address the problems that her all-white students had in really understanding racial prejudice. She divided her class of eight year-olds into two groups on the basis of eye colour.[126] For one day the blue-eyed children would be superior, the next day the brown-eyed children would be the elite.

Elliott showed how easy it was to turn her pupils into stereotypical prejudice groups. Within minutes the blue-eyed children were ridiculing their classmates, calling them "stupid" and shunning them in the playground. When the roles were swapped the following day the brown-eyed children exercised similarly prejudiced behaviour. In her subsequent career as a diversity trainer Jane Elliott's technique has been applied to a variety of workplaces, including General Electric, IBM and the US Navy.

Creating new group identities

Definitions of in-group and out-group are not based on rational data and can be manipulated very easily, so where you work can quickly create new perceptions of others in, for example people who work in another part of the function.

We all belong to multiple groups that we identify with, and it seems that we're also able to manipulate the boundaries of a group we belong to. The example of pedestrians and motorists is perhaps the easiest to understand. Your in-group is pedestrian when you're walking from the bus stop to the office, and the motorist who beeps you at the pedestrian crossing is your out-group. The reverse may be true when you are in a hurry driving to an appointment. Your in-group at one moment is your out-group the next.

In one study, subjects organised into teams of black and white participants were scanned using fMRI[127] while viewing pictures of a variety of people, from different racial groups. Both groups showed increased amygdala activity when viewing pictures of people of colour.

Participants were then reorganised into mixed teams of black and white people. On re-scanning, amygdala activity was found to be reduced; participants only responded to members of their out-group rather than by colour.

The conclusion then is that in-group affiliation is not hard-wired but can be manipulated. Which means the divisions between the parts of the HR function can be broken-down too.

Practical steps to avoid the traps of in-groups and out-groups

It takes work to avoid the dangers of the in-group/out-group traps. But it is worth considering whether this is the reason for tensions, misunderstanding and conflict rather than structural or process clarity. It can be valuable to identify and address the problems surrounding group identities rather than just rely on structural or process solutions.

1   Show that in-group/out-group distinctions can change

As with pedestrians and motorists above, the challenge for HR is to create one group across the HR function, or – better still – the whole organisation. The key is to find and focus on the common, unifying goals. Everyone travelling to and from work is a commuter, and we all want to get there as fast as possible. Across HR we're all working to implement the organisation's people strategy. Across the company we are all working to make the strategy successful.

2   Teach people how to walk in another person's shoes

The children in Jane Elliot's classroom were sad and afraid when they were suddenly thrust into the role of out-group member.

Recalling occasions when you've been in an out-group position, and remembering how painful that was, trains us in perspective-taking. People need to learn how to take the perspective of different groups within the HR function, and across the business. Formal skills training, regular practice, job rotations and cross-functional team work will all embed these skills.

3   Look for similarities between opposing groups

Fans of opposing football teams who may be prepared to do battle on the terraces are all equally passionate about soccer.

Members of different HR teams are all part of the function, and basic human needs for social connection transcend particular labels. How well do people know each other personally across the organisation? Do people understand each other's ambitions, values and passions? There's plenty of scope for HR to take action in building these crucial formal and informal connections.

4   Work on building security within departments and business units

People are more likely to stereotype and be divisive when they feel they have something to lose.

We've all had experience of workplaces characterised by power-plays and backstabbing, with departments appearing to compete with each other for their importance to the organisation. But you avoid this by helping each department to feel successful and secure.

If teams feel valued and valuable they are less likely to create divisions and seek comfort from inter-group differences and rivalries, and will be less likely to criticise other team members.

5   Share the insights of neuroscience

Include an awareness of the neuroscience of bias across the HR function. It takes effort to overcome in-group/out-group bias, but no amount of process-clarification will substitute for melding your groups together.

You'll not only see the benefits in collaboration within HR, but the understanding and behaviour will be an effective model for the business.

"So, are male and female brains different?"

Gender differences in the brain, and whether it matters

Whenever we talk with a group about neuroscience, we inevitably get a question about gender differences in the brain.

The short answer? There are some. The more complex issue is whether they make any difference to how people perform at work.

So, since this is such a thorny issue (and since every HR function gathers data about the gender diversity of their organisation) we thought it would be useful to summarise the current scientific understanding, and outline the potential implications for you in the workplace.

Differences between male and female brains

Israeli research has shown that distinctive differences between male and female brains can be seen in the womb[128] as early as 26 weeks.

A recent study that received a lot of popular press coverage mapped the connections in male and female brains[129] at different ages. It found quite noticeable differences, and that these differences became more pronounced as children matured into their teens.

The study by Dr Ragini Verma of the University of Pennsylvania looked at the connections in the cerebrum, which is above and towards the front of the brain and responsible for activities like thinking, and the cerebellum below and towards the back of the brain that is more responsible for taking action.

Each of these brain areas is divided into two hemispheres: the famous right and left sides of the brain.

In the cerebrum, male brains are more connected *within* the hemispheres, in females *across* the hemispheres. In the cerebellum it's the other way around, with male brains more connected across the hemispheres. Verma believes this reflects the cognitive skill differences between men and women which we discuss more below.

Nature or nurture?

But the question remains is this nature (our brains evolved to be different) or nurture (we behave differently according to our different social tasks, so our brains developed differently)? There are strong arguments for both theories. But first let's discuss some of the differences that have been demonstrated in how men and women perform and the studies that try to explain the sources of these differences in the brain.

As always, it's important to bear in mind that how you *apply* your brain is going to make as much, if not more, difference as structure and functioning.

Physical differences between men's and women's brains
Size: does it matter?

The brain in human males is on average about 10% larger than female brains.[130] But although the extra mass potentially gives males more processing-power, it doesn't necessarily mean that it is utilised, or that men are more intelligent.

Most scientists believe that the difference in size can be accounted for by the need to operate a larger male body mass. Despite this difference in brain size women perform just as well as men in intelligence tests (if you believe they measure anything reliable).

Differences in grey and white brain mass

Male and female brains are also constructed differently.

Researchers at the University of California-Irvine have found that men have 6.5 times more grey matter than women;[131] sometimes called "thinking matter," it makes up the brain's information-processing centres.

Women's brains have more than 9.5 times more of the interconnecting white matter which connects the processing centres.

"Female brains might be more efficient",[132] says Richard Haier, lead psychologist on the study.

Left-brain, right-brain and language

Men tend to process more in the left side of their brain,[133] women tend to use both left and right-brain.

"Females seem to have language functioning in both sides of the brain," according to Martha Bridge Denckla of the Kennedy Krieger Institute. And this activity across both hemispheres is thought to promote better intuitive skills, and women's better verbal communication skills.

But don't worry if you are a man reading this: we note your advantages below.

Evolutionary psychologist David Geary maintains that if there is a greater brain area dedicated to a set of skills, it follows that the skills will be more refined.[134]

"The frontal area of the cortex and the temporal area of the cortex are more precisely organised in women, and are bigger in volume," says Geary. Again, this difference may go towards explaining the advantage women have in language skills.

Cognitive differences between men and women
Processing language

Radiologist Joseph Lurito mapped the areas of the brain activated while participants of both genders listened to an audio-book.[135] Women, it transpired, used both the right and left hemispheres; men used only the left hemisphere.

Researchers at Yale studied the areas of the brain involved in active reading. In right-handed men, they found that just a small area in the left hemisphere (the left inferior frontal gyrus) was active for reading. For the right-handed women the pattern of activation was different: both frontal lobes were active and brain activity was more diffused.

These studies illustrate what appears to be a general difference in the functioning of men's and women's brains: men are more likely to use a small area of the brain, on just one side, for a particular task; women typically use more of the brain, on both hemispheres, for the same task.

Why the difference?

The evolutionary hypothesis for this is that women needed language and emotional skills to manage relationships between peers and their children whilst the men were away hunting. David Geary suggests that this behaviour, referred to as "relational aggression," may have given females a survival advantage[136] long ago.

"If the ability to use language to organise relationships was of benefit during evolutionary history, and used more frequently by women," he says, "we would expect language differences to become exaggerated."

Evolutionists suggest this is why the differences in "brain wiring" and skills developed. The theory is that women also use language to build relationships today, and this can be seen in studies. "Women pause more, allow the other person to speak more, offer facilitative gestures," says Geary.

Evolution has continued into present-day differences, which Geary suggests means women use language skills to their advantage: "Females use language more when they compete. They gossip, manipulate information."

Spatial skills

Another difference between the genders is in tasks that involve spatial navigation. Men are generally better at this than women.

The differences in "wiring" referred to earlier may also explain why men, whose brains are mainly connected *within* the hemispheres, can focus on things that do not need inputs from both hemispheres.

Hence the belief that men find multitasking more difficult and tend to focus on one thing at a time. In the cerebellum, the cross-hemisphere links related to action give men better motor abilities and physical coordination.

Map-reading and giving directions

Map-reading abilities are a perennial favourite in the gender-difference debate.

Women, it transpires, are more likely to rely on landmark cues[137] for direction ("Turn right at the Crown and Goose pub"). Men are more likely to use abstract concepts in navigation ("Go east for a mile, then turn north").

Those different strategies correlate with different brain regions. Neuroscientists have found that women use the cerebral cortex (mostly the right parietal cortex), while men use primarily the left hippocampus, a nucleus deep inside the brain which remains inactive in women's brains during navigational tasks.

Both methods of navigation work. But they're very different, and the brain areas involved are completely separate.

One theory is that their different spatial abilities served men well while they were hunting.

An alternative view is that nurture develops these differences in children.[138] Martha Denckla of the Kennedy Krieger Institute claims there is persuasive evidence that we build up our brain's representation of space by moving through space. And anyone who spends time around children knows that boys tend to get a lot more practice "moving through space" (chasing a ball, for instance) than girls do.

She believes that we could possibly erase this difference if girls were actively encouraged at a young age to do more physical games requiring co-ordination. She predicts that as more and more girls engage in sports traditionally reserved for boys (such as soccer), the data on spatial ability will show fewer disparities between females and males.

Processing emotions

Neuroscientists at Harvard have used fMRI scanning to study how emotion is processed in the brains of children[139] between the ages of seven and seventeen.

In young children they found that emotional activity was localised in primitive subcortical areas of the brain, specifically in the amygdala. That's one reason why a six-year-old cannot tell you she is feeling sad; the part of the brain that does the talking, the cerebral cortex, doesn't connect to the part of the brain where the emotion is occurring, the amygdala.

In adolescence, brain activity associated with emotion moves up to the cerebral cortex. The seventeen-year-old is able to explain what she is feeling, and why. But that change occurs only in girls. In boys, the locus of emotional control remains in the amygdala, which is why adolescent boys find it hard to talk about emotions – and for some that continues into adulthood.

Managing emotions

Women, on the whole, may also be better than men at controlling their emotions. Researchers have recently discovered that sections of the brain used to control aggression and anger responses are larger in women[140] than in men.

And indeed we're all aware that in stressful events men are more likely to adopt the fight / flight response while women favour "tend and befriend."

Cambridge neuroscientist John Coates claims that men and women tend to be stressed by different issues.[141] Women have the same levels of stress hormones as men but they are generally triggered by social rather than competitive stress.

What are the implications for the workplace?

The nature versus nurture debate continues. Meanwhile, increasingly sophisticated brain-imaging techniques demonstrate differences in male and female brain functioning even as their performance outcomes are similar. And none of this means that the application in the workplace favours one gender over the other.

It's also important to remember that male and female brains share a multiplicity of structures and functions, and are actually more similar than they are different.

What's more, there are many women with better-than-average spatial skills, and many men with excellent writing and language skills. And studies in neuroplasticity suggest that nurturing and training the brain offers exciting possibilities for enhancing what nature has provided.

"My 'feedback' is your 'criticism.' How can I get it right?"

How brains process feedback: what does and doesn't work

Feedback is the mantra of most people-management processes. Yes, it can be a bit tough to deliver, but surely that means it's worthwhile? And sometimes it's so good to get that irritation off your chest. Everyone just needs to learn how to take constructive feedback, right?

We've spent many years trying to train people to give feedback, and working with teams on creating a feedback culture. But at the end of the day, is there any evidence that it works?

Anecdotally, many people tell us it doesn't. They dread it. Or at least "constructive" feedback (which is a polite way of saying "negative" feedback) doesn't work when that's all they get. And they tell us they get very little "positive" feedback, if any at all.

Our own experience of managing people is that positive feedback, focused on what's being done right, can be effective. But the dreaded "constructive criticism" kind of feedback does nothing to improve performance.

When we stepped back and really analysed the results we were getting from the feedback process, we found they were at best neutral, and at worst damaging to individual confidence and work relationships. That sent us on a mission to understand why we're so attached to feedback and whether there's any scientific evidence to support it.

When is feedback effective – and when doesn't it work?

To start with, let's agree what we are talking about - because the term 'feedback' can mean different things to different people. A helpful definition of feedback[142] that we use is "information provided by an agent (e.g. boss, teacher, peer, parent, experience) regarding aspects of one's performance or understanding."

The psychological evidence

The most comprehensive study of performance feedback[143] found mixed evidence on the value of feedback: approximately 1/3 of the time feedback led to improved performance, 1/3 of the time it had no measurable effect, and in a 1/3 of examples it led to worse performance.

But the devil is in the detail, so it's worth exploring a little more:

- **Feedback can improve performance on simple**

tasks that people have experience in doing. An example might be completing a form or logging into the self-service portal.

- **Feedback can also improve performance on complex tasks.** But in specific circumstances where there are clear goals set by the employee: "My goal was to decide the structure and headings for the report. My boss had a couple of useful changes to the headings." The study's authors think this is because in these cases employees are focused on learning and goal attainment, and as a result worry less about protecting their image. They overcome their concerns about image in order to achieve their goal. For this to be effective, the goals must be established before the feedback is given. This is especially important in training, during workshops or coaching sessions.

- **Continual feedback may improve performance through improved motivation.**[144] However the research suggests that when feedback improves performance in this way the effect is dependent on a continuous flow of feedback, and motivation and performance suffer if the feedback stops.

It can even mean the individual is unable to perform without the continuous feedback. The study authors suggest that the cost of maintaining continuous feedback may outweigh the benefits, and could result in only shallow learning which may not be useful later. For example, this can happen in apprentice / mentoring-type situations where the trainee has got so used to "sitting next to Nellie" and getting constant commentary on their work that their motivation and confidence collapses when they attempt the work without "Nellie" alongside them.

- **Feedback can have negative results when given to employees engaged in complex, difficult or unfamiliar tasks.** In these situations the fear of looking incompetent shifts the person's focus from the job they're involved in to protecting their self-image, which has a negative impact on performance.

- **Feedback about attitude and personal traits doesn't work and damages performance.** So... don't bother trying to tell that team member about their constant chatter which is driving their colleagues mad. Better to ask questions that get them to realise themselves that it might be a distraction

Experiencing feedback as a threat

Neuroscience research has found that just saying the words "Let me give you some feedback" creates a threat response in the brain.

An understanding of threat and reward responses is central to understanding how people react, so we've developed the CORE model for easy reference. There is more detail on all of this in *Brain basics* in the Introduction but, briefly, CORE stands for:

Certainty: our confidence that we know what the future holds

Options: the extent to which we feel we have choices

Reputation: our relative importance to others (our social ranking)

Equity: our sense of fairness

Feedback can create a threat or reward response in any of these domains in social situations, but it's most likely to create threat unless it is very specific, deliberately positive and delivered in a brain-savvy way.

Negative feedback obviously impacts on a person's sense of reputation: they may feel humiliated or ashamed, and that can also lead to isolation from their colleagues. Feedback perceived as criticism creates uncertainty for an employee, which you'll recognise in responses such as, "So how should I be doing this?" And being told they're not performing to expectations limits an employee's options: they no longer know the right way to go about their work ("That's not how I like to work"). This probably feels unfair, so that's impacting on their perception of equity as well ("I should be able to decide the order I do things in").

When feedback does work

It is possible for feedback to have a positive outcome, if it's formulated with care, and given and received in the right frame of mind.

The right mindset for feedback

Carol Dweck's research on Fixed and Growth mindsets[145] suggests two very different sets of believes about performance which will determine a manager's attitude to giving feedback and a staff member's response to it. (You can read more about mindsets in the chapter *"If talent is our number-one priority, why don't we have a queue for our top jobs?"* and in *Talent mindset* in the *Leading yourself* section.)

People with a fixed mindset are characterised by their belief that performance is based on abilities fixed by their intelligence or talents. Managers with this view of the world find it hard to see the point of giving feedback: as they see it, an employee's innate talents determine performance, and trying to improve them is pretty much a waste of time.

Employees with these beliefs tend to dismiss feedback, and show less persistence and less learning from experience. They're more concerned about their reputation and comparing themselves with their peers. A fixed mindset gives them no mechanisms for dealing with setbacks and failure – they're more likely to give up than take risks on the perception of their performance.

The alternative set of beliefs is a growth mindset. People with this world view believe performance is based on hard work, experience and effort. Dweck's studies have found that people with a growth mindset work harder, learn from experience, and are willing to take more risk to achieve results. In one experiment, people with growth mindset beliefs paid more attention to learning when they had *gone wrong* than whether they scored the highest marks.

Managers with a growth mindset are more inclined to give feedback, provide stretch assignments, and offer coaching.

Giving the right kind of feedback

So, how would you craft your feedback to suggest the potential for improvement? You could change the emphasis from problem to solution: from "You're good at data but not communication," to "You've worked really hard on the analysis part; what's the best way of communicating your findings?"

The aim is to focus people on the effort that generated results rather than innate talent, and primes people to seek their own insights on an area that needs change.

What about "positive" feedback?

There is some evidence that feedback which fosters self-esteem can boost performance.[146] Getting approval feels good: it's a sign that you're part of the in-group. It's both highly motivating and rewarding.

But it has been well-documented that approval also reduces intrinsic motivation to gain mastery.[147] Approval may simply signal success rather than failure; unless you focus on how the person got there – the risk they took, or the effort they put in – there's no opportunity to learn.

It can also lead to comparisons, which can be divisive in the workplace. Our brain pays a lot of attention to assessing our social position,[148] and there is evidence that other people's success or failure can trigger envy[149] or schadenfreude (that secret delight in the misfortunes of others).

So what should you do about feedback?

Research on positive feedback has shown that supporting a sense of competence makes people feel good,[150] and that when people are motivated and engaged in their work, they do it well.

But our research shows that UK leaders, on the whole, are failing to maximise feelings of reward in their workforces.[151] When asked whether their leader gave them praise, positive feedback or recognised their contribution to the organisation, just 17% of employees said the feedback they got was always constructive; 42% said feedback was only ever negative, or that there was none at all.

But again, the devil is in the detail.

The Progress Principle study on how organisations sustain effective performance and high employee satisfaction[152] undertook a survey of 238 employees in seven companies over several months. From diaries kept by knowledge workers who recorded an event that stood out each day, it was apparent that they experienced three types of positive feedback:

> **Nourishing events** that were uplifting. For example, when a boss praised them or provided emotional support.
> **Catalytic events** that helped work tasks, such as resources or training being provided.
> **Progress events** involving getting feedback on how they were making progress in meaningful work.

Significantly, employees' "best" days featured progress events. Next most satisfying were catalytic events and the least-rewarding were nourishing events.

This means it's worth saying "Good job!" to people (nourishing events). It's even better to give people resources and training (catalytic events). But if you want to maximise the impact on motivation and engagement, comment on progress towards a goal that is important to someone.

When bosses praise progress, they remind employees that they're advancing and signal that it's noticed – all of which is consistent with a growth mindset.

So, the answer to the thorny issue of feedback seems to be:

- focus on positive feedback
- focus it on progress made towards goals people value
- encourage employees to assess their own performance, and especially how they can do even better at what they're doing.

How well are you doing on feedback? And how would your leaders score on giving this type of feedback?

"I dream about performance management that works."

Brain-savvy performance management

Press coverage of Microsoft's decision to abandon its "stack ranking" system catapulted the whole debate about performance management and ratings into the headlines for a few vociferous weeks at the end of 2013.

It probably came as a surprise to many HR people that a system popularised in the 1980s was still being used by a supposedly leading-edge company like Microsoft. And especially by a company that needs highly creative people bringing all their discretionary effort to work.

The system, often referred to in the US as "rank and yank" required managers to rank team members on a bell curve of performance. Only a limited percentage could be designated as top performers, and a set percentage also had to be labelled as low performers and targets for firing.

Many drew the connection between Microsoft's poor showing on a number of product launches and the hated stack ranking system. It drove a culture of politicking and backstabbing, forcing team members to compete against each other for ranking, and for managers to make arbitrary judgements to meet the percentages.

Looked at through the lens of neuroscience it was almost a perfect storm for closing down productivity, creativity and reward mechanisms in the brain.

And this is true of many performance management processes. The way most of them are executed creates a brain-fried rather than a brain-savvy experience for employees (brain-fried being maximum stress in the brain, far beyond what is useful).

There's nothing wrong with the goals of performance management

Most performance management processes aim for:

- Improved performance
- Fair promotion and pay practices
- Reliable legal documentation
- Measuring performance against goal achievement (usually for the purposes of allocating reward)
- Helping employees with career and skills development.

In some cases they also aim to help the most able employees perform even better.

There's nothing inherently wrong with the intent behind performance management. It's the tactics that make the difference. Neuroscience can point out some fundamental flaws that mean organisations may really be creating a no-win situation.

Here are some of the findings, and some ideas for how you could make your performance management process more brain-savvy and more productive.

Threat and reward – in neuroscience

Here we're not referring to the role of performance management in threatening the sack or rewarding with bonuses or perks, but the sense of threat or reward created in the brain which activates an avoidance state (in the case of a threat) or an approach state (in the case of reward).

The CORE model identifies the common factors that activate both reward and threat responses in social situations. They are:

Certainty:	our confidence that we know what the future holds
Options:	the extent to which we feel we have choices
Reputation:	our relative importance to others (our social ranking)
Equity:	our sense of fairness

These four elements activate either the "primary reward" or the "primary threat" circuitry of the brain.

The results are strongly felt. For example, a perceived threat to one's sense of equity – a chronically underperforming colleague being the only person to get a pay rise – activates similar brain networks to a threat to your life. A perceived increase to your reputation – your good work being praised at a team meeting – feels as good as getting a cash bonus.

The reaction happens in a nanosecond and is automatic, driving behaviour before we have a chance to rationally consider our response.

What makes the process threatening?

In performance management, a threat response might be triggered by:

- uncertainty about a manager's opinion of our performance
- a direction to carry out the role according to the manager's instructions, reducing options

- negative feedback, potentially creating a sense of shame and reducing connection with the group
- the power in the process resting solely with the line manager, creating a sense of inequity

Let's look at the elements of a typical performance management process and how the science can inform thinking.

Goals

A surprising number of organisations we speak to still have managers drafting their team members' goals. And if they do not completely draft the goals themselves they are the ones who decide the areas and the measures.

Goals written *for* employees will lack buy-in. Research on changing behaviour has shown that people need to have buy-in, and a vision of the future, to resist impulsive behaviour based on past habits.

Scientists in Germany found that vividly imagining the future activates the hippocampus[153] – the part of the brain responsible for memory and future visualisation – and the anterior cingulated cortex, the ACC, which is involved in reward-based decision-making. This resulted in a greater ability to delay immediate rewards and reduce impulsive choices, thus maintaining new behaviour.

Achieving goals means creating new ways of working and this will only be achieved if employees can overcome their automatic habit system by activating their prefrontal cortex, the planning and goals-directed brain area.

Having employees draft their own goals for agreement with their manager is an improvement. But giving immediate reward and reinforcement for a new behaviour is essential for shifting from old habits run by the basal ganglia, and creating a new habit which must be done by planning, priming and reinforcing using the prefrontal cortex. So, if you want an employee to use data in their presentations you need to get them to see the benefits, understand how they must act, and offer praise when they successfully adopt the behaviour.

Feedback

Perhaps the most brain-fried element of performance management is the whole notion that feedback will improve performance. As far back as 1994 psychological research was showing that 38% of feedback made performance worse.[154] In the light of that, it's a mystery how it ever became the byword for good management practice. We've never met anyone who thought feedback did much good for them. It mainly helps the person delivering the feedback, by giving them an opportunity to off-load something that's been irritating them.

A neuroscientific analysis demonstrates that feedback creates threat in all of the CORE social domains. So the person receiving the feedback is very unlikely to hear it, let alone be able to do anything constructive about it ("I told him, but he just didn't seem to take it in").

In addition, for the feedback not to fall on deaf ears the person delivering it *and* the person receiving it need to share the same mental model – the construct we create to help us make sense of the volume of incoming information. Which, given our diverse experience in the world, is highly unlikely.

Shifting mental models is hard to do, and very unlikely when there is little or no reward for the brain: "She said I need to develop my customer relations skills, but I think she's just under pressure to get our sales results up, and anyway her customer skills are terrible."

Personal change

The neuroscientific understanding of goals and feedback raises questions about how people *can* best be helped to change.

Research is showing we don't always approach work goals rationally. Rather, we think about our future self in the same way as we think about another person.[155] How well we know our self today will determine how we achieve goals and how much we listen to feedback, even positive feedback.

People need to have a clear mental picture of their future self and be sufficiently self-aware to know the degree of change that's possible.

Rating scales

Rating scales or rankings create in-groups and out-groups within the business. It's possible this might foster some healthy competition across the organisation, but there's no doubt it heightens tension and reduces collaboration.

Rewards

The assumption in performance management is that people will perform better if they are rewarded with more money. Research by behavioural economist Dan Ariely suggests performance actually decreases with higher levels of reward.[156] Money is both motivator and stressor: if rewards are very high the stress reduces performance.

What is often ignored is that socially-based rewards such as praise, positive feedback, public recognition and being given greater responsibility create a reward trigger in the brain of wellbeing that can be equally, or more powerful than an impersonal bonus. By ignoring the neuroscience of reward,[157] traditional performance management systems are missing out on the power of social reward and positive feedback.

Why does ineffective performance management persist?

Whatever the challenges and inadequacies, the current approach is familiar. And our brains like to be able to predict what's going to happen.

What's even more important to understand is that while current forms of performance management create a threat response for staff, and therefore may be largely ineffective, they are rewarding, and therefore brain-savvy, for managers. Managers have certainty about the timing, rating and the messages in the process; they have options about when and how the review takes place; they have power and their reputation is enhanced. They probably feel all this is fair.

They may only feel differently when the process is applied to them!

What to do? A brain-savvy solution

The brain-fried elements of performance management can be overcome by shifting the process in the direction of more CORE rewards rather than threats:

- Give employees control over process, timing, the data collected and especially who they ask for feedback and the goals they create.
- Managers and peers focus only on positive feedback.
- Teach employees to self-assess against well-defined standards so the manager's role becomes that of a performance coach.

The brain-savvy approach is to give employees options and control, coaching rather than criticism, and to focus on what is going right rather than what is going wrong.

"Are we missing out on free rewards?"

Brain-savvy reward strategies

When I worked in the City we had a saying that we "created our own prima donnas." Usually they were highly talented individuals who earned a lot of money for the bank and as a result their manager was terrified of losing them and indulged their every request.

The individual would get hooked on their own power and start behaving badly, which inevitably the manager would ignore. This would encourage more of the same until eventually the prima donna was fired because they went too far. It was a scenario where everyone lost.

The big issue was always the same: who's going to be the first manager to stand up to the prima donna? And it's a very similar issue to adopting a different culture and policy on reward. Which institution is going to be the first to adopt a more scientific approach to reward?

The beginnings of change

There's evidence that business leaders are beginning to pay attention to neuroscience research when deciding business policy generally. Business strategist Art Kleiner says the most widely-read articles he publishes are about the workings of the brain.[158]

Studies in neuroscience are raising questions about whether monetary rewards were ever the most effective way to motivate people. Not only could we be pulling the wrong lever, but we could also be overlooking alternative types of rewards which have minimal financial cost to our organisations.

We need the brains of our people to be working at optimum, and the prevailing reward systems don't encourage that. If HR understood the science of motivation and reward better, even if the system of monetary compensation proves too difficult to change in the short-term, other forms of reward might be introduced into the mix and begin to count more in the total reward package.

The science of rewards

"There's a mismatch between what science knows and what business does," says business author Dan Pink. To support his assertion, he cites consistent findings across many studies that financial incentives *inhibit* rather than promote creative problem solving and motivation.[159]

It seems that once basic needs are met, additional income does not affect job or life satisfaction. Happiness research has consistently found that the most satisfied people are those with the strongest social connections rather than the most money.[160]

And a 2009 review of 51 studies has detailed "overwhelming evidence" that financial incentives actually reduce motivation and pleasure at work.[161]

The reverse effect of bonuses

Dan Ariely's book title *Predictably Irrational* is probably an excellent description of the bonus debate. His research has shown that when groups are offered a monetary bonus for higher performance, those offered low and medium-level rewards perform better or just as well as each other.[162]

Amazingly, the group who were offered the highest bonuses did significantly worse, especially when the task involved cognitive effort.

In a further study Ariely demonstrated that when people were asked to perform in public, their performance diminished.[163] The research indicates that anxiety overrides the motivation to do well, and interferes with cognitive functioning and achievement.

The extraordinary benefits of creating "flow"

An environment where people are immersed in their work, and enjoy a deep and sustained focus on it, bringing all their skills and motivation to a task, is referred to as a state of "flow".[164]

Creating flow in a workplace is dependent on the balance between the perceived challenge and someone's perception of their ability. Too much challenge results in panic; too easy a task for a skilled employee results in boredom.

Achieving the optimum balance leads to a deeply satisfying experience at work: the activity itself becomes its own reward. What's more, those employees who are highly engaged and able to sustain their performance over time[165] not only show stronger commitment and have more job satisfaction but enjoy better health.

And the benefits of satisfying work aren't only enjoyed by the employees themselves. They make their companies more money.[166] A recent study of Fortune's *100 Best Companies to Work for in America* found that companies whose employees feel pride in their work and are happy with employee policies generate higher stock returns than comparable companies.

That works in reverse as well. Dan Ariely has tested the impact of meaningful work compared with pointless work and measured how financial reward impacts on both. He has demonstrated that just a minimal amount of acknowledgement provides motivation and meaning. But when people or their efforts are ignored, they need *more* money[167] to keep working.

The essence of work is... social

Economists, and most business people, assume that work is an economic contract: time and skills given in exchange for money. But behavioural economists and neuroscientists are now suggesting that work is actually a social contract.

Social relations are a primary need for human beings – as essential to us as food, water and sex. Matt Lieberman, founder of social cognitive neuroscience, says: "Social is not one of our programmes – it is our basic operating system."[168]

Research using fMRI has demonstrated that we are motivated more by social rewards than by monetary rewards.[169] The brain experiences physical pleasure when we are socially rewarded – when we give, when people co-operate with us, when we believe we have a good reputation or when we receive recognition.

Non-monetary rewards

There are other types of rewards for which neuroscience can produce measurable evidence of their effectiveness, though they are commonly ignored in discussions about rewarding employees.

Being treated fairly by others, for example, increases activity in the ventral striatum and ventromedial prefrontal cortex,[170] two key components of the brain's reward system. Positive feedback about one's social reputation also "lights up" these reward pathways in the brain.

We also frequently ignore the culture that people work in. Dan Pink proposes that increased satisfaction is associated with three factors:[171] having autonomy over one's time or work, enjoying a sense of mastery, and having a sense of purpose. There is evidence that self-directed decision-making encourages employees to thrive.[172] And efforts to help employees to move into that desirable state of flow pay dividends in satisfaction at a physiological level as the brain experiences a reward response.

Enhancing social contact in the workplace can also be very rewarding.[173] Mentoring subordinates or nurturing client relationships leads to an increased sense of personal engagement – as well as a better bottom line.

Simple strategies like encouraging employees in close proximity to make eye contact,[174] and smile have also been found to improve client satisfaction – probably due to greater social connectedness among employees. The improved relationship between employees influences their relationship with clients in a positive way.

The rewards of reputation

Because humans attach such importance to relationships, it seems clear that we should consider how reputation – our social standing compared to others – can be an effective reward.

Employees usually make such comparisons not across the whole company but within an identified peer group (in psychological jargon their "in-group"). If you're a CEO you will compare yourself with other CEOs. Traders will compare themselves with other traders, HR business partners with other business partners.

Research demonstrates that we feel envious if someone we relate to receives greater reward and recognition.[175] And this envy leads to reduced co-operation and empathy and even a delight in any setbacks that may befall the other person.

But concerns about reputation can be used positively. People feel rewarded when their reputation is enhanced through learning new skills, being praised publicly or having their expertise recognised. And social media can make this kind of instant-reward simple to implement.

Changing rewards – or remaining predictably irrational

Neuroscience evidence points to the need for a radical overhaul of the assumptions which underpin corporate reward strategies. Dan Pink tells us that employees expect to be given fair reward but beyond that additional money will not motivate discretionary effort.[176]

The challenge for business then, is to create reward policies that give *fair* reward in monetary terms combined with under-used brain-based rewards.

Will we rise to the challenge of the evidence, or remain irrational?

"Thanks for coming in to meet us: please tell us about..."

First-round interviews: how being brain-savvy can help

"Tell us about your approach to hiring: do you recruit with a growth or fixed mindset?"

"Interviewing, by its very nature, is stressful; what steps would you take to ensure that you're not triggering a limbic attack in your candidates?"

"How would you ensure that your brain's need for reward is satisfied at the expense of a threat for the candidate?"

If you're involved in the interview process for your organisation and you have no idea what these questions are about, then you might want to read on...

Recruiting with a growth mindset or a fixed mindset

Stanford University psychologist Carol Dweck has spent decades researching the impact of mindset: your outlook, the frame of mind you bring to a task.[177] She believes that it's not just our skills and abilities that bring us success but whether we approach our goals with a fixed or growth mindset.

How does it make a difference?

If you have a fixed mindset, you believe that talents are innate and static and as a result see effort as fruitless: "They've either got leadership talent / a hunger for sales growth / a feeling for client relationships, or they haven't." You're probably going to be looking for individuals who exhibit the skills and abilities that are required in the role from day one: "You'll need to be able to hit the ground running."

Obviously, this is going to make your recruitment process more difficult because you have a narrow set of criteria and a smaller pool of suitable candidates.

Recruiters who walk into the interview room with a growth mindset believe that talent can be developed, and see effort as the pathway to mastery.

They're going to be looking for potential: someone who might not have all the experience of the incumbent, but they're confident will have mastered the role in a number of months – and might also have a future elsewhere in the organisation. And, as a result, they can take advantage of a larger talent pool and a more varied group of interview candidates.

And what kind of mindset does your candidate have?

When you're more attuned to your own frame of mind you'll find it easier to explore what kind of mindset your candidate has.

And it's useful for you to know, because candidates with a fixed mindset tend to see effort as fruitless because talent is fixed. As a result, they will avoid challenges and give up easily in the face of obstacles: "If I have to work so hard at it, it's not what I'm suited for." They dislike any discussion of what hasn't worked and tend to feel threatened by other people's success: "Why are they staying late, they can't be very smart if they need to do that."

Candidates who come with a growth mindset, on the other hand, embrace challenge and are likely to persist in the face of setbacks. They see effort as the pathway to mastery and are ready to learn from criticism. They find lessons and inspiration in other people's success.

These are the candidates who readily answer questions about what they would have done differently, or what they learnt from a setback, and who might ask questions about training opportunities. They might refer to a leader who has been an inspiration, and they're probably also the candidates who will ask for interview feedback.

Managing interview stress

When interviewing is something you do regularly it's easy to forget how stressful the interview process can be for the candidate. Put yourself in their shoes and you'll soon understand that being probed and examined is bound to increase anxiety levels.

Some managers and interviewers still believe that applying pressure in an interview is a useful way of finding out how someone will perform in a stressful job situation. According to psychologist Jessica Payne, we perform at our best when we're mildly stressed.[178] So the situation itself is enough to create the ideal conditions: we don't need to pile on any additional pressure.

As an interviewer you need to consider what your intention is when interviewing. If it's to encourage a candidate to perform at their best, and feel confident to present all their talents and experience, you'll want to do your best to put them at ease.

Going limbic

In situations of extreme stress our prefrontal cortex, sometimes known as the CEO of the brain, is taken over by the limbic system (a complex set of structures which has the job of managing our emotions). This is situated in our mid brain and operates without our conscious awareness.

When we're overly stressed, our limbic system takes over, shutting down our prefrontal cortex and readying us for fight or flight. In an interview situation you see a candidate who just seems to freeze: you've asked them a competency-based question and they simply can't think of an example to give you.

How you handle this as the interviewer can be the difference between getting the best out of a candidate, or hammering their confidence and seeing the interview going from bad to worse. Asking the candidate to take their time, or acknowledging it can be difficult to think of an example can be all it takes to get the back on track – giving their prefrontal cortex the space to think about the question.

Who's being rewarded? A CORE analysis...

The CORE model gives some useful insights on the interaction between interviewer and candidate.

Essentially, we're social beings, and the motivation of our social behaviour is to minimize threat and maximize reward. (Even in an interview.) The CORE model identifies four areas where threat and reward are most commonly triggered: when Certainty, Options, Reputation and Equity come into play.

Sharing some certainty

In an interview, it's obviously the interviewer who holds all the aces. They have a huge sense of certainty: they know exactly how long the interview will last, what questions they will ask (well, hopefully) and what skills and qualities they're looking for etc.

So anything the interviewer can do to give the candidate some sense of certainty will help alleviate the sense of threat they're experiencing. This could start before the day of the interview by sending out information to the candidate about what they can expect: who will be on the panel, any supporting materials you'd like them to bring, how long it will last.

In the interview, always start by giving an overview of what you will be covering – think of them as the key stages and outline them with the candidate. Sometimes you will see them physically relax as their brain experiences the "reward" of recovering a degree of certainty.

Being aware of your options

The second threat/reward trigger is the degree to which we feel we have any options in any given situation. No options make us feel trapped and powerless.

Again, it's the interviewer who can choose which questions to ask, and when. The candidate has no choice but to do as directed and to answer the questions they're given. It's quite a satisfying, "rewarding," process for the interviewer to be proceeding methodically, but for the candidate, with no choices about how the interview will be conducted, it can only feel threatening.

This may be an instance where it's a bit more difficult to create some options for the candidate. Perhaps, if there are a number of selection activities, you can give them some choice about which they tackle first – but this isn't always possible.

Boosting reputation

It goes without saying that, in this situation, the interviewer is much higher status than the candidate in relative terms. If you can find ways of boosting the candidate's status they are more likely to answer questions fluently and you'll find out more about their true selves.

This can be achieved quite simply by, for example remarking on their impressively varied CV or most recent achievements, or congratulating them on having graduated from a particular university.

Ensuring equity

Finally, it goes without saying that equity is crucial. You won't want to discriminate against a candidate on grounds of sex, age, or gender, or *between* candidates by treating them differently.

Look for ways to make your process transparent, consistent and fair. Even if your process is challenging, as long as the candidate perceives it as having been fair, they will take away a positive impression of you and the organisation.

So what can we learn from all this?

For us, it's all about being more conscious of how our brain works and then using what we know to support what we're doing (in this case, interviewing).

Knowing, for example, that we perform best when we're only mildly stressed, and setting up an environment that fosters this. And being mindful of our own brain's desire to seek rewards, and looking for ways to give that boost to the candidate. These all make for a more brain-savvy interview process.

Why would you do all this?

Because it's important to model the kind of behaviour you want to be selecting for, and would hope is exhibited throughout the organisation.

Because encouraging a candidate to perform at their best helps to ensure that you don't miss the best candidates.

And because whether you hire this candidate or not, you want them to go away feeling they've had a positive experience, and that your company is a great one to work for. After all, you will interview far more people than you will ever select to join the organisation, so all those candidates will be going forth and spreading positive (or negative) views of the enterprise.

So, thanks for coming along today and taking the time to meet with us. Successful candidates will be invited back to the second stage of our interview process, where we will explore the impact of bias.

We'll be in touch.

"Welcome back: it's good to meet with you again..."

Second-round interviews: avoiding bias in selection

Good to see you again. We're so glad you've chosen to continue our dialogue.

You'll remember from our last meeting that we explored the topics of growth versus fixed mindset. We also discussed the impact that stress might have on your performance in this interview process, and how our desire to minimise threat and maximise reward might impact on our behaviour as your interviewer.

At this second meeting, we'd like to explore the issues of unconscious bias in this selection process.

We're all familiar with the idea that interviewers make their minds up in the first four seconds of meeting a candidate. The obvious inference is that we should ignore this reaction and base our decision on the objective process that follows.

But hold on a minute: let's explore what's happening here and see if we might miss out on some valuable information. This reaction goes back to the "sabre-tooth tiger" era: on meeting someone we immediately evaluate whether they're friend of foe. We actually do this in much less than four seconds. It takes milliseconds. We're basically deciding: "Will this person eat me or can I eat them?"

Today, since we no longer get eaten by sabre-tooth tigers, this seems a little extreme. However, for interviewers, our advice would be: always listen to this intuition, and then dismiss it whilst you continue with your *objective* interview process. If indeed that's possible, in view of what follows.

What is decision bias?

Research by Daniel Kahneman shows we have two thought systems.[179] One is a fast, instinctive and emotional brain system and the other a slower, more deliberate and logical system. Often when we make decisions our intuitive system jumps to conclusions or takes shortcuts that the rational system doesn't question.

There are reasons why this can be very helpful: in many situations, such as interviews, we need to take in and process lots of different information in a very short space of time. The candidate may give us chapter and verse in response to a question, but as interviewers we need to listen well and not jump to conclusions before we have heard all they have to say. To take a simple example: if they talk about a change project; it's easy to assume that they have good experience of leading change.

There are more than 150 types of decision bias which could impact decisions. These are some of them that may come into play during the interview process:

Confirmation bias

This is our tendency to favour information that confirms our pre-existing beliefs or hypothesis. It's one of the reasons why we'll find it is so difficult to let go of our initial hyper-fast impression. We make this judgement and then we look for information to confirm it. We know that the candidate has attended a top university, so we may assume that they are super-smart; we may be positively biased towards their application and throughout the interview process even if the evidence from selection activities tell us otherwise.

False consensus effect

This is the tendency for us to assume that our own opinions, beliefs, preferences, values and habits are "normal" and that other people share them[180] – particularly if we think that person is similar to us. So this is a bias that can favour candidates we've already tagged as "fitting the mould." Or candidates that we like personally.

The more "like us" they are, the more we will assume they share our views – even down to having the same preferences in food. So take care if you find yourself noting that you share experiences with the candidate (you both spent a gap year in South East Asia, or you both went to the same university) and assuming "They must be similar to me – they'll fit in perfectly with the team."

This is clearly not logical but our desire for shortcuts blinds us and we make these assumptions unknowingly.

Negativity bias

This is the psychological phenomenon by which we pay more attention to negative rather than positive experiences or information.[181] We remember them more easily, or call them to mind more frequently, and respond more to them.

So if your interview candidate shares one piece of negative information – they failed a module at university, or a project didn't meet its targets – we will remember and focus on it in our decision-making, despite all the other positive evidence we may have gathered.

So when a recruiter reflects: "I like this candidate they have great experience in recent years, but I'm concerned about that project that stalled in their first role," that could be negativity bias at work.

Physical attractiveness stereotyping

Many studies have shown that we're biased to believe that physically attractive people also possess many other socially desirable personality traits.[182] We assume they're happier, more outgoing, more successful, kinder...

And yet your sales director, who's no oil painting, is one of the most successful, positive team-players in the whole organisation. But you could have overlooked them at recruitment.

What's the solution?

Unfortunately, we are all subject to these unconscious biases – and many more. So the best way to combat them is to be aware of them. That may involve taking a slightly more formal approach to interviews, and keeping your natural self in check.

It's also helpful to have a number of assessors involved, with varied backgrounds, and to avoid sharing informal views about the candidates throughout the process, until you're making your final evaluation.

And you might be interested in participating in some of the Harvard-sponsored Project Implicit online tests,[183] which explore thoughts and feelings outside of conscious awareness and control.

> So, as your interviewer today, a couple of final questions for you to ponder: "How brain-savvy is your interview process?" And having attended both interviews, we'd like to ask: "What will you do differently in your next interview?"
>
> Once again, thanks so much for coming along. We'll show you back to reception.

"Why are people so resistant to change?"

The threat response and change – how to make it more rewarding

If there's anyone in HR today who's not involved in change, you can skip to the next chapter.

Oh, you're all still here? Yes, that's what I thought. Change management is a top priority on the HR agenda, and for most businesses getting projects to deliver is crucial. But the figures are not good: according to research by *The Economist* around 70% of change programmes fail or only partially succeed.[184] For organisations that's an unacceptable cost.

Why are we failing? By and large, it's not because plans are under-funded or poorly conceived: in *The Economist's* report, lack of buy-in from people was cited as the reason for the failure. Studies in neuroscience are showing us why change is so hard and why resistance is so entrenched. They are also pointing the way to what HR can do to introduce new ways to make change programmes work.

More of the same-old...

What we often hear from HR leaders is that resistance to change is not direct. At an intellectual level most people agree with the change proposition, but time and again they revert to their old ways of working, or even fail right from the outset to make the shift to new roles and work methods. Incentives and threats serve only to drive resistance underground: most people in the department continue to work in the old way whenever the boss's back is turned, or find a work-around so they can keep using the old system.

Why do they do this? There's no *logical* reason for people to continue working in the old way. But before we leap to judgments, it's worth reflecting on the number of times we've dug in our own heels when change has affected us personally. So what can neuroscience tell us about what's happening?

Developments in functional magnetic resonance imaging (fMRI) technology have allowed scientists to watch responses at a neurobiological level. And the studies show that people's responses to change are remarkably similar: change creates the same sort of painful experience in the brain[185] to being punched or breaking a bone.

Why is change painful?

We find it hard to change because our brain responds to patterns, and likes to create them:[186] they are short cuts which reduce uncertainty and save brain-processing energy. Routine or regular activities are run by the basal ganglia which is an energy-efficient part of the brain. You don't have to work out how to open a door every time you come to one, and many parts of our job are similarly recognisable and task-efficient.

Doing something different to the norm sends an "error" message to the brain[187] which alerts the amygdala, the emotional centre of our brain which creates a flight-or-fight response. This is processed as a threat in the brain.

The prefrontal cortex can override this more primitive emotional centre – which is why we *don't* always fling down our pen and march out of the office whenever someone suggests we do something differently. But the override process takes a lot of energy and soon becomes fatigued.

Set up a reward-response

Traditional change management pays no heed to this understanding of the brain's functioning. Bonuses and incentives, or coercion, will not overcome this biological reaction, and nor will *selling* the programme more persuasively – which usually amounts to *telling* people, but in a better way.

The way to get past the threat response is to help people to decide for themselves that the new approach is what they want. Involvement in the change, being asked to contribute and having some control over how the change is introduced, all create a reward response in the brain. This can go a long way to offsetting the threat created when people are experiencing change.

Analyse the threats and rewards

We've been working with organisations to adopt a brain-savvy approach which applies the findings of neuroscience to the change process.

Our CORE model addresses the issues of Certainty, Options, Reputation and Equity which research has found are the central issues most likely to create a threat or reward response in social situations, like the workplace. (For more about this model, turn to the *CORE principles* chapter in the *Introduction*.)

The model helps understand that a threat to any of these elements will result in poor motivation, sub-optimal brain functioning and resistance to change – just at a time when employees need to be performing at their best. The model can help you to identify which of the CORE elements is threatened by the proposed changes, and reduce resistance by creating more reward responses.

Our Leaders' Change Charter

We've also developed a simple checklist for leaders which we call the Leaders' Change Charter. The Charter helps to manage change with the brain in mind. It helps your people to recognise the benefits of the change for themselves, and get involved in the process. What distinguishes it from the familiar "change buy-in" approach is that it goes beyond box-ticking and more sincere attempts at collaborative involvement, by being informed by an understanding of the basic threat and reward responses.

The steps are:

- Involving people in the design of the change strategy and the details of how it will work.
- Using good questions to encourage personal insight, and facilitating an understanding of what the change means for each individual personally, and how they can set their own goals within the broad strategy.
- Encouraging people to generate their own ways of working in line with the new approach.
- Providing training which enables people to build on their existing skills, and develop skills which match the new work patterns.
- Helping people to be solution-focused rather than problem-focused.
- Giving positive feedback and celebrating success.

This is a new way of working for many leaders. They may feel as though they've handed away control of the process, that it's all a bit time consuming and undirected, and there's not enough focus on disseminating information and telling people what to do.

But the results will be seen in better take-up of the change, with less personal pain and organisational resistance. The data is clear: we can continue to fail at change, or we can adopt a more brain-savvy approach.

"Once upon a time there was an HR leader..."

The neuro-power of stories

There was a chicken farmer who was a very keen rock climber. One day, climbing a challenging rock face, he came to a ledge where there was a large nest with three eggs in it: eagle eggs. He knew it was wrong but temptation got the better of him and he carefully put one of the eagle eggs into his rucksack. And when he got back to his farm he put the eagle egg into his hen house.

That night the mother hen sat on the huge egg, the proudest chicken you ever saw. In the fullness of time the egg hatched and the eaglet emerged. It looked around and saw the mother hen and squawked "Mama."

And so the little eagle grew up with its brother and sister chicks and learned to do all the things that chickens do: clucking, scratching in the dirt and flapping their wings.

One day many years later, the eagle-who-thought-he-was-a-chicken happened to look up at the sky and saw an eagle soaring overhead. "What's that?" he asked in awe: "It's magnificent!" "That's an eagle," said the chicken. "The King of the Birds. But we're only chickens – we're birds of the earth."

And so the eagle lived and died a chicken because that's all it believed it was, and all it thought was possible.

Why are stories so effective?

This is one of our favourite stories for when we're facilitating workshops. We use stories to pass on ideas and messages in a way which talks to the unconscious as well as the conscious mind. We know we've got it right when the next group of participants tell our story back to us: someone has passed it on to them already.

Every culture uses stories to pass on knowledge and wisdom. They're powerful tools for influencing, and once you know how our brain responds to a story, it's easy to understand why. Neuroscience is beginning to uncover the evidence of how our brain reacts to stories in a very different way to receiving information from a PowerPoint presentation, for instance.

What happens when we listen?

When we're watching a PowerPoint, with words and bullet points up on the screen, the language-processing areas of our brain – Broca's Area and Wernicke's Area – are activated to decode the meaning.

When we're listening to a story these same areas are activated, but also the areas of the brain that relate to elements of the story, for example, visual processing or the emotions. So in the story above the emotions about success and purpose are aroused in the listeners.

What's more, when people tell stories to other people, stories that shape thinking and pass on wisdom, the brains of their listeners synchronise with the storyteller's. A Princeton study found that similar brain regions are activated in both listener and the story-teller,[188] including the insula, which is thought to provide emotional context and integrate information, and the frontal cortex, responsible for analytical and control functions.

Even more remarkably, the study also identified a subset of brain regions in which the responses in the listener's brain *preceded* the responses in the speaker's brain. These anticipatory responses suggest that listeners actively predict a storyteller's words. This may be to compensate for a noisy background, or ambiguous meaning. But the Princeton research found that the more extensive the join-up between a speaker's brain responses and a listener's anticipatory brain responses, the better the listener understood the story.

Thinking in narrative

Neuroscientist and psychologist Mary Helen Immordino-Yang has found that when we hear inspirational stories, more blood flows to the brain stem:[189] that part of our brain which makes our heart beat, regulates our breathing and keeps us alive.

It seems that we experience a story's inspirational message at the very core of our biological survival mechanism.

It's also possible that the reason stories are so powerful is that we think in narrative all the time[190] in the default system. These are the parts of the brain where we think about other people, and are so-called because we default to thinking about ourselves or others within a few seconds of not being engaged in a task.

The default system's way of expressing thoughts is usually a narrative – a story we are telling ourselves. So there is a consistency in how we "talk" to ourselves and how we tell stories.

Broken down into its simplest form, a story is a connection of cause and effect. And that's how we think. Whether it's about buying groceries, what's happening at work or thinking about our friends, we make up stories in our heads for every action and conversation: "If I don't prepare for the management meeting I won't have anything sensible to say and then they will think HR aren't pulling their weight."

In contrast to this "self-talk," it's been found that our conversations with other people are *not* primarily instructive, or directive, or concerned with conveying information that people need. They are 65% personal stories and gossip[191] – and that goes for men as well as women. Storytelling is how we relate to other people.

Matching our experiences

When we hear a story, we want to relate it to our existing experiences. That's why it's so effective if storytellers use metaphors, such as "her words cut like a knife." While we're busy searching for a similar experience, we activate a part of our brain called the insula, which connects us to that same feeling that the storyteller is describing.

The social value of information

UCLA's Matt Lieberman has been studying what happens in the brain when people hear an idea that is destined to spread successfully:[192] the kind of insight which they will pass on to someone else, and which they relay in such a way the second person will also pass the idea on. (In HR terms, this is about communicating those strategic insights or solutions to problems that we would want our listeners to tell their teams and networks.)

Lieberman and his colleagues designed an experiment to explore what is going on in the brain when we first encounter these kinds of important ideas.

The expectation was that the research would find areas of the brain activated that are associated with memory and deep encoding: the areas that are used to hold onto critical information. In fact, those parts of the brain did not stand out in the results. What they found was strong activity in the brain's default system – where we think about ourselves and other people.

We're not just thinking about ourselves

Before this study, it was assumed that when people are exposed to new information (a new "story") they're assessing whether the information is sufficiently useful to them to pay close attention and try to remember. The experiments showed that we bring our social concerns into play when we assimilate new information.[193] People are testing whether the information is of value to other people who are important to them, and not just whether it's important to themselves.

Lieberman calls this being an information DJ – people don't just think about whether the information is useful to them, but who else it will be useful to. They have other people's interests in mind when they first encounter it. And the more important they feel it is, the better able they are to pass on the information in a way that also resonates with others.

Lieberman suggests that the brain's rewards systems are activated, increasing the person's sense of reputation within their group. What this means for us at work is that the more understanding our leaders have of what will appeal to their audience, the more likely their listeners are to pass on the right information which will appeal and spread.

Encoding stories

Other research which supports Lieberman's findings includes a Canadian analysis of 86 studies which shows there's substantial overlap in the brain networks we use to understand stories and the networks we use to understand other people[194] – especially when we're trying to understand other people's thoughts and feelings.

Since the regions activated are associated with the ability to simulate the minds of other people, it appears that to be an effective influencer you need to spontaneously think about how you would communicate information to others in a useful and interesting way when you first hear the information yourself. This is called the encoding stage.

The findings also add to emerging literature on the link between the default system and social communication more generally.

Synchronised understanding

For instance, during natural verbal communication it's been found that when a listener's brain activity in the default network mirrors the speaker's brain activity,[195] there is greater communication and understanding between them.

The brain areas activated were the same key regions found in Lieberman's research, including the medial prefrontal cortex, and the precuneus/posterior cingulate cortex, all part of the default system.

What does this tell us about effective communication?

The findings have important implications for the dissemination of ideas, values, and culture.[196] It suggests that it depends more on the influencer's social-cognitive abilities, use of emotions, and motivation, and less on IQ-type intelligence.

None of the brain regions involved in storytelling make use of the brain regions associated with higher-level abstract reasoning and executive functioning.

So the next time you want to be an effective influencer, make sure you're putting yourself in the shoes of the people you want to convince. And if you're struggling with getting people on board with your projects and ideas, tell them a story which has the same ending you're trying to achieve.

Stories are a powerful way to plant ideas into other people's minds.

5 Leading talent, engagement and learning

Neuroscience is giving us lots of new insight on how to better engage, develop and build a talent culture. In reading these chapters you will challenge your thinking about current practice and learn how to create successful practice and design of programmes and policy.

"Emotional Intelligence: our leaders aren't convinced."

The persuasive science of EI

Emotional Intelligence (EI) is much better understood and accepted by HR people than it is throughout the businesses they work in. Daniel Goleman's books have developed a huge following, and HR leaders have seen the usefulness of his concept in developing leaders and guiding behaviour in organisations.

But corporate leaders are resistant. Perhaps because, as the post-war business consultant W Edwards Deming said, "The problem with business is that it is afraid of dealing with the business of people."

It's not just a passing fad

Emotional Intelligence has a respectable history in scientific understanding. Darwin believed that emotional expression was essential for survival. In the 1940s psychologist David Wechsler, and later Howard Gardner, did groundbreaking work in developing the theory of multiple intelligence.[197] And in a paper published in 1990, psychologists Peter Salovey and John Mayer defined EI[198] as:

> "The ability to monitor one's own and others' feelings and emotions, to discriminate among them and to use the information to guide one's thinking and actions."

Daniel Goleman's influential article "What Makes a Leader?"[199] was published in the 1998 Harvard Business Review, in which he presented the results of applying EI within business. Goleman challenged the long-held belief in business that intellect and rationality are central to success. They do matter as "threshold capabilities," he said, but he described them as "the entry-level requirements for executives."

The model that he used for describing emotional intelligence is one that many practitioners went on to apply in their businesses.

And yet so many of the leaders we talk to today, and not a few HR professionals, still work on the assumption that IQ – that is, intellectual ability, or "business smarts" – is the key to top business performance. Any other types of intelligence are of secondary importance, in their view.

And here we have in a nutshell the problem of resistance in organisations: the relegation of EI to the silo of "soft skills," a poor relation to skills in finance, strategy and IT that are seen as essential to business survival.

The evidence for Emotional Intelligence

When you're hoping to persuade business leaders trained in IQ-type intelligence, one of the great advantages of neuroscientific concepts is that they're supported by research data.

You don't want to know everything so we'll just give you the big chunks of evidence behind current thinking on *interpersonal* intelligence, (the capacity to understand the intentions, motivations and desires of others), and *intrapersonal* intelligence, the capacity to understand oneself.

From a neuroscience perspective these two are intimately linked.

It's hard work thinking about other people

The brain areas which help us to understand other people, the default or mentalizing systems, are largely the same ones[200] that enable us to think about ourselves. And this implies that the better we are at using this mentalizing circuitry to understand ourselves, the better we are at understanding other people.

But when we're activating the mentalizing circuits we close down much of the rational, executive-functioning prefrontal cortex. So it's not possible to be doing a task or thinking about[201] a new product design, for example, and also be thinking about the impact of that on others.

The mentalizing system is quick to switch on[202] – Lieberman suggests it kicks in within about 20 seconds if we're not focused on cognitive tasks – but it performs poorly when people are stressed or processing large amounts of information.

What this tells us is it takes effort, focus and concentration to understand other people. When these are lacking the mentalizing system does not come on line, or does not come on line efficiently. But in business the ability to understand the *impact* of information on people – on employees, on customers, on competitors – is a critically important leadership skill.

How well do we understand other people?

Lieberman found that when people know something themselves (like being able to recognise a tune, or knowing the capitals of obscure countries), they are poor at predicting whether other people will know the information too. Only something like 2.5% of people accurately predicts what others will know.[203]

This can make it easy for business leaders to skip vital steps in bringing people along on a new strategy: they may assume "we're all on the same page" when they're not.

Emotions in business

Business leaders may be inclined to believe that they should leave their emotions at home, and that how they feel is a personal matter. But a better understanding of our ability, or inability, to control our emotions will show how they are highly relevant to workplace performance and decisions.

Threat or fear activates the amygdala, an area in the brain that releases the transmitter glutamate, which in turn activates other regions in the brain stem and hypothalamus. This starts a stress-response reaction and the release of cortisol into the bloodstream has a widespread impact on the body.[204]

Cortisol redistributes energy to critical parts of the body, like the heart, and away from non-critical parts of the body like the digestive system, which is why it's hard to eat before major presentation, or a difficult meeting. If active for long periods it will also take resources away from the body's immune system.

Why *connecting* with people makes business sense

There's no point devising a bold new business strategy if you can't communicate it and get it implemented. But "being a good communicator" may feel soft and vague to a sceptical business leader.

Sandy Pentland at MIT invented a wearable electronic sensor to measure exactly what good communication involves,[205] in real time. His "sociometric badge" captures *how* people communicate, not *what* they say. In his study the more successful people were more energetic; they talked more, but they also listened more; they spent more face-to-face time with people and picked up cues from them; they drew people out, and got them to be more outgoing.

Pentland's data identifies what makes for effective communication and connection between people, such as in a team meeting, or presenting a proposal. Pentland's findings support the notion that these types of social factors like tone of voice, body language and energy are as important as intelligence.

Using EI

Of course what neuroscience alone cannot cover is the *application* of the insight it gives.

So you may develop an understanding of yourself or others, but you still need to apply that understanding to the work environment. And this is where many EI development programmes fall down.

Too many HR professionals and business leaders tell us they attended an EI programme that provided great insight but no application. Tools and embedding to the job are crucial to achieve results; otherwise they may think this EI stuff is just a lot of "soft stuff." So whilst the research can help you convince your sceptics, you need to go the next step and provide brain-savvy training to apply the insight. More about that in the chapter in this section, *"We're spending enough money – why isn't our training and development working?"*

"We're spending enough money – why isn't our training and development working?"

A different type of audit: make connections, anticipate resistance and allow time for learning

Re: Memo to all managers: Training 101
Dear Training Manager
Please can you clarify a few points for me about the 101 training.
Why have I been asked? Who is the training for? Who else will be on the course on the dates you have invited me? What will I learn? How is this relevant to my job? Could I learn this without needing to go on a course outside the office? What are the outcomes I can expect from the training?
Sorry for all the questions but I am really busy.
Yours...

Learning and development practitioners say they're being more commercial and business-focused. But we still hear that programmes aren't producing the behavioural changes expected.

Training budgets are too tight to allow for this kind of wastage. But how can you decide the kind of changes you need to make to achieve breakthrough? Fortunately there's a body of well-supported neuroscientific evidence which can tell you what will work – and what won't.

Some of the points that make up brain-savvy training design may already be part of your well-run programme. But understanding the science behind learning and behavioural change will mean you can audit your own programmes effectively, and make sure you're getting the best return on your investment.

Why wouldn't people *want* to learn?

Obviously you want the people attending your programmes to be ready to learn, and – even more importantly – ready to change their behaviour as a result of what they learn.

The question of motivation to learn and change kicks in before anyone is even invited to the training. And a significant issue is that you're asking a participant to realign their group identity.

"Who else is going to be on the course?"

Humans are essentially social beings and one of the first things we do is categorise people into in-group (people similar to us) and out-group (people who are different).

Training interventions will create new in-groups: the cohort or alumni of the programme.

If people perceive that by taking part in the programme they're separating themselves from a valued in-group then they'll be reluctant to participate. But people will feel good about attending a programme with high-potential colleagues, or being offered a place on a course where numbers are limited, or with high profile colleagues. Those can be powerful motivators as they create a new valued in-group, with their training cohort.

One of the aims of the programme may be to mix up people from different functions across the organisation. Evidence shows that the boundaries of people's in-groups *can* change if you present information that challenges their preconceptions: front office people can learn something from service functions, sales people can learn from accountants. In order to overcome resistance to group-change you need to create an awareness of the benefits of introducing participants to a valuable network.

> Key questions:
> - How does the programme cut across existing in-groups?
> - How could you make that seem an attractive scenario?

"Why do I need to change the way I work?"

You're asking people to change. This activates the CORE triggers and literally creates pain in the brain.

Change usually creates threat but there are ways to create reward feelings, like learning in a community or the enhanced reputation from being more skilled. Your pre-programme communications need to mitigate threat and maximise reward to ensure your learners will be in the right state of mind: their brains receptive to new learning and change.

Make sure that participants understand that being invited onto this course isn't implied criticism of how they're currently working. Better still, create a sense of reward by enhancing the reputation of those who acquire new skills and work in new ways.

And communicate the WIIFM ("what's in it for me) at a personal level. Research has shown that people need to have a clear vision of the future to help maintain behaviours and goals .

Key questions:

- What are the benefits for those who attend?
- Will attending the programme reward their CORE elements?
- Do people understand the goals of the programme and has time been spent ensuring they're personalised?

"Will I actually *learn* anything"

The leaders you want to support will be wise enough to understand the difference between "being taught" and actually learning.

New learning is obviously a key element of any programme. And the science of how we learn is compelling but sometimes counterintuitive.

Work by Jessica Payne at the University of Notre Dame shows the brain learns best when it is mildly stressed, has a good mood, and has had a good sleep.[206] A positive for one of these states means learners are more likely to have a positive state in the others.

Think about it: if you've been awake most of the night going over your presentation to the CEO you're not going to feel at your best, and that tends to put you in a bad mood so you're sure that you'll mess up, and then you get stressed about that and... you get our point.

It's hard to order up a good night's sleep beforehand for your programme participants. But you can structure programmes to span a night: even one-day workshops can be scheduled for an afternoon and the following morning. The research indicates that it's during sleep that new connections are made and when new information is linked to existing knowledge.

"Are we going to be abseiling down cliffs?"

Research into the optimal 'Flow' state has shown the ideal conditions for work and learning are a balance between the level of challenge in a situation and the participant's perceived ability[207] to carry it out. This is Payne's mild stress.

If either is too low, people coast; if too high, they panic. In any development or training programme stress needs to be reduced, but only to the point of flow.

So, no jumping off cliffs – either physical or mental – but exercises which stretch participants just beyond their comfort zone.

Course content could look very similar to what you've run before, but it will be carefully designed to anticipate the capabilities of the participants and will need excellent facilitation that can dial the intensity up or down depending on the individuals in the group.

Don't try to cram it all in

When training budgets are under the pressure and we all have to do more with less, the obvious response is to cram more content into less time, work longer hours on the course and keep the pace brisk.

There are two key pieces of research which should inform your decision-making on the intensity of your programmes.

It's well-known that synapses in the brain (the connections between neurons and other cells that allow for the transmission of information) grow when they're learning. But more recent research has shown that in the short-term, synapses get even stronger than previously thought but then quickly go through a transitional phase where they weaken.[208]

Previously, educators and scientists believed that learning was cumulative; in neuroscientific terms the synapses started small and got progressively bigger and stronger. But it now seems that synapses that have recently been strengthened are peculiarly vulnerable, and more stimulation can actually wipe out the effects of learning.

It's also been shown that that when people have to process complex information, giving them time to reflect, if only for a few minutes, makes their decisions much better.[209]

We've all had course participants joke about "brain overload" at the end of a long day's training. It's real. More training during this phase is actually counterproductive. There's no point trying to cram more information into the timetable: you're wasting your resources.

How to structure for maximum behaviour change

The neuroscientific evidence is clear: for generating long-lasting memory, spaced-out training works best. Well-designed programmes deliver training in small chunks, and provide time for reflection. And for anyone who thinks reflection is a waste of training time, active reflection methods can be developed.

The mood of the programme also has a significant impact.[210] A positive mood improves processing of new information, memory consolidation and creates better insight or "Aha!" moments.

Telling people what they should know doesn't generate behaviour change. Creating insight and then embedding the insight through the use of tools and goals is more effective. Only by consolidating insights will new neural connections be built.

Occasionally you may need just to impart knowledge. But if you want behaviour change, participants must work out for themselves what it means for them, and set their own goals.

Key questions:
- Are you creating the right atmosphere?
- What spacing do you have?
- Are key ideas being generated through insight rather than instruction?
- How are people reflecting on the learning?
- Can facilitators vary the pace and intensity.

Will this create behaviour change?

These days most programmes are delivered over more than one session and use multiple channels like video, podcasts, reading, experiential learning and so on.

If you want to create more than a brief feel-good factor, you're aiming to create new habits. A brief word on how they're created. *Habits* are the job of the basal ganglia which controls automatic behaviour. After a period of time people get comfortable doing the same tasks, the role is predictable and a task becomes a habit. To acquire new habits, new skills or ways of working, people need to identify new cues, and create routines and rewards for themselves.[211] and persist until they do the new behaviour automatically.

We use social learning software to support the embedding of new behaviours; these virtual communities can both provide support and act as a pressure group.

Key question:
- How long will your programme support and reinforce new behaviours?

Creating brain-savvy training programmes improves retention of learning and means people develop new behavioural habits and gives a better return on your training investment.

How do your programmes stack up?

"Why do we put training into buckets?"

Training for the role rather than core skills

I was with a client a while back discussing how our approach to leadership development uses neuroscience to help leaders improve their performance.

The client was telling me his goal was to get his account managers to become better people managers. In particular he wanted them to coach their teams more effectively.

My response was that this should be easy. If they are trusted advisors to their clients they already know how to ask powerful questions to help people have insight, hold the mirror up, and challenge assumptions – all the skills a coach needs.

Great account managers know how to ask questions that deepen the client's understanding of what will work in their company. When the client is asking for the impossible they know how to describe why it won't work in a way that doesn't offend. And great account managers draw out the assumptions the client is making and sometimes challenges them to ensure the campaign is successful.

My client was excited about framing his leaders' role and skills in this way, recognising that he would gain more acceptance for what he was asking them to do with their teams.

Our brain is wired to work flexibly

There's strong scientific evidence for the effectiveness of this approach.

A recent study has explored the "flexible hub" theory of the brain in relation to transferring[212] skills. "Flexible hubs are brain regions that coordinate activity throughout the brain to implement tasks – like a large internet traffic router," suggests Michael Cole, author of the study. By analysing activity as the hubs connected during the processing of specific tasks, researchers found unique patterns that enabled them to see the hubs' role in using existing skills in new tasks.

The process, known as compositional coding, allows skills learned in one context to be re-packaged and re-used in others, shortening the learning curve. By tracking and testing the performance of individuals the study showed that the transfer of these skills helped participants speed up their mastery of new tasks, and use existing skills in a new setting.

Using this to design training

Are your leadership or HR capability programmes taking account of the flexibility hub in the brain?

Too often we segment learning into buckets. A programme for improving performance with the team. Another programme for improving client relationships. A third for self-development.

What we could be doing instead is taking a holistic view about the core skills leaders or HR need that can be applied in all sorts of situations. Like the examples above, we often use the same skills in both client and internal situations but call them different things or learn them only in one context.

Abilities such as asking good questions, listening to the content and the emotion, testing assumptions and finding solutions are all skills that apply to both managing people and clients.

As leadership experts we would do well to review how we structure and market our programmes. Helping leaders to build core skills which apply across all the roles a leader plays could gain acceptance more quickly, speed up developing competence and also save costs.

But there are two crucial elements I believe must be included.

Use the neurophysiology

The first is that you have to give leaders the insight that the skills serve more than one role, or that they already have the skills to apply in the new situation.

And the second is giving them an understanding of the physiology of applying skills – understanding that skills come with feelings in the body and linking the two is crucial for effectively using them. Leaders will need to be flexible enough to adopt that physiology in different scenarios to adapt their skills effectively. I see many leaders who have a distinctive physiology for clients and quite a different stance and body language with their own people.

Helping leaders to be aware of their physiology, and that they can adjust it by doing this rather than that, is a crucial skill in itself. How many leadership programmes teach that insight?

"Will our training produce the kind of leaders we want?"

It's about the design: a quick fix won't change behaviour

If your answer is yes, and you have got your leadership development right, lucky you! If your reaction is to turn the page you're probably having an avoidance reaction.

Your brain has experienced the title as a threat. You don't want to believe you've been throwing your budget away on ineffective programmes. But as a professional you're just going to skim through in case we say something reassuring.

Well, you'll be reassured if you work in the telecoms sector. If you work in financial services or manufacturing you might think, "At last – some hard data on what I've suspected for ages!" Or you might want to sit down.

Despite hard times companies have been spending well on leadership development.[213] The Chartered Management Institute's report for 2012 showed spending of between £1400 and £1700 per annum per person in a manager role. And research by The Conference Board and Right Management in 2013 found that companies globally expected to increase their spend by 39%.[214] But is it money well spent?

Clients tell us they have sophisticated development programmes, many delivered by high-ranking institutions costing much more than the CMI averages, but they're failing to achieve changes in behaviour.

We believe them! Because we have the data.

Brain-savvy leaders

To gauge the standard of leadership in different industries, in 2013 Head Heart + Brain commissioned the *Brain-savvy Leaders* study of more than 2,000 UK workers[215] about their bosses. The questions were based on the key criteria that define good leadership, based on the principles of neuroscience.

We believe that if leaders work with an awareness of how human beings operate, working *with* the brain rather than against its biological processes – that is, they are brain-savvy – they will be more effective and better leaders for their organisations.

The questions we asked people were about how their leaders lead them. The survey measured a variety of factors, from the amount of autonomy employees are given, to the clarity and openness of communication about job responsibilities and targets, to the quality of feedback and the fairness of leaders.

So here's a summary of the data, then our view on what you can do if your leaders are struggling.

The results

Our survey showed that:

- The telecoms sector has the most brain-savvy leaders
- The most brain-fried leaders in the UK are in financial services and accountancy. With leaders in manufacturing coming close behind them
- Leadership in the civil service rates just above the UK average
- A quarter of leaders in health are failing to manage change correctly and fall well below the UK average
- Retail, transport and education perform below the UK average in leadership

Of course our survey can't predict *your* leaders' behaviour. You may work in the Telecoms sector and be finding it hard to recognise your leaders by these measures. The only way to be sure is to get your team to complete the survey and gather the data.

The survey covers the areas clients tell us they want to improve in leadership development, and yet employees are not seeing the benefits. It's apparent that some sectors are suffering a crisis of leadership. The surprising thing is that these are sectors spending hundreds of thousands of pounds on leadership training. So what is going wrong?

What do we need to change?

Our research tells us the problem is more about the structure and design of their programmes rather than the content. Programmes are not designed to be compatible with how the brain learns and how behavioural change actually happens.

With the best will in the world, no one ever changed their behaviour because they were shown a new model, attended a lecture, or the CEO told them to change. That's just not how behavioural change works.

You wanted a one-workshop solution? Neuroscience demonstrates that effective learning and behavioural change is complex and multi-layered.

Here is a brief summary of the evidence on how individual learning works and behavioural change happens. You can use it as a check-list to compare with what you're doing in your development programmes.

Insight

People change when they have their own insight. Far too many programmes are focused on imparting information without encouraging the development of insight through questions, reflection and applying the content to their own experiences.

WIIFM – What's in it for me?

People need to understand how the information or behavioural change is important and why changing makes sense to them personally. The WIIFM is critical, even if we're generally a little more subtle about how we describe it.

Mindset

Programmes need to work at the level of beliefs and mindset, not just behaviour. In our view too many programmes expect change to happen even if people hold the same beliefs after the programme as they did before. If you believe people are born with certain traits like empathy or tough-mindedness no amount of training will convince you that you can develop those abilities.

The brain is just not "wired" to be able to do that. To apply the learning the leader must *believe* it makes sense for them to do it, preferably over the long term.

Coaches could be including belief-audits at the start and end of their programmes and programmes should be designed to examine beliefs not just skills and behaviour.

Make it personal

To learn, leaders also need to generate their own version of the knowledge, to apply it to their role.

According to Columbia University's Kevin Ochsner, 70% of what we do is habitual.[216] And Hebb's Law, from the "father of neuropsychology" Donald O. Hebb, is commonly summarised as "neurons that wire together fire together".[217]

We need to create new neural connections if we want leaders to adopt new behaviours, and that happens when an insight is applied, discussed, written about and goals are created.

Self then others

Eighty-five per cent of the areas of the brain that are used to think about ourselves are also used to think about others.[218] So leaders will find it very hard to apply learning to their teams unless they can apply it personally.

We've spent some time working with the top 200 leaders of one of the largest sections of the civil service. They were doing great work transforming their leadership but many of them were still approaching the learning as something "out there" which was going to be applied to other people. First it needs to be "in here," and part of the leader's experience.

Learn then teach

Because other people's opinion of us matters to us, learning in a social context can make the learning stick. And Matt Lieberman has shown that learning something so that we can teach others makes it stickier still.[219]

Social learning adds an emotional element to the process and generates personal motivation for the leader. So if you want your leaders to pass on their learning to their teams, deliver development in this context and you'll shift the dial in the right direction.

Spacing and reflection

As we discussed in *"We're spending enough money - why isn't our training and development working?"* Programmes that are crammed full of material and giving little or no time for application and reflection may be *reducing* learning not increasing it.[220]

And further research has found that when people process complex information, giving them time to reflect makes their use of the information more effective[221] and their decisions much better.

Do you space out learning, with time to reflect and apply it to people's roles?

Create new habits

Finally, personal change needs to be embedded.

One day programmes and one-off training seminars look attractive for the budget, and for time-pressed executives. But too many programmes stop too quickly before new behaviours have been made into habits.

Habits are run by the basal ganglia. To establish a new habit people must create a cue[222] to tell them when to perform the behaviour, plus a routine and a reward for doing it. Then persist until it is ingrained. Leaders must keep up the practice until the new behaviour is automatic, like asking questions before stating their opinion, or listening to the words and the tone.

Designing-in habit creation is critical to successful development. Social learning platforms, that allow a group of leaders to discuss their successes and challenges, can be used to support the process. The community provides both support and a social pressure group which helps people to stay on track with their goals and intentions.

How do your leadership programmes rate against these brain-savvy criteria?

Even if you work in one of the better-performing sectors according to the overall results of our survey, we didn't find any sectors that were doing well across *all* the criteria, so you will be able to identify areas where your programmes can improve.

And for insights on how to audit your training programmes you may also want to read the chapter in this section *"We're spending enough money – why isn't our training and development working?"*

"Is the future of learning programmes virtual?"

Beyond faceless cost-saving:
the real advantages of virtual learning

The more we talk to clients, the more we realise that the future of learning and corporate leadership development programmes is going to be changing. Radically.

We believe that virtual programmes will become much more common. Maybe not replacing all of your development programme, but certainly significant elements of it.

Why do we think this? A number of reasons. Some are factors that are pushing leadership and learning professionals to change. Some are factors that are pulling them towards a more effective way of delivering learning and development.

Push factors

On the push side there's the never-ending pressure on cost.

And maybe even more important is the pressure on leaders to do more. Taking days out to go on workshops is just too much of a luxury for most executives. Virtual programmes or virtual elements also allow people to learn when it suits them. And they allow for differences in learning preferences and attention.

And generational differences shouldn't be ignored. Younger executives are used to "just in time" learning, rather than the traditional "just in case" programmes. Virtual programmes can provide a variety of channels and types of material available when people want them, and available over and over again if people want to revisit.

Pull factors

But it's the pull side that we believe will create the biggest difference to leadership and learning programmes.

We've studied the neuroscience of learning and behaviour change and there are many elements that point to greater benefit from virtual programmes over traditional learning programmes.

Sadly, much of this is ignored because virtual learning acquired a bad name from early e-learning programmes that were little more than a book or manual loaded online with a test at the end.

How people learn

The neuroscience is telling us that people learn best when:

- they have control over when and how they learn
- the learning materials are designed to create insight, not just impart information
- when they learn in a community and have interaction with others and
- importantly, when the learning engages their emotions and they're convinced it will help them personally be more successful.

For long-term behavioural change people need to embed the learning by applying it, and using it in a number of ways until it becomes habit and part of how they automatically work.

Getting the best results

You can of course build all of these elements into a more traditional programme. But the push elements (time pressures, generational differences...) mean we need to become more creative about learning and behavioural change.

And technology is helping us to produce virtual programmes that engage and manage learning more effectively.

We've been experimenting with virtual learning and have found that for best results you need to:

1. Communicate with potential participants to identify the WIIFM ("what's in it for me") features. And participants need to come to the programme with a sense of responsibility for their learning.

Some things that we've found work well are to ask participants to select a sponsor from within the organisation, and to make a personal learning agreement which will help them to keep on track with their learning.

Communication needs to introduce people to the technology, which itself needs to be simple, engaging and intuitive.

2. Design the programme to be virtual from conception, rather than just upload the face-to-face programme. There should be three elements to each module of content: knowledge, processing and application.

Knowledge takes place during the learner's own time and is usually a video or some reading. Or it could involve research, such as interviewing leaders from other organisations or other parts of the business.

Processing is usually a webinar, when the group comes together to process their learning. They may be asked to present their insights and views on the material, or discuss how they can apply their learning and what it means to them personally.

This deepens understanding. And hearing how others are applying the learning creates additional insight and motivation.

Group work also helps to build relationships across the cohort, maintains personal connection to the programme and ensures the webinars are interactive and continue the learning.

Application takes place in the workplace and is where the learning is applied and put into practice.

Once the programme is underway, participants work with others, in pairs or small groups, to coach each other or apply the tools and insight to business issues and day-to-day work.

We've been using a social learning site which also houses the materials. Other methods can be action learning sets, business projects, and monitoring how learning is being applied through journal-writing.

Part of the by-product of this stage of the programme is that people begin to learn from each other. And as future modules roll out, different individuals are able to contribute aspects of their expertise and experience. Learning from each other builds confidence and commitment, and ensures the programme immediately pays back to the business.

Keeping this stage social also builds in pressure to meet the expectations of the group in applying and sharing results, as well as providing group support.

Active facilitation

An important role of the facilitator is to monitor the activity of the group: seeing where their interest and curiosity is taking them, and where they're struggling and might need more input.

Again, a social learning platform helps here if it allows participants to access materials, add their own content, comment on content, ask questions of others in the community and follow colleagues.

One of the other important things we've learnt is to keep learning groups small – no more that 12 to 14 people for each webinar – so they receive focused attention throughout the programme.

Getting started

The biggest block to virtual learning appears to be the attitude of learning professionals. And this is understandable: we all like what is familiar. We were sceptical when we started looking into it.

So for our experiments we started with our own learning group: testing ideas on ourselves before using them with clients. To champion virtual learning effectively in your own organisation you might also find this a good way to get started.

And along the way we've been looking to other areas of learning for ideas and confirmation of our own discoveries. We found the Khan University (which provides free online tutorials[223] in maths and science) particularly inspiring. We're sure you'll find more inspiration for yourself once you get involved.

"I keep telling them they should be using coaching..."

Coaching vs telling: here's the evidence of what works

It's interesting looking at ideas that "seem obvious" but just don't get traction. And coaching is one of them. Many companies use external coaches to work with their senior people. But HR often find it hard to persuade those senior leaders to use the same coaching techniques with their own teams.

Companies we work with still have many leaders who are wedded to the old "command and control" style of management. Basically, they like telling people what to do. And why not – they're busy people, they were usually promoted because they were good at their jobs, not because they were good at "people stuff," and they're paid to keep their eye on the bottom line. So let them just tell their teams what needs to be done, so they can get on with it.

Well, if that's the most effective way of passing on the necessary skills and information, so be it. But let's look at the evidence on which technique works best – coaching or telling – especially during times of complex change.

Making maps and forming habits

It's all about how we absorb and organise new information.

Brains work by making connections and associations: linking what is happening now and what has happened in the past, both conscious and unconscious memories. The result is a kind of map of connections in the brain; no two maps will be the same, even though two people's brains will have used the same biological process to map the same information. Just to give you an idea of the complexity of the work that's going on here: your brain map is creating over a million new connections *every second*.

The brain likes order, and tries to connect new information to what is already known,[224] in order to categorise it. It is also a prediction machine. Predicting how something will happen and getting it right creates a sense of reward in the brain.

Neuroscience evangelist and inventor of the Palm Pilot Jeff Hawkins says that our ability to make predictions, based on the connections our brain makes, is what differentiates us from other animals.[225]

When we first encounter something, we're relatively slow to understand it. Like reading this article, we need to get the foundations in place first. Learning a new skill (that is to say, creating the map for it) takes a while before it becomes familiar – maybe a few minutes or maybe days, depending on the complexity. The more embedded the maps are, the more we free up mental resources for acquiring and understanding new information.

We call this process of creating maps "forming a habit." And the process of shifting activity from the high-energy, relatively inefficient prefrontal cortex down to the more efficient habit-forming areas is the basic operating mode for the brain.

All of this happens also when we learn something new or receive new information. Before we can use it, it needs to be fitted into our mental map and then over time we can use it on autopilot: a new habit has been formed.

So with this understanding as background, let's look at the impact of *telling* someone to change compared with *coaching* them to change.

Telling versus insight

One of the key premises of coaching is that people work things out for themselves. And the difference between being told and having insight is all about creating new mental maps.

If you're thinking about something like how a new process will work, or the reaction of your team to a new strategy, you're creating a mental map. These new thoughts are energy-consuming from a brain perspective so you might find this work being done when your brain is freed up from other activity: you're just stirring the soup, or walking the dog. This type of thinking often results in what we call an "Aha!" moment – that flash of insight when a new map, or part of a map, is formed.

If you're *told* how to carry out the new process, or what the strategy means for your job, you still have to create that mental map, but without the help of "Aha!" moments when everything suddenly falls into place. So it's all a much more laborious process.

To take any kind of action based on what they are told people have to *also* be given the opportunity to think it through for themselves. Making it a two-step process. If the coach-manager asks the kind of questions that prompt insight people can make the connections and create their map in one step.

Threatening advice

The other factor which makes telling so ineffective is that it's more likely to set up a threat response, because the listener's predictions and connections aren't set up for this new information. This difference in perception creates an error message which turns people away from the new information and increases the likelihood of resistance.

Managers who tell rather than coach are not only wasting their own time and energy, they're potentially making it *more* difficult for employees to accept a new idea.

Are your managers and coaches creating insight, or telling people what to do?

Creating motivation to change

You'll know the burst of motivation and energy that comes with a moment of insight, but which can quickly dissipate if it's not reinforced. (It seemed like a good idea at the time, but... well, it was probably impractical...) It's that reinforcement which hardwires new connections and potentially triggers new behaviour. But this type of thinking and action is hard work for the brain because it takes more energy, so people may avoid it or give up too soon before a deep map is formed.

So coaching that reinforces insights through creating goals and opportunities to practice the new skill is more effective then telling someone what to do and expecting them to do as they're told.

Are your managers focusing people on creating goals and persuing them?

Moving to action

Conventional wisdom, in many businesses, is that if people understand rationally why they need to do something they'll get on board with the process. But only 30% of what we do is under our conscious control[226] rather than being habit and automatic, and that includes how we do our job. Because habits operate outside of our conscious awareness, logical thought will not be enough to initiate change. This is why telling people what needs to be done and then leaving them to it doesn't work.

Several things need to be in place to achieve behavioural change. UCLA's Matt Lieberman says we must go beyond the conscious "reflective" systems where goals are created,[227] and manage the triggers for the old behaviours in our unconscious "reflexive" systems. Goals designed to act in the new way tend to be created in the conscious reflective system but we need to also control the unconscious habit system by managing triggers that generate the old behaviour.

The focus of Elliot Berkman's research is goal-setting and achieving new behaviour, and his studies suggest there's a sequence for creating new habits of behaviour:[228] cue; when to act; routine; the steps to take; reward.

Only if people are coached to be able to redirect these well-rooted behaviours, by managing the triggers that prompt them and by building in rewards for the new behaviour, is change going to happen without lots of additional effort.

Are your managers working with both systems? Are they helping to create new behaviour by creating new habit routines and the rewards? Are there strategies to manage the triggers that will prompt old behaviour?

We are social

It's easy to forget, at work, that we are all primarily social creatures.

"Social pain" – a public reprimand or stringent direction of someone's work – is experienced in the same way as physical pain, and the memory of it remains more vivid. The frontal cortex is drained as the limbic system hijacks all of the energy of the unfortunate staff member and impairs their ability to think clearly ("My mind went blank..."), making it even less likely that telling will be effective.

Leaders need to understand how the brain actually works in order to appreciate what will be most effective – coaching or telling. We'll leave you with some questions you might put to an unpersuaded leader, which may generate their own insight:

- How did someone react when you told them to change?
- When has telling someone to do something differently worked?
- What have been the benefits for you of encouraging insight in others?
- What good surprises have you got from asking questions, rather than telling?

"They just need to copy the role model?"

It's not just about showing how, but understanding why

We know modelling is an effective way of learning new skills and behaviours, from children modelling their behaviour on their parents and siblings, to apprenticeship schemes.

Leadership development has adopted role modelling as the way to break through some of the challenges of passing on requirements to future leaders. The thinking goes: "If we can point to the role models, tell people who they are and suggest new leaders copy what they do, our leadership problems will be over." Of course we're exaggerating, but you get the point...

Are role models a good idea?

We believe in the power of role models. Our Success Profile® process is a methodology for identifying what the most successful people do and how they do it. The profile can be used to show other leaders and more junior employees what the very best do, how they think about their role and the most important factors for success.

But going from knowing what someone does and successfully adopting that capability is quite a big leap. For example, our work creating Success Profiles across many organisations, in countries all around the world, has found that the difference in the success of the most successful is not *what* they do but *how* they think: the purpose they bring to the role and the beliefs that they hold.

You need more than a name

For many organisations knowing what those beliefs and purposes are can be difficult and it is very difficult for others to observe role models and guess what drives their behaviour.

Knowing *how* someone behaves is not enough. You have to also understand *why* they behave that way. The "why" drives the behaviour. Only with the "why" will the behaviour be authentic; based on common beliefs, not just aping actions.

Time and time again we've seen that acting out the same steps as the role model doesn't work. People have to believe in what they're doing: believe that it's effective behaving in this way; believe that they can do it; believe that they can adopt these attitudes and behaviours and still be themselves – not pretending to be someone else.

This is the true challenge for leadership development. How do you develop leaders who adopt the successful "why," and not just the "what"?

How does this happen in the brain?

Our beliefs on this are supported by some of the latest findings in neuroscience.

Work by Matt Lieberman at UCLA has focused on[229] the role of mirror neurons versus the area known as the default system. This is associated with mentalizing, the ability to understand others and to "guess" what they are thinking, their goals and motivations.

The default system is the area of the brain where we think about ourselves, and it largely overlaps with the areas activated when we think about and try to predict the actions of other people. Useful for our cave-man predecessors when "am I safe with this stranger?" was so closely linked to "is he going to try to steal my food?"

Two parts of the brain at work

This is the processing that comes into play when we ask people to role-model a leader in the business, and put themselves in another's shoes in order to understand how to be successful.

Essentially the brain has two systems for understanding other people: mirror neurons and the default system (or mentalizing system). Why we have two systems is a bit of a puzzle since the brain is a very efficient organ and duplicating a function takes up a lot of brainpower and energy.

Mirror neurons are quite a new finding and scientists are still learning exactly how they work. Current knowledge suggests they're active when we perform a goal-directed action and when we see someone else performing the action. Lieberman undertook research to find whether there were differences in how the two brain systems react when we see and think about other people's actions (which is what we're doing when we are modelling our behaviour on someone else's).

What happens when we're observing behaviour?

When we observe a role model there are different interpretations going on:

> *What* they are doing

> *Why* they are doing it, and

> *How* they are doing it

For example, if a leader is describing their strategy to expand the organisation's retail outlets to China, these different aspects might be:

> What: formulating the plan for the number of outlets

> Why: to create a new revenue stream in a growth market

> How: finding properties and staff in the cities with the most customers for the product

When you want to model behaviour, the most important question to be answered first is the *how* question: "How is this leader behaving?"

This is essentially what HR are asking future leaders to do: to look at *how* the senior role model acts. But as we've observed, there is more to success and authentic behaviour than *how*.

Which parts of the brain work on the different questions?

Lieberman's research aimed to understand the different brain activity occurring in these three aspects of an action. The experiment looked at understanding the different brain regions involved in *what* someone is doing compared with *why* they are doing it and *how* they are doing it.

Participants were asked to watch video clips of someone performing a task. Having established how the task was being executed, they were then asked to determine either why the activity was happening or what was happening, and their brain activity was observed.

Lieberman found that different parts of the brain processed the different aspects of the task. The mirror neuron system activates for *what* and *how*; *why* is answered by the default system, the area which thinks about ourselves and others and understands motivation. This system typically doesn't activate except when *why* questions are posed. This is important for us to understand: it's the area that needs to be activated in order to role-model.

How does the research help us?

The default system is quick to switch on; Lieberman suggests it activates within about 20 seconds if we're not focused on cognitive tasks. But when the default regions are active, the cognitive, analytical regions switch off, and vice versa. This suggests that these two modes of thinking compete with each other.

Mirror neurons are robust under cognitive load, when the brain is busy processing data or stressed, but the motivation-understanding default system can't operate well when people are stressed, undertaking cognitive tasks at the same time, or trying to process large amounts of information.

It takes effort, focus and concentration to understand other people's motivation (*why* the leader is proposing this retail strategy). When they're in short supply the default system doesn't come online, or doesn't operate efficiently.

Re-directing our role modelling

So people who spend a lot of time in rational cognitive thinking may be out of the habit of switching on the default system, or at least tuning in to it when it is switched on. We all know people who take little time, or make little effort, to understand themselves or other people. What can leaders do to make their motivations (the "why") clear and relevant for the future leaders in their teams? And how can HR help future leaders understand their senior role models better?

Help must be given balancing their attention between cognitive thinking and thinking about other people. And the research tells us that successful role modelling needs to focus on purpose and beliefs, not just behaviours. To do that an organisation needs a model of success which includes them. They may be communicated in writing, or senior role models may unbundle their own beliefs and purpose. So asking leaders to understand their own purpose and beliefs and share them is a vital ingredient of a successful role modelling strategy as part of your leadership development approach.

"A nice hotel, plenty of coffee, role-play exercises… what have we missed?"

5 ways to make your Development Centre work

Assessment Centres have been around since the 1920s when they were introduced by the military to improve the officer selection process: less of the "Was his father in the regiment?" and more "Let's see how he might perform leading men into battle."

"Development Centres" are a much more recent by-product which grew out of the desire to help talented individuals within an organisation understand their strengths and get a sense of what they need to develop to take the next step up the career ladder.

Because of this shared history, or because "development" sounds more palatable than "assessment," we tend to talk about Assessment and Development Centres as though they're the same sort of thing. But their aims and their outcomes are very different, and organisations that bundle them together do so at their peril.

What's the problem?

In theory, a couple of days spent in a nice hotel finding out about our strengths and development areas sounds like a great idea… from an HR point of view. More commonly the initiative is met with terror and suspicion: particularly ironic given that your target audience is the best-and-brightest in your organisation and your aim is to motivate and inspire them.

Let's face it: assessment, even if it's for development purposes, is bound to trigger a massive threat response in the brain. Examined in a CORE framework, concerns about Certainty ("Does this mean my promotion's on the line?"), Options available ("Why now?"), our Reputation ("Will I make a fool of myself?") and the Equity or fairness of the whole process ("They're going to be watching us 24/7 for the entire weekend?") are bound to be triggered.

So how do we get it right?

There are effective ways to neutralise these threats and make your Development Centre as effective as you need it to be.

After many years of running these centres we believe that the best are designed by keeping just five brain-savvy principles in mind:

1   Be clear about the intent and purpose of the Centre

Aim for clarity and transparency all the way through. If the activity is about assessment, then be honest and call it an Assessment Centre. Sometimes stakeholders think that by calling it a "development centre" the initiative will become more palatable to participants. This couldn't be further from the truth: the future leaders of your organisation aren't going to be impressed by deception and will very quickly recognise the true intent.

Bring any hidden agendas amongst the stakeholders out into the open and get them resolved. A good test to identify the aim of the programme is to ask, "Who will own the data and what will it be used for?" If the organisation is going to be custodian of the data produced by this centre, and intends to make decisions based upon it, then this smacks of assessment. If the individual will own the data, and they are empowered to use it to move forward on their own development goals, then the intent of the programme does look more like development.

Once this is clarified, communicate it. And be consistent. This is extremely important in creating the right tone, and positioning the programme correctly. Pay attention to the language used to describe the centre, share as much information as you can to give people certainty, and be open to answering any questions they may have.

We've found it useful to run question and answer sessions prior to running Development Centres: they go a long way towards giving participants a good understanding of the purpose of the initiative, as well as certainty about what it will involve and a sense that the process will be fair.

2   Make it personal and relevant

In order to pay close attention to something, our brain needs just the right amount of two important neurochemicals: dopamine and norepinephrine.[230] To increase dopamine levels in a learning situation, the content needs to be relevant to the learner. They need to be able to see the value of focusing their attention on the content: "This is really relevant to my HR business partner role and I can see that this will definitely impact my performance if I can master this."

One way to increase relevance is to make the learning scenarios as real and personal as possible. Identify the real challenges that the role holders face, and design activities to explore and practise these. Use the language and culture of the organisation, and ground all the exercises and simulations in what really happens in their roles. Getting the group to work out who should get a place in the lifeboat might be fun, but bears no relevance to their work.

3   Create a multi-sensory experience

Consider different ways you can present your information. Remember that participants will have different learning styles – some will be reflectors, some will be activists, other will want to discuss. Give hand-outs and text references for those who like to read. For those who like to learn experientially, include development activities introducing new skills that can be practised during a later stage of the programme.

We know that memory is located in different centres of the brain,[231] not (as was first thought) in one specific centre. This means that the more sensory triggers that are attached to information when it's disseminated the more likely it will be stored in multiple parts of the brain and the more memorable it will be. So tell stories, add humour, colours, videos anything... to embed the learning.

4   Coach to develop insight

Because this is about development, we encourage participants to coach themselves. (See the chapter in *Leading the function* on the value of feedback to find out more about why this is important.)

One-way feedback from a coach sets up an immediate threat to a participant's reputation. "I'm being judged... I got that wrong... everyone can see I got that wrong..." The format of the Development Centre should be framed from the beginning as a two-way partnership between the coach and participant, with the coach facilitating self-reflection and insight.

For example, in a role-played meeting with a business customer, we would stop the action and ask the participant what feedback they would give to themselves at this point. "What did you do well? What might you have handled differently?" Then we start the action again and get them to practise their new approach. In this way, we trigger a reward to their reputation and get them to take ownership of their development.

This tactic has the added advantage of giving the participant an opportunity to discuss and integrate new skills immediately.

Both psychological and neuroscientific research shows that the key to optimising learning and building long-term memory is to create "ownership" of learning content.[232] This ownership – or "generation of own learning" – occurs when an individual is motivated to understand, contextualise, retain and apply knowledge in their own way.

So it's very effective if the learner is encouraged to take in the new information and personalise it, transforming it by giving it meaning for themselves.

They might be invited to compare this information with their existing knowledge, volunteer an example where this new insight might be useful to them, participate in role-play, or otherwise think about this information in a "deep" rather than a "shallow" way.

5   Create a learning environment

A successful Development Centre will encourage participants to try out new things and approach challenges differently. But all this can only happen in a "safe" environment.

Many factors contribute to creating a safe setting which will support learning:

- Consistent language: right down to the name labels ("coach" rather than "assessor").
- The physical space: you need to think about creating an environment that is similar to work but also symbolically different. This will send signals that this is about development rather than the day-to-day job. Consider simple things like arranging chairs in a semi-circle, setting up the main room without furniture, and organising roleplaying scenarios in a conference room which resembles an office.
- The mind-set of the coach: it's the little things that give the game away. Copious notes, for example, send signals of assessor rather than coach, as does any kind of rating scale or feedback form.

So there we have it, five principles to keep in mind to get your Development Centre right. Designed and positioned well within the organisation you are likely to have participants telling you that this has had significant impact on their performance and how they think about their role. Get it wrong and you could motivate them to attend an Assessment Centre elsewhere...

"If talent is our number-one priority, why don't we have a queue for our top jobs?"

Change your talent culture and develop the pipeline

There isn't a CEO in the country who wouldn't say that talent is a key focus for them. They tell their employees, they tell their board members and they tell their shareholders: "We want to attract, nurture and develop the best talent..." "We depend on our people..." "People are our competitive advantage..."

And CEOs consistently tell *us* that talent is in their top-three priorities and it has been for years. So why aren't the issues being solved?

Why don't their organisations know who the successors are for key jobs? Why don't they know how to develop them, why don't they have a pipeline of great people ready to step up for new roles, and why don't they have successors in place? Have we all been approaching the issue of talent in the wrong way?

In the chapter *"I know I'm smart..."* in the *Leading yourself* section we look at some of the new thinking about how people learn and develop, and how their mindset can be switched to one that's most productive for today's business climate. (Those described as having a fixed mindset will believe that people are born with abilities or intellect that are pretty much unchangeable. While people with a growth mindset will use stretch assignments, feedback and development opportunities to grow talent.)

Here we're looking at the collective mindset of an organisation, expressed through its talent strategy. Is it hindering success, and what can you do to create real changes?

What's the mindset of your organisation?

The prevailing mindset of your organisation is revealed by the language you use about people, and the processes that you use to identify, assess and develop them. For example:

- Is talent commonly described as a selected, static group? Talent is a fixed trait that some people have.
- Do you rely on measures of intelligence and other attributes? Measuring fixed abilities that people are born with.
- Do you offer stretch assignments with measures of progress? Giving people assignments that create growth

in skills and experience.

- Are mistakes seen as learning? Debriefing projects and extracting what can be applied for greater success next time.

In the past, talent strategy in most businesses was firmly based on a fixed mindset: find talented people and keep them in the company.

Managers defined potential leaders as people who were similar to themselves. They worked with a team developed in their own image, and the prevailing belief was that progression was based on intelligence and only the brightest would rise through the various grades and rites of passage.

Managers fostered by this kind of culture will be heard to say things like, "She's really smart: went to a top university, got the grades, flew through our entrance exam..." Or, "He's so clever he out-thinks everyone else: he's our go-to guy for new projects."

Why Fixed needs to be fixed

If the dominant mindset is fixed, change is seen as risky, painful and hard.

One of the dangers of a fixed-mindset approach is that it can create fear and threat, and in extreme cases even be abusive. Instead of learning, growing, and moving the company forward, leaders worry about being judged, and these feelings cascade through the company making it hard for courage and innovation to survive.

Managers who hold a fixed mindset will find it hard to see the point of development programmes, feedback and coaching. They see talent as a static trait. The implications for their talent strategy are clear: you need to find those naturally talented people, and then work to hire or retain them. Much else is a waste of money, effort and resources.

Why you should go for Growth

If the collective mindset of the organisation is set to "growth," the prevailing belief is that change is an opportunity to learn and grow.

The views of growth-mindset managers about the members of their teams tend to centre on how they approach their work. The ones who are viewed as high potential and worth investment will be the ones identified as hard workers who try new things, take risks and learn from their mistakes.

You'll hear them saying things like, "He messed up but he learnt from it." Or, "You have to admire her guts: this is the third assignment where the stakes were high, but she came through."

These managers will be more inclined to give feedback, provide stretch assignments and coaching. You'll see that they themselves have a readiness to be a novice again and to review their performance in the light of new standards and changing business needs.

The thing about these individual managers' beliefs is they add up to a culture about talent, and that culture in turn becomes the way people are managed, assessed and developed.

Same thing, different intent

The same activity in a talent strategy can be creating growth or fear, depending on how it's presented and judged.

For example, in a growth-mindset culture stretch assignments are seen as recognising potential and giving an opportunity for development: "There are unique opportunities to learn in an emerging country." But in a fixed-mindset culture they can be seen as tests of capability, or rites of passage: "We must test her out in an emerging country where she can show her smarts."

To create a growth-mindset culture, talent initiatives need to be set up in a different way. How you support and develop the people will be subtly different:

- Give feedback, but include coaching for success and change rather than observations of what was done "right" and what their weaknesses were.
- Assessment interviews: ask about how the person would tackle a new assignment, how they would measure their success, what would indicate to them they were doing well.
- Look for examples of seeking to learn, overcoming obstacles, seeing mistakes as learning and resilience to setbacks.
- Present 360-type feedback and other kinds of assessment not as a static picture but as a snapshot in time with indicators for change and growth.
- Back this up with coaching to make the change.
- When introducing learning opportunities, be they formal programmes or on the job, present skills as learnable rather than "who's good at this?"
- Don't talk about filling a gap in their skillset, but about opportunities to master skills.
- Make the manager's role a resource or performance coach, not as the judge of performance.

A talent strategy based on growth will look across the whole workforce; it will seek out people who have a history of growth rather than just qualifications, high IQ or who've been educated in the right places; it will provide opportunities for job rotation and development of skills; and it will encourage employees to take on stretch assignments, new challenges and new roles. Weaknesses will be seen as opportunities to learn and coaching will be embedded in every manager's role.

Overall the strategy will convey the idea that the organisation values trying and dedication, not just ready-made talent.

The research on managers' mindsets

Research by Peter Heslin, who frequently collaborates with Carol Dweck, measured managers' mindsets.[233] Their employees were then asked how much the manager helped analyse performance, gave useful feedback, acted as a sounding board, inspired confidence and supported new challenges.

Fixed-mindset managers did little or none of this.

They also found that managers with a growth mindset noticed improvement in their employees, whereas those with a fixed mindset did not: these managers appeared to be stuck in their initial impression.

In Heslin's study, employees evaluated their growth-mindset managers as providing better coaching for development. He also found a link between mindset and the *way* managers coached.

Managers who had or adopted a growth mindset were more willing to coach and give quality suggestions for improvement. When managers were trained to adopt a growth mindset they were able to change. This lasted over time and the managers' ability to coach got better.

Tackling the difficult conversations

There is also evidence that mindset impacts the way people deal with difficult conversations in work relationships.

Managers with a growth mindset are more likely to speak up and try to solve the issue. Managers with a fixed mindset tend to shy away from a conversation thinking there is little point in confronting issues if people can't change. The more difficult the problem the less likely the manager is to deal with it.

All this has a significant impact on performance management, engagement and other HR processes. It also suggests that shifting mindset is a prerequisite to successful training in handling difficult conversations, and similar issues.

Why the mindset matters in business today

For managers to have an impact on an employee's mindset they should be praising effort rather than achievement. Plus encouraging risk, debriefing learning, and noticing progress.

Here are the key features of good praise.

Don't focus your praise on intelligence

The psychology of self-esteem encourages parents to believe that building it means praising intelligence. At work, employers speak admiringly of "being smart."

Dweck says this doesn't work in high-change, high-challenge environments.[234] She believes what you *should* do is give people the tools to become confident learners.

Dweck found that when intelligence was being praised, people in her study didn't opt for a challenge – they wanted to work on something they knew they could do. When a hard challenge was given they lost their confidence, and their performance on an IQ test actually declined over the course of the study.

Those praised for effort performed better, were more confident about taking on difficult tasks and their performance improved.

Praise the *effort* rather than the result

Dweck says we need to praise the effort and struggle undertaken.[235] "Someone said to me recently: 'In your culture, struggle is a bad word.' And it's true: we never say 'Oh I had a fantastic struggle today,' but we should."

The predominant organisational culture is usually that tasks should appear to be accomplished effortlessly, demonstrating that the employee is operating with ease and complete mastery of their area of expertise. Any kind of additional effort or stress usually remains well-hidden, after hours, and it's the seamlessly-completed project that gets singled out for commendation.

But Dweck says managers would do their staff a greater service by noticing and commenting on their efforts and the challenges they have overcome. "That was a phenomenal struggle" sends a signal that effort is valuable and admired.

She says managers should praise persistence in the face of setbacks: "That was really difficult and it didn't stop you." Praise finding a strategy, and trying out new strategies: "That was a good idea to look for new ways to contact our customers." And praise for being up for challenges: "Wow, you chose a really tough one, that's fantastic – you're going to learn a lot from that."

Encourage employees to take on challenges she advises: to enjoy effort, and bounce back from setbacks. Then they will build their *own* confidence and self-esteem by knowing how to deal with work, and they'll become challenge-seeking and resilient.

Can mindsets change?

If you're now sitting with you head in your hands saying: "I can see all our managers have a fixed mindset: our talent strategy is never going work," you're falling into a fixed mindset yourself!

You can turn this around.

Dweck says that when you leave mindsets alone they are stable: people's beliefs are not challenged and so they continue to think and act like they always have. But she has experimented with changing fixed-mindset beliefs to growth-mindset beliefs with some success.[236]

The interesting part about Dweck and Heslin's research for companies is that simple changes can influence the mindset of employees and their managers. In their work they trained managers to shift their beliefs in a short workshop which included exercises like thinking of times when they learnt something new, identifying people whose performance had changed for the better, and pointing to examples in the company where people had learnt from challenges or initial failure and gone on to be successful.

Running simple but powerful workshops can turn managers' beliefs from fixed to growth, and the evidence seems to be that the change persists.[237] Workshops can be as short as 90 minutes. Giving managers' exercises to do which get them to notice growth in themselves, and others, are highly effective in shifting their beliefs.

After the training Heslin and Dweck found their managers coached more, gave more performance suggestions, and noticed the efforts of their employees. They checked the shift in beliefs six weeks later and the growth mindset was still in place.

So, to move beyond the fine statements in the annual report and develop a truly effective talent culture within your organisation, understand the mindset of your managers. And to develop adaptability, learning and growth make the shift to praising effort, risk-taking and the willingness to take on a challenge.

"Not another staff survey..."

4 steps for creating effective engagement

Engagement of staff in the business is a hot topic. But do HR functions really care about it, or has it become just another process to run: "It's the survey season again." Rather than being an issue that's central to HR and business results.

Clearly something isn't working, as all the data says our workforce is not engaged.

The brain-savvy survey

Head Heart + Brain commissioned a poll of more than 2,000 UK employees to ask them about their leaders.[238] The questions were based on neuroscience criteria about how a leader engages their team. The index measured various factors, from the amount of autonomy employees are given, clarity about job responsibilities and targets, to the quality of feedback and the fairness of leadership.

Here are some of the highlights from the data:

- Only *60%* of employees have a clear understanding of their role and purpose. One factor essential for an engaged workforce is knowing what is expected and that they are on the path to achieving it. *40%* of employees don't have an answer to this basic question.
- *57%* of people have autonomy over only the small things in their job or none at all. Autonomy is a huge factor in having a sense of control over work and helping to provide meaning.
- Leaders are failing to maximise feelings of reward at work. When asked whether their leader gave them praise, positive feedback or recognition of their contribution to the organisation, just *17%* of employees said the feedback they got was always constructive. *42%* said feedback was only ever negative, or that there was none at all.
- We asked employees if their leaders are always fair. *36%* said yes. But a worrying *58%* said "only sometimes." The problem for leaders is that it's very hard to re-establish a damaged reputation for fairness.
- On a happier note *82%* said they get on with their colleagues or they are a close team.
- However, fewer than one third *(32%)* of employees are fully engaged with their job. And over one in seven UK workers *(14%)* say they aren't engaged with their organisation at all.

So what will work?

Engagement isn't a fluffy extra: it leads to a real improvement on the bottom line.[239] Some research suggests by as much as 28%.

But having a survey that tells you what is going on doesn't go far enough. HR professionals often shy away from going beyond the survey because it's hard to define what will make a difference.

There are well-researched factors which impact engagement. The Conference Board found that across all the studies reviewed, and for all locations and age groups, there was agreement that the relationship with the immediate line manager is the strongest of all drivers[240] on employee engagement. So focusing on this relationship potentially gives the best return.

Our research would also suggest that having leaders who work in a brain-savvy way results in better business outcomes. Good leaders create engaged employees who in turn produce business results.

There are, in our experience, five basic requirements for leaders wanting to develop an engaged workforce.

1   Know and trust the team

Successful leaders build trusting relationships with each team member and amongst their team. You might want to read more about how to do that in our chapter *"How trusting should we be as an organisation?"*

The bottom line is you get what you expect. If you assume your employees will steal the stationery you will probably be proved right; if you trust them they will live up to your expectations – and you keep more of the stationery.

A brain-savvy leader uses their powers of observation and questions to stay attuned to what's going on in their team. They ask questions about what employees are feeling – not just what they think, or about progress on the task.

They know they must also be mindful. By which we don't mean they will be meditating, but taking time to read the cues on what motivates their people. They'll be particularly aware of how their interactions with team members can cause them to feel either threatened or rewarded.

Mindful leaders know they need the brain of each person in the team to be in "reward" mode for them to be able to access their creative, decision-making and problem-solving skills. The brain-savvy leader knows that when their staff are in "threat" mode they will find it harder to manage their emotions and there's a risk of the team starting to unravel and definitely not being engaged.

2 Get out of the way

This is otherwise known as giving autonomy or Options in our CORE model, and means allowing the individuals in a team to tailor the *way* they work to their preferences and abilities.

For example, some people leave things to the last minute, they need the pressure to get creative, while others work well ahead of schedule so they can plan for interruptions and crisis. Some want feedback; others prefer to make their own way and feel micro-managed if the leader interjects too much.

The brain-savvy leader asks their team members about the app-roach they prefer, and then, if possible, adapts to meet their needs. If the leader has to assign both the goal and the method for reach-ing it, it's possible to create some choice by enabling the team to make decisions about more peripheral aspects of the task. For example, if everyone has to attend a weekly meeting, individuals can take turns leading the meeting, or setting the agenda, decid-ing the length of the meeting and the format. Studies show that making even small choices creates a sense of autonomy.

3 Exercise your superpowers

This isn't the kind of strength that raises buildings or works for S.H.I.E.L.D. but brain-savvy leaders do use the superpowers identified by neuroscientist Matt Lieberman.[241] The most import-ant of them is the understanding that as humans we are social beings first and foremost: we gain a sense of reward from doing things for others or engaging with others.

Other superpowers at a leader's disposal include the knowledge that humans experience social pain in a very similar way to physical pain: social rejection like being ignored or left out of projects really hurts. But the memory of this pain continues much longer than if you had broken your leg or stubbed your toe. The leader's superpower: the ability to spare them that pain!

Another astonishing power is our ability to read other people's minds. We have a separate brain system just for understanding other people, and we use it to predict their goals and motivations. The social thinking network, or default network as we usually call it, is totally separate from the intellect network. It's quieter when we're thinking intellectually, but starts working whenever we're not involved in cognitive work.

And we can even prime other people to think socially, just by mentioning social factors, such as saying "how might our clients feel about this?" just before a meeting. And we can make them absorb information more effectively, for example just by telling team leaders that this is going to be information they'll need to pass on to their teams. They will take in the information through a filter of what will be useful to their team.

Of course, every superhero has their destructive kryptonite, and Lieberman says ours is our failure to realise just how important "social connection" is to us. In a work context it tends to be seen as a "nice to have." Many leaders still think of social needs as, explicitly or implicitly, less important than rewards such as salary. This is a mistake, and in terms of creating engagement it's a costly one. It's possible that if leaders made just this one shift in thinking all their other engagement issues would disappear.

As a leader, focusing on the quality of the relationship between you and employees, and between employees, is a superpower. No leader or individual can be successful on their own. Our need for social connection is a primary need. We'd say that Maslow got his "hierarchy of needs" wrong.

4 Being predictable

Brain-savvy leaders are really strong at managing themselves, and particularly their emotions.

They know when they've been stressed by their journey to work, and how to make sure they're calm by the time of the team meeting. They'll know that they need to take a break before a team meeting if they've had a tough time with the CEO, otherwise they'll pass on their stress to the team and everyone will be in threat mode. They also understand about social contagion and that their body language and moods will pass to the team, for good or ill.

Is all this describing some completely fictional leader? Or a wish list that your organisation's leaders will never achieve, no matter how much training you give them?

Well, your business *has* got brain-savvy leaders. Here are some clues as to where you'll find them:

- Those pockets of the business that have really amazing scores when you do your engagement surveys. They contain a brain-savvy leader or two.
- The sales team that's doing really well and isn't driven by internal competition. Probably a brain-savvy leader in there too.
- The business unit that keeps finding different ways to innovate, to save costs or improve products. There's a brain-savvy leader around in there.

What's so super about brain-savvy leaders is that their powers mean the teams they manage are highly engaged, and we know that a business of engaged teams has better financial results, better retention and better overall performance.

"Can we make work more fulfilling?"

Understanding the see-saw between task and people focus

Is it reasonable to expect personal fulfilment at work?

Philosopher Alain de Botton believes we shouldn't expect too much, based on his observations of the professionals he got to know[242] while researching his book *The Pleasures and Sorrows of Work*. Many of them were unfulfilled, but he does believe that work usefully occupies our time and stops us worrying about far bigger issues like the inevitability of death and the pointlessness of existence.

Whether or not work serves no greater intellectual purpose than to stop us thinking about much more unpleasant things, research by recruitment firm Randstad confirms that fulfilment is a sought-after but unattainable aspiration for many employees.[243] They have found that 10 million people are professionally unfulfilled in the UK; higher than other European countries like Germany and France, and also higher than in English-speaking countries such as Canada and Australia.

This lack of fulfilment comes with costs for employers to the tune of a staggering £14bn in absenteeism. Plus the effects of staff turnover, lost productivity and dissatisfaction with the organisation, and presumably its leaders.

But are we setting our standards too low? Is de Botton himself mired by a lack of fulfilment and interpreting his findings in a way that underestimates the potential of leaders to create an environment where fulfilment can be achieved at work? In my view it is the leaders who will make the difference here. No leader can make an employee fulfilled, but they can create the environment.

The importance of leadership

Leaders not only hold the key but probably also cause the problem. We have low expectations of their effectiveness in this area, we only develop and hire for half the requirements in leadership, and our leaders have become lazy. The result is a lack of fulfilment.

Leaders have got into the habit of telling people what to do. It is after all far easier than taking the time and effort to set a purpose, engage people in the goals, get to know people and their ambitions and manage the myriad "people issues" that will be created by engaging the team's view. But like any habit this "telling" style has a rational reason for its existence.

The brain will always try to take the most energy-efficient route. Behaviour which is repeated is moved to the older parts of the brain, the habit centre or basal ganglia, where it is available out of conscious awareness, saving energy and processing-power in the newer prefrontal cortex. A "telling" style of leadership is a habit that has been formed in business. This may be why we hear much more about a socially-connected, purposeful leadership style in newer businesses like Facebook, where old habits have not had a chance to take root.

So what new habits should leaders adopt, and what's the evidence they will work?

Include social considerations in the strategy

The brain is designed to solve both intellectual and social problems. A study using fMRI (functional magnetic resonance imaging) asked managers to consider strategic and tactical workplace dilemmas while they were in the scanner.[244] The best strategic thinkers showed more activity in brain regions associated with empathy and emotional intelligence; the insula and anterior cingulate cortex.

This finding suggests that good business strategy may include considering the social implications of the strategy, which could lead to more satisfying and potentially rewarding work for employees.

Balance thinking

Matt Lieberman, who runs the social neuroscience lab at UCLA, suggests that leaders who are poor at managing and understanding social interactions are missing important opportunities.[245]

He believes a human's ability to understand other people is unique. The brain circuits with which we do this are largely the same areas that enable us to think about ourselves, a process scientists call Theory of Mind or "mentalizing." This combination of processes suggests that the better we are at understanding ourselves the better we will also be at understanding others.

Our brain circuitry acts a bit like a see-saw. When we are thinking about ourselves or others and activating the mentalizing circuits, we close down[246] much of the rational, executive-functioning prefrontal cortex. So it's not possible to be creating a business strategy, for example, at the same time as thinking about the impact of that strategy on people.

Many leaders appointed for their goal-focused abilities get out of the habit of ever noticing the implications for people. This habit can only be shifted by taking time to reflect on the team and putting yourself in their shoes.

Stop telling people what to do

The difference between being told and having insight is all about creating new mental maps. If leaders tell people what to do they still have to create the mental map for themselves to take action. Engaging people in problem-solving or creating insight[247] through powerful questions means people create the map in one step; they also have an interest in their own idea. Also telling is likely to set up a threat response.[248] This in turn moves people away from the new information and increases the likelihood of resistance. Working out the implications for themselves increase insight, motivation and produces brain-based rewards, which is fulfilment.

Connect socially

This is more than walking about smiling tentatively at your team. Connect by getting engaged with what they are doing, asking questions about how they are feeling (not just the task they're involved in), and involving the team in developing the tactics on projects and the implementation of strategy.

The science shows that social needs are primary in the brain:[249] something that many managers forget at work. Social pain activates the same regions as physical pain,[250] when someone is put down, or their ways of working are controlled, or they are told publicly what to do, a threat response is activated reducing their ability to think clearly.

Avoiding this negative style of management, and working with a new understanding of the brain enables leaders to create an environment where employees can connect to their work and each other: essential ingredients for fulfilment.

Oh and leaders may just get an unexpected bonus: a sense of work fulfilment for themselves from their new habits.

"How trusting should we be as an organisation?"

The science of trusting your people, and why it matters

A while ago we were working with a leadership team, and in the course of a workshop they got into a debate about trust. Opinions were split, with the senior leader insisting their role was to mitigate risk by putting policies in place and policing people to ensure the company was safe. He cited the examples of people taking excess holidays, overspending on expenses and not working when home-based.

His starting premise was people are not trustworthy: if they can they will cheat the company. Others in the team held a different view which could broadly be summarised as "If you trust people, they'll respond honestly."

It was clear the issue could have significant ramifications for policies the company was developing, and especially for their culture.

The debate got me thinking about the neuroscience of trust and how our personal starting point may determine the level of trustworthy behaviour we see demonstrated.

Trust has been shown to be a core component of employee engagement[251] by many studies, including the Edelman Trust Barometer. HR are often the key players in developing policy and custodians of the cultural norms that will promote or inhibit trust.

Understanding the biology of trust and the science of what creates trust is an important element in guiding policy and advising leaders. So what has neuroscience got to add to our understanding of trust and engagement?

The moral scientist

The work on trust has been led by neuro-economist Paul Zak at California's Claremont Graduate University. Zak has found that countries characterised by high levels of trust between citizens are also the most economically successful.[252]

The trust molecule

Zak started out looking at morality and thought that oxytocin, the neuromodulator hormone commonly associated with mother and child bonding, might be an element in morality. He subsequently focused on trust as a more tangible belief system to study. The studies carried out by Zak were designed to understand how the human brain determines when or when not to trust someone.

Participants took part in the Trust Game designed to study individuals' propensity to be trusting and to be trustworthy, and their oxytocin levels were monitored throughout. The researchers found that when participants felt they were trusted, their brains responded by producing oxytocin,[253] and when participants were shown increased levels of trust their brain produced even more oxytocin.

Most significant however, was the finding that the rise in oxytocin levels resulted in participants behaving in a more trustworthy way.[254] The researchers concluded that people who feel trusted *become* more trustworthy as a result of increased oxytocin levels in their brain, leading Zak to call oxytocin "the trust molecule."

Conditional and unconditional trust

It transpires that qualified trust operates quite differently to unconditional trust.[255] Different parts of the brain respond; the cerebral cortex, signals the ventral tegmental area to release dopamine into the amygdala, the prefrontal cortex and the nucleus acumens. These regions of the brain make up the reward system. Conditional trust selectively activates the ventral tegmental area, a region linked to the evaluation of expected and realised reward. Whereas unconditional trust selectively activates the septal area, a region linked to social attachment behaviour. The interplay of these neural systems helps create reciprocal exchange.

Trust and empathy

Experimenters also found that changes in oxytocin were related to levels of empathy, and could be used to predict people's feelings of empathy.[256] Zak believes it is this emotion which connects us to other people and triggers moral behaviour, an element of which is the desire to be trusted.

We want to help people, this makes us feel good about them and so we act well towards them. This is not a new idea, neuroscience is now supporting the proposal that Adam Smith made in his 1759 treatise, *The Theory of Moral Sentiments*: that we are social beings and therefore share the emotions of others, and if we do something to make someone happy we share those emotions too.

The darker side

But what about when people feel distrustful?

Zak and his team have discovered that when male participants are distrusted it results in a rise in levels of a hormone called dihydrotestosterone[257] which increases the desire for physical confrontation in stressful social circumstances. Men, it seems, can react aggressively to not being trusted. And women? Women are what Zak calls "cooler responders," although this is not yet fully understood or verified.

And some recent research has found a darker side to oxytocin, and one that it's useful to be aware of.

Research from North Western University has found that the hormone can *increase* emotional pain.[258] Oxytocin seems to be the reason that stressful social situations, like having a bullying boss or extreme stress on a business project, can trigger fear or anxiety long past the event. If a social experience is stressful or negative it activates the lateral septum, which is known as the oxytocin pathway. That in turn amplifies fear and anxiety and intensifies the memory, making people susceptible to feeling fear in similar stressful situations in the future.

Hopefully, oxytocin also intensifies positive social memories and therefore increases feelings of well-being, but that research has not been done yet.

The implications of trusting (or not trusting)

When there's a breach of trust the brain's conflict detector (the ACC) activates the amygdala. But high levels of trust are associated with *decreased* amygdala activity and reduced fear. Trust therefore frees up the brain for other useful activities, such as creativity, planning and decision-making.

If HR leaders want to increase trust in the workplace the best place to start is at home: by being trustworthy and by trusting people more.

There is evidence that this works at both a conscious and an unconscious level. At a conscious level staff want to honour your trust in them, but trust also works on a deeper, neurological basis, at an unconscious level which has the potential to create a snowball effect of trust. Showing people that you trust them increases their oxytocin levels and that makes them potentially *more trustworthy*. They then also show more trust in you and that in turn raises your oxytocin levels, causing you to be more trustworthy and to show more trust in them.

There are examples of companies adopting these types of policies, such as Netflix having no requirement for employees to have holiday-time signed off.[259]

HR departments who display constant distrust, through policy or personal actions, may be producing the reverse snowball effect. At best people will keep doing what they were doing anyway and will definitely not be engaged.

And the leadership team we were working with? It's a work in progress, but education is a powerful thing!

6 Leading yourself

How to develop your creativity and insight, be more resilient, stay focused on your goals... Harnessing the insights of neuroscience to maximise your personal performance.

"I know I'm smart…"

Talent mindset: what do you believe about your abilities?

Do you find yourself stuck doing your job the way you always have? Are you well-suited to your role: it matches your talents and abilities, and you like to be in a role you can succeed at? Or do you like a challenge, and prefer to take the risky role rather than the sure bet? These types of thoughts and strategies may be the result of your mindset. And you might want to review that mindset and your own beliefs in the light of research on talent and success.

Understanding your psychological world view

Stanford psychologist Carol Dweck has spent her career researching learning, and in particular exploring the "mindset" for success. She describes a mindset as someone's entire psychological world, where everything has a different meaning depending on their beliefs. Her studies show that people tend to have one of two sets of beliefs that create their mindset about work, learning and their own abilities.[260] (As you read on, you might find it useful to consider your own approach to learning and challenges.)

Fixed mindset

Dweck describes people who hold a belief that talent, ability and intelligence are something you are born with as having a "fixed mindset." And you'll notice that much of our language about ability and performance is framed by this mindset: "He's very bright," "She's so talented," "She's a natural leader," "He has a gift for languages."

People coming from this mindset believe you either have it or you don't. And there are a range of behaviours which reflect this world view. First rule of a fixed mindset is look clever – at all times and at all costs. If you're not going to look clever, don't do it. In the face of any setbacks, hide your mistakes and conceal your deficiencies, because mistakes and deficiencies are permanent and that's going to be a black mark against you.

In studies, Dweck has found that people with a fixed mindset say, "The main thing I want when I do my work is to show how good I am at it." If this is you, you probably change jobs when the standards or requirements change, and you're always looking for roles that match your demonstrated abilities, where you know you can shine. Because you're bringing what you believe to be your innate, natural talents, you'll tend to tackle the new role in a similar way to how you worked in the last one, moulding the role to your strengths and ways of working.

We frequently see these traits in senior leaders who introduce the same strategy that worked for them in their last company (irrespective of whether time has moved on, or the organisations are different.)

Employees with this mindset believe their performance is a result of their talents. They're concerned about their ranking and reputation, and are quick to compare their performance with peers.

But they actually exhibit less persistence and less ability to learn from experience. Their mental framework provides no mechanisms for dealing with setbacks and it can mean they're reluctant to take on tricky assignments. Their readiness to change jobs can be less about enthusiasm for a new challenge than unwillingness to persist with current problems when their performance may show up as less than excellent.

Growth mindset

In contrast, people who have a 'growth mindset' believe that talent, abilities and intellect can be developed. Their number-one rule is learn, learn, learn: they're the people leaning over your shoulder when the new software programme's being demonstrated, the first ones to sign up for an optional seminar, the person who went on a course as part of their last holiday.

Growth mindset people say things like, "It's much more important for me to have a challenge than to be rated the best person." They do care about rankings, but they care even more about having an interesting, challenging role where they're going to be getting into new areas and working with good people. For these people it is not about intelligence and talents; even if they have those traits in abundance, they are the start point rather than the end point. Mistakes are part of learning; deficiencies are part of being human and indicate you need to work harder; they find out what they can do to learn, who they can learn from and where the testing opportunities are.

Dweck's studies show that people with a growth mindset work harder, learn from experience and are willing to take more risks[261] to achieve results. After a test, they're not the people fist-pumping their high score but the ones grabbing the paper and saying, "Hang on, where did I go wrong?" (a trait demonstrated in one of Dweck's experiments).

You can recognise who's who in the workplace: fixed mindsetters are quick to claim the plaudits, share the news of successes, and propose rolling out the same plan again. They're impatient of introspection and would tend to say, "If it aint broke, don't fix it." You'll never hear them say, "Tell me where I went wrong." It's all, "Let's move on..."

But growth mindsetters are definitely the people you want on a team if things haven't gone well: a major setback will be re-framed as a powerful learning opportunity. They're open to people moving into new roles they have no experience of, and they're ready to put themselves into unfamiliar but interesting situations.

Yes, you can change your mindset

If you recognise the qualities of growth mindset as the way you'd like to be, you're already on your way. Here are some simple steps for coaching yourself, which you can also adapt for leading your team.

Step 1: Learn to hear your fixed-mindset "voice"

As you approach a challenge you're very likely to hear the voice in your head saying things like, "Are you sure you can do this?" "You've never tried this before." "It's going to be really embarrassing if you fail and people realise you thought you could do it." "Maybe this just isn't for you."

If something goes wrong for you the voice might be saying, "This would have been easy if you just had the talent for it." "This happened last time, you're never going to get this." "It's not too late to back out, and try to regain your reputation." "Now everyone knows your limits."

If you come in for some criticism you might hear yourself saying, "I couldn't deliver the results without backup." In relation to the person delivering the criticism, you might tell yourself, "They really don't know what this job involves." If your boss is giving you some very specific, constructive feedback, you may be hearing, "I'm disappointed in you: I thought you were capable but now I see you're not."

Step 2: Your interpretation

Everyone is going to be presented with different opportunities, face different challenges and setbacks, and come in for some criticism. It's how you *read* them that's your choice. Fixed mindset: it's your talents or abilities that are lacking. Growth mindset: you need to work in a different way, try something new, make more effort, expand your abilities.

Re-frame your inner voice, and consciously check yourself when you catch that type of internal voice. Replace, "Oh god, I can't do this," with, "It's always really scary in a new role, but in three months I'll be on top of it."

Instead of, "Keep your head below the parapet for this one: it's not going to do your career any good," try replacing it with, "If I don't try, I automatically fail and where's the dignity in that?"

Privately brainstorm a list of times when you've been successful. Write that list down, and keep it to hand. Update it. Visualise seeing yourself successfully completing the project, and get a feeling for how it's going to be on the other side of it. And seek out the right kind of positive, open-minded people to support you. For a setback: instead of "You just haven't got what it takes," give yourself: "What's so wrong with trying? Successful athletes have to practise and fail to eventually get to the top."

Identify what you're passionate about and put your effort there. And keep a record of the milestones of your progress. If you're getting criticism, instead of pushing it away make a real effort to view the situation from their perspective. Consciously tell yourself: "If I don't take responsibility, I can't get better. I can always learn something."

Step 3: Follow-up with the growth action

Build the habit of creating growth-mindset explanations, and learn to act on your new voice. Consciously ask yourself: "What would the growth mindset action be here?" It will feel uncomfortable at first. It really helps to write down these ideas and intended actions to make them more tangible. And keep a note of your progress: seeing results is highly motivating.

Carol Dweck has found that people *can* change their mindset and beliefs, and that techniques like these are effective in making and maintaining the change.

You'll find more details about her work in the section *Leading talent, engagement and learning*, where we look at how the mindset of managers influences talent strategy, and how to turn your organisation into a growth mindset culture in the chapter *"If talent is our number-one priority, why don't we have a queue for our top jobs?"*

"I'm great! Why do I need self-awareness?"

Self-knowledge makes for better performance

Self-awareness sounds like a quality to have in a marriage partner, but in business... does it really matter?

A recent study by management consultants Green Peak Partners with John Hausknecht of Cornell University found that executives who drive hard for results may destroy value in a firm, while leaders who have high levels of self-awareness are able to build teams that are high-performing.[262]

"Our findings directly challenge the conventional view that 'drive for results at all costs' is the right approach," says Green Peak's J.P. Flaum. "The executives most likely to deliver good bottom-line results are actually self-aware leaders who are especially good at working with individuals and in teams."

What *is* self-awareness? Looking at the science behind self-awareness leads to a plethora of studies of human consciousness. And scientists, just as much as philosophers, enjoy lengthy debates about the differences between the two. But here is one useful explanation: consciousness is awareness of our body and our environment; self-awareness is recognition of that consciousness. It involves not only understanding that we exist, but understanding that we are aware of our existence.

Or to put it another way: to be conscious is to think; to be self-aware is to realise that you are a thinking being, and to think about your thoughts. And you can read more about that in our chapter on thinking *"So, I need to think about my thinking?"* in the section on *Leading purpose*.

The self-awareness part of the brain

Numerous neuroimaging research projects have shown that thinking about ourselves, recognising images of ourselves and reflecting on our thoughts and feelings are all forms of self-awareness[263] demonstrated by activation of the higher brain, the cortex.

These studies demonstrate a clear pattern: when people see pictures of themselves or see themselves in a mirror, the regions in the right prefrontal and parietal cortex on the lateral surface of the brain are active, in addition the parietal region which responds to seeing your own face.

But self-knowledge is more than knowing yourself in the mirror or recognising your picture.

A Dartmouth College study showed participants words such as *polite* and *talkative* and then asked them if the word described themselves or the US president. The researchers recorded brain activity, and the results showed similar patterns of activity as in the mirror test, but also activity in the medial prefrontal cortex and the precuneus rather than the lateral surface. Which indicated that recognition and *thinking about* ourselves happens in different brain regions.[264] Descartes' conception of the separation of the mind and the body seems to have its parallel in the brain's systems of processing.

Ninety-four per cent of all studies of self-reflection have identified activity in the medial prefrontal cortex:[265] it is the only brain region reliably associated with questions of "who we are."

Building self-awareness

We tend to believe that the self we are aware of and think about is composed of personal beliefs, goals, and values. But how do we gain self-awareness? Nietzsche believed it was through the people in our life and our interactions with them forming our beliefs and memories: we become that mix.

Other similar theories include the "social construction of reality"[266] which suggests over time we create mental representations (mental maps) of our actions that determine the way we interact with the world and each other. These beliefs and actions become a habit. We tend not to question our own beliefs and assumptions and in turn they determine what we notice and what we don't. Our thoughts and actions can be limited by the unexplored mental maps and assumptions.

When assumptions are brought to the surface and questioned, new alternatives can be considered, more choices are on the table, and movement from one way of seeing an issue to another becomes possible. It's this awareness that provides insights that enable us to learn and change.

Different mental maps, based on different underlying assumptions, shape management philosophies and guide the way people within the organisation think and behave, resulting in different expectations of employees and leaders.

The influence of our group

But are these ideas all our own? Think, for example, about our response to fashion. We like to think we look at a trend and decide for ourselves whether it's right for us. It might be the fashion for ties the same colour as business shirts, or for women a fashion for black and white patterned shirts. To start with we often resist: we're not going to go along with the herd. But how often does it happen that after a few weeks or months of seeing everyone else wearing those ties, or those shirts, you find yourself buying into the trend: it is "right for you" after all.

Having our beliefs and values unconsciously influenced by those around us[267] is, UCLA's Matt Lieberman argues, a way of creating harmony in a group. The self exists primarily as a conduit to let social groups supplement our personal urges and impulses with socially driven behaviour.

Social interaction implants a collection of beliefs about ourselves and what constitutes a worthwhile life, and we use these to monitor our "performance" in the world. Self-awareness peaks when "socially internalised impulses" and "self-interested impulses" live in harmony.

This would suggest that at work success means we adopt the norms and values of the business rather than finding a business that has the same values as our own.

Awareness depends on feedback

A similar view was also suggested by the founding fathers of sociolology and social psychology, Charles Cooley and George Herbert Mead in the 1900s, in their "reflective appraisal generation" approach,[268] which might be summed up as "What I think you think of me." Challenging the conventional view that we look inward to determine what we think about ourselves, they proposed that we rely upon the feedback we receive both verbally and in non-verbal behaviour.

This is partly why processes like 360 feedback are so popular; they give us a legitimate means of collecting detailed information on what others think of us and how that integrates with our interpretation of other feedback we have received which forms our self-view. 360 feedback provides us with additional data to flesh out our self- knowledge.

How we develop self-awareness

Matt Lieberman and Jennifer Pfeifer studied adolescents to test this idea that we create our self- knowledge by adopting the views of others. They worked on the assumption that adolescents would have more need to actively think about the views of others[269] to be sure about their own view of themselves.

Every parent despairs at how easily teenagers seem to be influenced by their peers in everything from fashion sense to study habits, but up until this time no-one had looked at 13 year olds' brains to understand how they formed their sense of self.

The neuroscientists asked adolescents and adults to report on both a direct appraisal of themselves: "I am smart" and a reflected appraisal: "My friends think I am smart".

They expected to see activity in the medial prefrontal cortex when asking the direct appraisal question "Are you smart?", and this was the case for both adults and adolescents. With reflective appraisal "Do your friends thing you're smart?" they expected to see activity in the default or mentalizing system and this was also the case. (The mentalizing system is associated with thinking about the mental states of *others*.)

The adolescents showed strong activity throughout the mentalizing system, including when they were making direct appraisals of themselves. The adults did *not* mentalize when thinking about themselves; their mentalizing system activated only when thinking about others views. These results suggest adolescents brought to mind the reflected views of others rather than their own internalised views; adults had internalised their self-awareness whereas adolescents had to draw on the views of others to know themselves.

The importance of an outside view

In psychology these activities – self-knowledge and knowing how others see us – are generally seen as different processes, and in business we tend to build development programmes based on this psychological assumption. But when we are learning to understand ourselves as adolescents they are intertwined in our brain.

What the science suggests is that instead of trying to know and understand ourselves by examining our innermost thoughts, we might find it more useful to pay attention to what other people tell us about ourselves, both directly and non-verbally. Perhaps there's something to be learned from teenagers and we should define ourselves less by our uniqueness and more by an identity formed through our interaction with those who are important to us. As philosopher Alain de Botton says, "Living for others is such a relief[270] from the impossible task of trying to satisfy oneself."

Looking inwards or outwards

So what are the implications of this for HR, and particularly for leaders' self-awareness and self-reflection?

We often characterise leaders as embodying unique, authentic characteristics. Steve Jobs advised graduates[271] to avoid letting the "noise of others" override their own voice. But the data would suggest this is poor advice; rather than battle for inner awareness it would be better to help leaders integrate into their group and to let the "self" work through others.

It's an idea also supported by the Servant Leadership movement.

Rather than exercising leadership through the strength of their unique beliefs and values, the servant-leader shares power and understands the needs of others first.

Not only can it prove to be more effective for the organisation's bottom line, but in terms of self-reflection it can be especially fruitful in the early days of leadership when feedback from others is helping an emerging leader form their own awareness. Leadership development could be focused more on helping "socially internalised impulses" and "self-interested impulses" live in harmony for the benefit of the business.

"Am I good enough?"

Self-esteem or self-compassion:
how to develop a high-status mindset

> *"Everything that happens to you is a reflection of what you believe about yourself. We cannot out-perform our level of self-esteem. We cannot draw to ourselves more than we think we are worth."*
>
> **Iyanla Vanzant**

One of the success factors that emerged in our HR Leaders research was high levels of self-esteem; the high-achieving leaders we interviewed believed in themselves and what they were doing and had confidence that they could make a difference.

It's an attractive idea that seemed ideally suited to the nineties and the noughties – truly believe in yourself and all will be right. It certainly took hold in child-development circles: no more winners and losers, no more humiliation of being the last kid picked for the soccer team.

But the evidence emerging from the wealth of psychological studies on the subject is fairly contradictory, and a growing body of data suggests that trying to boost your self-esteem, or that of children, is difficult if not impossible. So what useful insights can neuroscience offer, and how can it help you manage your levels of self-esteem?

Understanding our sense of self

Researchers have used fMRI[272] (functional magnetic resonance imaging) scanners in self-reference experiments to understand how people process thinking about themselves. For example, the brain scans were compared when people were asked to make a judgment about the statement, "I am a good friend," compared with a neutral statement such as, "Water sustains life."

The studies have shown that self-referential activity is processed in the medial prefrontal cortex, a sub-region of the frontal lobe where higher-order cognitive functions are processed. This is the locus of the brain's "default mode" network, first identified by Marcus Raichle[273] in 2001, working at the Washington University School of Medicine. He observed that it's less active when the brain is working on a task or cognitive processing and more active when thinking about ourselves or others, and linked it to the neurobiology of self, that is thinking about ourselves.

Self-esteem and status

Many scientists believe that self-esteem is closely linked or even identical to reputation or social status, and is a vital part of our personal interactions.

Humans hold mental maps of the social hierarchies that are important to us: our families, work groups or regulars at the pub. Our status is our position on a map relative to everyone else around us. Studies have shown that we create a representation of our own and someone else's status in our brain when we communicate,[274] which influences how we interact with others.

We're aware of everyone's position in the social hierarchies we belong to, and make efforts to maintain or elevate our own position. And the organisations we work in set up well-defined hierarchies, and usually try to motivate people with the promise of moving upwards.

The trouble with social ranking is when it's challenged. At some point we all experience a downwards shift: someone doesn't laugh at your joke, the boss disagrees with you publicly, or you don't get the permanent appointment after "acting up" in a role. At these times the low self-esteem "involuntary defeat response"[275] kicks in. We turn tail, looking and feeling as though there's no fight left in us.

You know your reaction when you feel defeated: you undervalue yourself for a while, and keep clear of conflicts. "I'm just keeping my head down and getting on with the job." Scientists believe this reduction in activity to challenge or improve our place in the hierarchy is a self-protective behaviour. Keeping your head down at work after a failed project, for example, gains you time to regroup and avoids the potential for falling further in the hierarchy.

Hormones that help our self-esteem

Studies with human and non-human primates suggest that changes in the levels of the neurotransmitter serotonin, linked to feelings of wellbeing and happiness,[276] play an important role in regulating self-esteem and our sense of place within the social hierarchy.

Research indicates that high serotonin levels in the brain produce a sense of high self-esteem[277] and social status, while low serotonin levels produce low self-esteem and social status. High serotonin levels are associated with calm assurance, which leads to smoothly controlled movements. Low serotonin levels are associated with the irritability that leads to impulsive, uncontrolled, reckless and even violent behaviour.

Social feedback creates fluctuations from our baseline serotonin levels, and these fluctuations help determine our current level of self-esteem and social status. Serotonin fluctuations help us to negotiate social hierarchies,[278] to move up as far as circumstances permit, and to be reasonably content at each stage.

This suggests that a high or low level of self-esteem and serotonin isn't innate and permanent. Successful people may suffer a fall in social status, self-esteem, and serotonin levels when they lose their job or have a setback. Equally, success within our social hierarchy elevates our self-esteem and serotonin levels, and each elevation further raises our social expectations, perhaps spurring us to try for a promotion or leadership role we would not have considered when we were lower down the ladder.

The level of serotonin encourages us to strive for more and provides us with a way of coping, helping us to be content to play a group role that's consistent with our current limitations.

The winner effect

But like most things balance is critical. Cambridge neuroscientist and former Wall Street trader John Coates found an increase in self-esteem or status is one of the greatest feelings[279] and drives confident behaviours. Dopamine and serotonin levels go up, linked to feeling happier, and cortisol levels go down, lowering stress. Testosterone is increased; helping people focus, feel strong and confident.

An increase in status increases the number of new connections made in the brain, and broadens perspective and the processing of information with less effort. People with higher status are better able to follow through with their intentions; they have more control, more support, and more attention from others. Being in a high-status state helps make the social connections that the brain finds rewarding, which in turn puts you in an upward spiral toward even more positive neurochemistry.

This may well be the neurochemistry of "the winner effect." However Coates also found that too much of this "high" tipped traders over the edge and created a downward-spiral of low-self esteem and poor trading decisions.

Re-think the competition

You can elevate your self-esteem and status through winning against others[280] or "playing against yourself."

Thinking about yourself and thinking about others largely use the same circuits.[281] So you can harness the power of "beating the other person" by making that "other" yourself. Playing against yourself gives you the chance to feel ever-increasing status, without reducing the status of others. Competing with yourself to improve your skills, learning new things and striving to achieve mastery are all aspects of increasing self-esteem and status. And if you think about people who are most successful they tend to do this – they often have hobbies like marathon-running where they compete against themselves all the time.

Self-esteem or self-compassion?

You may find the idea of working to boost your self-esteem, and the risk of going "over the top" with the winner effect, doesn't sit well with you. In which case you'll be interested to know that a growing body of research, including studies by Berkeley psychologists Juliana Breines and Serena Chen, suggests that *self-compassion*, rather than self-esteem, may be the key to managing the impact of setbacks[282] and social status changes, and unlocking our full potential.

Self-compassion is a willingness to look at our mistakes and shortcomings with kindness and understanding. It includes accepting that as humans our social status will move both up and down. When we are self-compassionate we neither judge ourselves harshly, nor feel the need to defend and protect ourselves. Studies show self-compassion leads to high levels of personal wellbeing, optimism and happiness,[283] and to less anxiety and depression.

Self-compassion may *feel* good, but what impact does it have on performance? In their studies, Breines and Chen asked participants to take either a self-compassionate or self-esteem enhancing view of a setback or failure. For example, when asked to reflect on a personal weakness, some were asked to "imagine that you are talking to yourself about this weakness from a compassionate and understanding perspective. What would you say?"

Others were asked to focus on boosting their self-esteem: "Imagine that you are talking to yourself about this weakness from a perspective of validating your positive qualities. What would you say?"

People in the self-compassion group were more likely to see their weaknesses as changeable. "I know I'm not that great at maths but I can learn and get help to check my calculations." Self-compassion actually *increased* their motivation to improve and avoid the same mistake again in the future.

And this increased motivation led to better performance. For example, in one study participants who failed an initial test were given a second chance to improve their scores. Those who were directed to take a self-compassionate view of their earlier failure studied 25% longer[284] and scored higher in the second test than participants who focused on bolstering their self-esteem.

Self-compassion seems to be powerful because it is not judging.

You can confront your flaws and failures, get a realistic sense of your abilities and decide what to do differently next time.

When your focus is on protecting your self-esteem, you can't afford to look at yourself honestly and acknowledge the need for improvement, because it creates a threat to self-esteem or social status that triggers avoidance and a tendency to move away from the issue.

The key to success is to learn from mistakes and keep moving forward. Self-compassion gives a means of approaching mistakes without feeling threatened.

"How can my memory of the event be completely different to everyone else's?"

How memory works, and what you can do to get around its limitations

The brain can do extraordinary things: process vast amounts of data and carry out complex tasks at the same time: reading music while playing a musical instrument, having a conversation while driving a car... So it almost comes as a surprise to come up against some of the brain's limitations, not least of them relating to memory

Many of these limitations aren't well-understood, and as a result we often expect more of ourselves than our mental capacity will ever be able to deliver.

How working memory works

Working memory is the information we can consciously hold in our minds at any one time, including the phone number you just looked up. It enables us to hold information so we can work on it, like doing calculations or working out a time zone difference. It's a part of our consciousness we can be aware of at any given time. We can't turn it off, and nor would we want to.

We need it for solving problems using pieces of information, for making decisions and for making sense of new knowledge, as well as for remembering shopping lists. And some complex problem-solving, such as working out what time it is on the other side of the world when clocks in the UK have gone forward or back an hour, can tax our working memory very quickly.

Educational psychologist Peter Doolittle says there are four components to how it works:[285]

- it stores immediate experiences
- it stores a little knowledge
- it allow us to reach back into long-term memory and pull that in when we need it
- it mixes all of these together, linking present experience to past experience to achieve a current goal

Working memory *capacity* is the ability to use these components to fulfil a task, whether that's making a cup of tea or remembering the last word you wrote in a sentence. "Life comes at us, and it comes at us very quickly," says Peter Doolittle. "What we need to do is take the amorphous flow of experience and somehow extract meaning from it with a working memory that is about the size of a pea."

The limits of the pea

To illustrate the limits of working memory, try solving these arithmetic problems in your head: add 145 and 287. Or multiply 47 and 56. You *can* do it without pen and paper, but it takes a lot of effort and for most people it feels beyond them.

Yet these types of problem are easy compared to the things your brain manages every day, like calculating how to catch that ball that's coming towards you, or keeping on your feet in the middle of a gale. To achieve these physical feats your basal ganglia has to do a multitude of much harder calculations each second, to judge the right amount of force to be applied by various muscle groups. These are considered "non-conscious" tasks, and the unconscious mind manages them effortlessly because it has many more resources available to it, and is much more energy-efficient.

With its more limited resources, how many things can we hold in working memory at any one time? Most people have an idea that the magic number is seven, but research using *fMRI (functional magnetic resonance imaging)* shows that the average is just *four* completely independent pieces of information.[286]

The more we can hold in working memory, the more information the brain has to work with and the more connections and links can be made. People with high working memory capacity tend to be able to reason well, have high levels of writing ability, are good storytellers and do well on IQ tests.

Improving working memory

Sadly, working memory is limited in capacity, duration and focus, and all too easily distracted by a conversation at the adjoining desk or your own internal dialogue in a meeting. We can remember those four things for 10 to 20 seconds unless we do something with the information. To remember for longer, we need to deploy coping strategies: talk about the new information, process it, or apply it to some useful purpose.

So, when we're listening to a presentation we're more likely to remember it if we process what's going on in the moment, by asking ourselves questions like: "Do I agree with this?" "Are these assumptions right?" "What's missing here?" or "How does this apply to me?" The more we practise this type of active learning the more we'll see improvements in our working memory. Doolittle says: "What we process we learn."

Another way of helping memory is to record new learning in images, which are easier for the brain to recall. Use images when you are making notes, or even keep the points you want to remember as pictures which you can use to help you recall information: for example you may visualise yourself "filing" new pieces of information in an imaginary location, such as top left-hand drawer of a chest of drawers.

Memory training for children

Researchers in Japan tested whether training could increase the working memory[287] of primary school-age children, and also tested for changes in their IQ scores.

Children aged six to eight were trained for 10 minutes a day for two months. They were presented with a sequence of numbers or a number of words, with a one-second interval between each. Their recall was tested with questions such as: "Where in the sequence was the number four?" or "What was the third item?" Students had to practise holding the item sequence in working memory, and with practice increased the number of items they could recall from three to eight.

Changes in IQ scores correlated with the improvements in working memory: IQ increased by nine per cent in the group that had been given the memory training. And the training effect was even more evident in slightly older children: those who'd had memory training gained 12% in intelligence scores.

The feel good factor in memory improvement

It seems that improving our working memory capacity feels good: in other research it's been found that performing working memory tasks increases the release of the neurotransmitter dopamine,[288] which is associated with reward experienced by the brain. A Stockholm study trained people for 35 minutes a day for five weeks, with a difficulty level close to the limit of their individual memory capacity. Afterwards, all the participants had increased their working memory, and fMRI scans showed that the training had increased the density of dopamine D1 receptors in the cerebral cortex that transmit feelings of euphoria and reward.

These types of findings have resulted in the design and marketing of lots of brain-training programmes which claim to not only improve working memory but also reduce cognitive decline. It's being suggested that working memory can be expanded by attentiveness training, music, and some specially-designed games. But studies to date aren't conclusive.

Re-writable memory

In surveys, most people say they believe that once a memory is formed it remains the same. They expect memory to be a bit like a video camera capturing everything and storing it on disc. But memory is not a device that makes fixed recordings. Cognitive psychologist Elizabeth Loftus describes memory as more like a

Wikipedia page that you can go in and re-write,[289] and which can also be re-written by others.

Loftus has worked with the US army's "survival school" which prepares solders for the experience of being captured. Participants were shown a photograph of a man who was identified as the one who had conducted a hostile interrogation of them, and were asked questions such as, "Did your interrogator give you anything to eat? Did he give you a blanket?"

The trick was that the photograph was of someone completely different. But 84% of soldiers who were fed this misinformation later identified the person in the photograph as the perpetrator. All of them were mistaken.

Vulnerability to misinformation

The soldiers' memories for other details could also be affected by misinformation. Some of them were fed misinformation about a weapon that was supposedly present during the interrogation. Later, 27% claimed to have seen the non-existent weapon. Others were fed misinformation about a telephone in the interrogation room; over 90% of them claimed to have seen it

In other studies Loftus has demonstrated how even subtle changes of language can re-write memory. People shown simulated accidents estimated higher speeds and said they had seen non-existent broken glass if the word "smash" was used instead of "hit."

Research shows that people are especially vulnerable to memory mistakes when an event is stressful, and even highly-trained individuals – such as combat-trained soldiers – are susceptible to memory revision.

Experiencing and remembering

Behavioural economist Daniel Kahneman has shown that we perceive things in two ways: as the "experiencing self" and as the "remembering self."[290]

The experiencing self makes assessments in the moment, but the remembering self creates a coherent story about events in retrospect. The remembering self is a storyteller and creates a story which becomes our memory: this is what we get to keep from our experience.

Kahneman says the remembering self is helping us to make decisions going forward and, ultimately, determining how satisfied we are with our lives. We don't choose between *experiences*, we choose between *memories* of experiences. Even when we think about the future, we don't think of our future normally as experiences. We think of our future as anticipated memories.

The importance of endings

If something bad happens at the end of an event it ruins the memory of the experience. So, for example, if we go to a concert and really enjoy the music but trip and fall on the way out, our memory of the concert is tainted by the fall. For the remembering self the fall is integrated into the concert memory.

Kahneman says the ending is a critical part of every event. An experiment asked people undergoing a medical procedure to report on their pain every 60 seconds. Those patients who experienced more pain at the end of the operation later reported worse overall pain than they had in fact reported during the procedure.

We can use this insight to great effect in our working lives by ensuring that any bad news is delivered at the beginning of a presentation, and ensure positive memories by making sure good things happen at the end of an event.

Memory vs experience

The experiencing and remembering selves act as different entities, says Kahneman, and this can cause confusion. The remembering self keeps score, maintains the structure of our life and is the one that makes decisions based on the memory we chose from an experience.

And our idea of the future is shaped by anticipated memories. We often do things intentionally to create a memory, and then consume the memory; booking holidays is all about the anticipation of the experience we want, and the months of planning a wedding is summed up in the photograph for the mantelpiece.

Kahneman says that a sense of happiness or satisfaction can be very different depending on whether we are recording an experience, or how someone *thinks* about the experience – their memory of it. This has implications for HR policies on engagement and job satisfaction. Your survey is almost certainly collecting data on the *memory* not the *experience* of engagement. There are apps that can help you to collect data on what people are experiencing in the moment, and using these types of measure may give you very different results.

Incorporating experience feedback

Of course, collecting immediate data recording the in-the-moment experience of your engagement programme might make you feel better if it returns more positive scores. But it won't alter the effectiveness of the programme unless you can establish a better match between your participants' experiencing and remembering selves.

Based on the research evidence, it may be possible to influence the takeaway memory which will be acted upon by having participants feedback on their experience along the way, refer to their experience scores when summarising the programme, and share with the rest of the group their positive outcomes and how they may change their future practice. Oh and it should help if they have a positive experience at the end of the programme.

Influencing memory or experience

The differences between the experiencing and remembering self influences how people define what's important for them at work. In the moment, people will usually say social connection and relationships; when asked to think back on what is important to them, they will say money. We may well be satisfying *memory* rather than *experience*, and the significance for HR policy is profound.

If we could link these experienced and remembered assessments better, it's possible that organisations could be more effective at meeting employees' real needs and designing more effective policies.

Developing a better understanding of how memory works can improve bottom-line results in terms of productivity and performance. There is clear, and useful information available to inform business decisions. And on an individual level, if we understand the limitations of our own memories we can set reasonable expectations for ourselves, and develop workaround strategies to help us improve our own performance.

"Would I pass the marshmallow test?"

The success factors of self-control

An underlying assumption about success in business is that we have to control ourselves and our emotions: the office is no place for getting shouty or teary. For most of the last century emotion has been a dirty word in organisational culture and the British stiff upper lip is seen as the pinnacle of control.

Emotional Intelligence has at its heart the ability to understand the emotions of others and manage them in ourselves. So what's the science behind emotional control and how can you use it to enhance your success?

The power of delayed gratification

Walter Mischel's "Marshmallow Test,"[291] the famous long-term study begun back in the late 1960s, is probably still the best-known example of emotional control, and demonstrates the close link between self-regulation and later success in life.

The Stanford research used a simple but effective test to measure pre-school children's ability to delay gratification in order to win an additional treat: a marshmallow. The children were presented with a marshmallow and it was explained to them that if they could resist eating it for 15 minutes while the researcher was out of the room, they would be rewarded with a second marshmallow when the researcher returned.

Videos of the tests show the perfect agony of restraint; the most successful children had strategies for distracting themselves from yearning for the immediate treat. Following up with the participants years later,[292] Mischel found that the children who had been able to resist outperformed their peers on several scores including academic results, income and social success.

Like the marshmallow children, adults who are good at meta-cognition – that is, they understand their own thoughts and feelings – are also better able to direct attention away from whatever's immediately attracting them and stay focused on their goals

Mischel and his colleagues believed the test measured self-control, but later researchers have questioned whether it also depended upon factors such as intelligence that might be a factor in later success.

Beyond self-control

Angela Duckworth, University of Pennsylvania has correlated

performance on delayed-gratification, marshmallow-type tests to both home-based ratings of self-control and measures of intelligence. It transpires that the ability to control and wait does not predict anything on its own.[293] Higher self-control at age four was a predictor for higher standardised-test scores, higher grade point averages (GPAs) and lower bodyweight in ninth grade (14 year-olds).

Duckworth and her colleagues believe that grade point average at school is a better predictor of future success because it reflects a combination of overall ability and a willingness to work hard in school. Self-control is related to people's ability to work hard to achieve their long-term goals.

It's also interesting that a study has shown that people who have the greatest self-regulation,[294] especially those with good emotional resilience, are also more productive at work. So there's a clear business case for teaching people these techniques. If you feel you're prone to succumbing to short-term temptations you might want to understand more about some of the self-control techniques.

Brain responses to social interactions

As social animals we're primed to relate and engage, but every social interaction has its stresses and different things can push our "hot buttons" and trigger negative behaviour: a sudden outburst, a harsh comment, a rush of sadness.

What's happening in the brain is that the prefrontal cortex is taken over by the limbic system,[295] a set of structures in the brain responsible for our emotions and the formation of memories. In extreme cases "going limbic" can result in the amygdala hijacking our thinking brain, resulting in "freezing," and memory blanks.

Memories and emotions are intrinsically linked, and remembering an experience which has a strong emotional element can activate a limbic response. This might be positive (your first kiss), or negative (an embarrassing incident at work). Emotional control or regulation is about understanding your triggers and avoiding them, or dealing with the consequences in an effective way.

Priming your mind

It's possible to manage negative triggers by using priming, which is the implicit memory in which exposure to a trigger increases the response to a later stimulus. For example, if you decide to buy a particular make of car you seem to see them everywhere. Your brain is unconsciously primed to be on the lookout for it.

We can prime our brain in a negative way. Think of a "bad morning:" you've slept badly, you missed the alarm, you spill your coffee on the way into the office and then find you've left behind some important papers you were working on at home. "This is not going to be a good day!" you say to yourself, and – not surprisingly – it isn't. Your brain has been primed to be on the lookout for everything that goes wrong.

You could, of course, prime your brain differently to notice the positives in your day.

Social contagion

We practice self-regulation every day in our home and working lives, with varying degrees of success. For example, scientists have discovered – rather shockingly – that our stress permeates out through our skin and "infects" the people sitting close to us.[296] It's a distressing thought-picture, particularly for any parent, but it highlights our responsibilities: don't infect the team!

Self-regulation techniques

Stanford psychologist James Gross has developed a model for emotional regulation, assessing the pros and cons[297] of the different techniques.

Avoidance takes several forms, from not getting into emotional situations by avoiding the person who annoys you, distracting yourself by reading a book, or focusing on something else, such as work. The successful "marshmallow children" employed variations of these techniques.

Suppression embodied in the attitude of British stiff upper lip can be injurious to your health: raising your blood pressure and heart rate. It also uses up more brain energy and fails to deal with the cause of the emotion.

Reappraisal involves looking at the situation in a different light and interpreting events in a more positive way. It can be a successful strategy, dealing with the root cause of the emotion and reducing amygdala activity.

Mindfulness is a meditation technique that has been shown to reduce the reaction to emotional triggers and also has several health and concentration benefits. Taking the time to become more mindful through a meditation practice can have long-term results.

Gross makes the point that all of these techniques require practice, and like a muscle the more we practice the more the ability develops. This occurs whether it is a supportive technique, bringing with it multiple benefits like mindfulness, or a negative technique such as suppression which can have unintended consequences.

So when a colleague asks for space to think about an issue that is stressing them, respect the request. And ensure you are training yourself and your leaders in the supportive techniques, because you can be assured we are all quite adept at the poor ones.

"I set goals, but making progress is hard."

6 ways to keep going with your goals

Making a list of goals feels organised and inspiring. Or it can feel daunting and completely unrealistic. In our chapter *"Goals... how do I set them up right?"* in the section *Leading purpose*, we cover six ways you can set yourself up for success when you're deciding on your goals. But if we're not careful, just going through the process of setting the right goals can become the end in itself.

What we need to remember is that the aim is to *achieve* the goal, so we need to keep our focus firmly on action. So here are six strategies to help you stick with those goals until you achieve success.

1 Create opportunities to take action

People rarely fail to achieve their goals because they're too difficult. Failure is usually a result of not taking action or seizing opportunities.

It seems blindingly obvious of course, but it's surprising how often we're able to create a substitute sense of achievement by focusing on a completely different task. Doing the immediate tasks for the internal client rather than taking the next steps towards the goals. Like answering a query on Talent rather than designing the new talent process.

Taking action towards your goal may involve planning when and where you will take each action, in advance. Studies show that this kind of planning will help your brain to detect and seize the opportunity when it arises,[298] and increase your chances of success. And that also refers to timescales: if there's no sense of urgency goals can get pushed back and motivation wanes.

Planning in advance works better than just having a good intention. Research has found that "if-then" statements, or implementation intentions, work well for many people.[299] For example: "If I am going to be more influential then I will read up on the business results." "If I'm going to lose weight then I will eat fruit not dessert." "If I want to influence the CEO on diversity then I will collect the data." It's an approach which activates automatic parts of the brain and needs less willpower.

2 Understand your motivation and rewards

People have one or other of two broad motivation preferences.[300] Either they like to move *away* from a problem: their goals are focused on avoiding what they don't like. They leave a job because they don't like their current boss. Or they move *towards* a vision of the future: their goals are focused on attaining something new. The move to a new job will give them additional skills and experience of a new sector.

This idea about different motivation preferences has been around for some time in neuro-linguistic programming (NLP), and now neuroscience has shown there are actually different parts of the brain activated, depending on your preference. Understanding what kind of motivation works for you can help you structure your goals to suit your preferences, and keep you motivated.

Keeping motivated is also dependent on setting up brain-based rewards. You have to trick your brain into seeing goals, and progress towards your goals, as rewarding. You can do this by associating perseverance with reward. Break the goal into small steps and give yourself a treat after each step is completed.

Dopamine is a powerful part of the brain's reward system,[301] and stimulates a feeling of pleasure. Every time you complete a goal or make a significant step towards it, visualise yourself getting that reward of dopamine. Just imagine a squirt of chemical being released in your brain! It is possible to trick your brain into giving you a dopamine boost by looking at everything you do as a small achievement. It's the equivalent of the computer-game's "Yesss!" or counting the Likes on your LinkedIn comment.

Harnessing the power of belief is also effective.[302] Neuroimaging has shown that *believing* something alters brain function. If you believe in achieving your goals the brain aligns to notice opportunities to take the right actions. So make sure you *believe* you can meet your goal.

3   Give yourself a break

If you slip up while you head towards your goal it's not the end of the journey: you can always re-set your intentions. There's often a tendency to think that a setback signals our inability to achieve our goal. We don't like to be wrong, and this feels like failure.

Nineteenth-century psychologist William James suggested that a habit is like a folded piece of paper:[303] when it's opened out, the paper will fold itself back along the same lines. To get it to fold in a new way you have to make new creases that are deeper and sharper than the old ones.

In the same way, deeper "habitual" neural pathways need to be made which will replace the old ones. If you backslide, recognise that new habits take time and effort to be instilled, and plan how to get back on track rather than focus on the setback. And make sure to look for any lessons in what happened, and incorporate them into your plan.

4   Keep track of your progress

Achieving any goal also requires honest and regular monitoring of your progress, to allow you to adjust your behaviour and take a new approach if your original plan isn't working. If you don't know how well you're doing, you can't adjust your behaviour or your tactics to be more effective.

Sometimes we manage to avoid checking our progress because we don't want to know the answer, but we need to make the check frequently: weekly, or daily, depending on what you need to achieve. Another useful technique is known as mental contrasting,[304] which involves thinking about the difference between where you are now, and where you want to be. It tends to have a motivating effect by focusing your mind on what you need to do to achieve your goal. Thinking "I really want that promotion by next year" means you're more likely to do the preparation before a team meeting, rather than making vague commitments to contribute more.

A year can seem a long time, and hard to visualise. Psychologists Johanna Peetz and Anne Wilson have shown that mental contrasting can be even more effective when you link the progress you need to make to any significant dates[305] (or "temporal landmarks"), such as your birthday or Christmas, between now and your goal completion date.

Peetz and Wilson also suggest that these "episode dividers" could be used to manage how you feel about a setback. If you've gone off-track with your goal plan, you should pay attention to significant dates and events between the failure and today. Highlighting those past events ("This time last year, I hadn't received my promotion yet") could make it easier to believe you're about to start a *new* phase towards the goal.

5   Develop tenacity

What's going to be needed is a willingness to make a commitment, and persistence in the face of difficulty. Psychologist Angela Duckworth calls this quality "grit,"[306] and defines it as perseverance and a passion for long-term goals. (You'll find more on this in our chapter in this section on mental toughness *"Life's tough: what's the key to thriving?"*)

Duckworth has found that grit is a trait that can be learned and strengthened using effort, planning, persistence, and good strategies. She expresses the process as a formula: *Achievement = Skill x Effort*. Studies show that people with grit stay in education longer and achieve higher results[307] in tertiary education. It has also been shown to be a more powerful predictor of which military cadets will make it through their first challenging year at West

Point than IQ, leadership skills or fitness.

6 Strengthen your self control

To stay on track towards your goal requires self-control: in order to achieve *this*, you mustn't allow yourself to be distracted by *that*. It can be useful to think of self-control as a muscle which, like any other muscle in your body, needs exercise to prevent it becoming weak and ineffective. There is evidence that regularly exercising self-control increases control.

To build willpower, take on any challenge that requires you to do something you would rather not do. Give up your favourite chocolate bar, learn a new skill or go for a run each morning. When you find yourself wanting to give in, or just not bother, be determined and *keep going*. And if that sounds easier said than done, you will be supporting your self-control training programme by starting with one activity, making a plan, and using the if-then construct to deal with challenges: "If I have a craving for a cake, I'll eat one piece of fresh fruit." As your self-control strengthens, you will find it easier to take on more challenges.

No matter how much you develop your willpower its capacity does have limits and if you put temptation in your path it will have to work harder to resist. And this kind of brainpower can be depleted by hunger or tiredness, with consequences for the most serious decisions. One study has demonstrated that parole judges' decisions[308] on whether prisoners with the same crimes and sentences will be given parole are significantly linked to the time of day and how long it is since the judge has eaten.

The effects of brain fatigue aren't generally noticeable to us over the normal course of a day. But it is possible to observe reduced brain activity in the areas responsible for inhibiting impulses, and more activity in the brain's reward centre, meaning we will respond more readily to immediate rewards, and pay less attention to goals.

So don't challenge your self-control: don't buy cakes if you want to lose weight, and don't expect to make good business decisions after a hard day. And be aware that most people are over-confident in their ability to resist temptation, and that it's easier to stop behaviour completely than to "have just one."

"How can I get out of this rut?"

How behaviours become habits,
and how you can make new ones

Habits are automatic behaviours that allow us to do a lot more than if we had to think about everything we do. Some 70% of what we do is automated in this way, and given how useful this can be, how can you form useful habits and stop those that have ceased to be useful?

First of all, it's important to distinguish between your *intention* to adopt a new habit or achieve a goal, and your *plan* to do so. Around the first of January every year most of us have very clear intentions, but rather vague plans.

And brain science tells us it's more effective to focus on what you *do* want rather than what you don't. According to Hebb's Law, "neurons that wire together, fire together," so focusing on breaking the old habit may actually strengthen it. Focusing on creating a *new* habit forms new neural networks in the brain and gives you the best chance of embedding the behavior as a habit.

Business writer Charles Duhigg proposes a three-stage process for creating, or changing habits.[309] It involves developing a plan that contains a cue, a routine and a reward.

The habit model

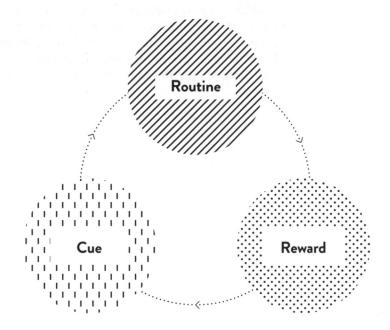

1   Your cue

Habits are triggered by cues – triggers or signals that tell us to act in a certain way. To create a new habit, we need to also create a cue: something that tells us to take the next step. Working on the cue will help make or break a habit.

For example, if you want to connect more with the team you may decide to spend 10 minutes each morning walking around the office, instead of sitting doing your emails. Your cue might be hanging up your coat: that's when you start your walk-about.

Identifying a good cue can be crucial. They tend to fall into one of the following categories:

- location
- time
- emotional state
- other people
- immediately-preceding action

One method which has been shown to be effective is to create "behaviour chains:" using your current routines instead of trying to fight them. (Hanging up your coat is your current behaviour, which is now linked to the new behaviour of walking around and talking to the team.)

Experiment with different cues until you find the one, or more than one, that works for you.

2   Routine

Define the steps you will take: the actions that you are trying to form into the habit.

It helps to write down your routine so you know the exact steps. For example, if the routine is to talk to the team informally three times a week, you might block out these times in your diary so that other meetings can't be put in.

The concept of "if-then" planning is built around a routine and helps to plan for issues that might knock you off course. (You can read more about this in the chapter on goals in this section: *"I set goals, but making progress is hard."*)

For example, instead of just having the intention, "I will have more informal conversations with the team," your if-then intention might be: "If I walk around the office at least three mornings a week then I will talk to the team informally." Studies have shown that this can be very successful in helping to form new habit routines.

3   Reward

This is important to embed the new behaviour into a habit. And it's probably the reason why just repetition doesn't work.

Rewards need to have some key characteristics. For example, if you are trying to get into the habit of going to the gym, choose a cue such as going as soon as you wake up: get dressed straight into your gym gear. Your reward might be the endorphin rush you'll feel once you get into it, or a smoothie after your workout.

Then *think* about that smoothie. Allow yourself to anticipate the reward: the anticipation is actually more important to the brain than the reward itself. Rather than trying to make yourself enjoy the routine your aim is to get your brain to crave the reward.

Many studies have shown that a cue and a routine on their own aren't enough for a new habit to last. Only when the brain starts expecting the reward – craving the endorphins, or the smoothie – will it become automatic. Your cue, in addition to triggering your routine, must also trigger a craving for the reward.

The reward attached to connecting more with your team might be having a better understanding of what's going on in the office, and a greater sense of control. Anticipating that sense of control could be what maintains the new routine.

Creating habits for organisations

The habit model can also be a useful way to implement sustained change at an organisation level.

The cue: when introducing a change such as implementing a new process or policy, a well-communicated cycle can act as the cue to trigger the behaviour required. Linking the cycle to existing business events that are well-embedded, such as the business planning cycle or end-of-year results, can make it easier.

The routine: again, the business cycle can provide a routine that people begin to follow. And routines can be reinforced through training to improve elements of the new policy or process.

The CORE model can guide this reinforcement. For example, provide Certainty about the steps to be taken, Options within the policy, enhanced Reputation to early adopters, and Equity in availability of resources and a sense of fairness in how the whole policy is implemented.

The reward: you need to build in rewards at an organisational level. They can be of more than one type, and tailored to different groups: work units, teams or groups of specialists. Again CORE can be a useful way of thinking about them, such as reputation rewards like a Coach of the Year award, or team rewards which feel equitable.

Social rewards are particularly brain-rewarding, and you can harness the power of social connections to build them. You could create cross-functional teams that work together to implement the new approach. Or reward managers for the quality of their adoption, or set up healthy competition between groups. Use measures such as the health of the talent pipeline, or the speed of career progression across business units, and report on them to reward efforts within the organisation.

What about lapses?

Even with the best intentions, lapses will happen. Who hasn't started at the gym regularly, then gone on holiday and fallen out of the routine? Or introduced a new way of working across the organisation, only to have it trail off after a month or two when you – or the organisation – are under stress?

If you want to avoid lapses there is one more crucial ingredient: belief. "For a habit to stay changed, people must believe that change is possible,"[310] says Charles Duhigg. "And most often, that belief only emerges with the help of a group."

For example, social learning communities can help learners support each other to adopt new behaviours. Groups create accountability and belief, which are crucial in helping you stick with new habits.

So if you want to improve your connection with the team ask yourself who can give you encouragement and feedback? If you want to make a habit of going to the gym is there someone who could be your exercise partner every morning? Or could you hire a personal trainer you'll feel compelled to report your progress to?

The more positive reinforcement you can surround yourself with, the easier it will be.

Give yourself a break

New habits, no matter how well-supported, can be very fragile. It's as well to be prepared for when you relapse. Dan Ariely calls this The "What-the-Hell" Effect.[311]

Imagine the scenario: you've been incredibly disciplined about getting to the gym each day, but today you miss a session. Or, you've been making time to walk around the office each morning but yesterday you were late and didn't do it, and today you forgot…

So now you're ready to trash the whole new habit plan – it's not working. Not only do you not go to the gym but you eat chocolate biscuits all day.

The solution is to examine your plan and find exactly where things started to go wrong. Look for small things that changed your cue or your routine. Remember, a habit is a formula our brain automatically follows: when I see a CUE, I will follow the ROUTINE in order to get the REWARD.

So the message is: have a good plan, make sure there are anticipated rewards that are cued regularly, and don't beat yourself up, or be too hard on your organisation, if you lapse.

"I need to get creative. Easier said than done."

Brain-savvy techniques to boost creativity

"If you can dream it, you can do it. Always remember this whole thing was started by a mouse."
Walt Disney

We have looked at what happens in the brain during the creative process in our chapter in the *Leading purpose* section: *"What's the truth about being creative?"* Now it's time to roll up our sleeves and look at your own creativity and problem-solving.

Walt Disney, founder of the Disney film production empire, described his creative process as "imagineering," a combination of imagination and engineering. And the method he evolved at the Disney studios for turning dreams into reality suggests an intuitive understanding of how the brain works.

The Disney process had three distinct stages:[312] Dreamer, Realist and Critic, which each took place in separate rooms with distinctively different environments and props, and allowing for a variety of physical postures to encourage the style of thinking for each stage.

The dreamer physiology

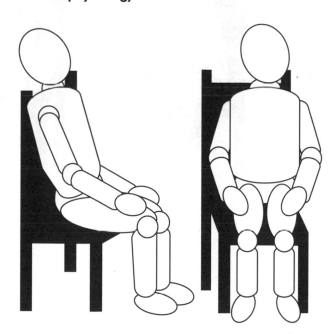

At Disney this stage took place in comfortable surroundings away from the hustle and bustle of daily work. People would take a relaxed posture: lying back, eyes unfocused and looking up. It was all about free-ranging thinking, brainstorming and making loose connections between ideas. Allen Braun and Siyuan Liu of the US National Institutes of Health have tracked the brain activity of rappers doing freestyle improvisations, and their research has found that when rappers are in full creative flow[313] the areas in the brain that make decisions are largely inactive. But the medial prefrontal cortex, which is responsible for learning associations, context, events and emotional responses, is extremely active.

"We think what we see is a relaxation of 'executive functions,'" says Braun, "to allow more natural de-focused attention and uncensored processes to occur that might be the hallmark of creativity." The Dreamer stage typically puts you into a relaxed, positive mood which is associated with having a broader perspective and making more connections and associations.

The critic physiology

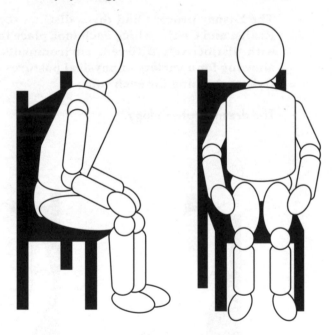

The realist physiology

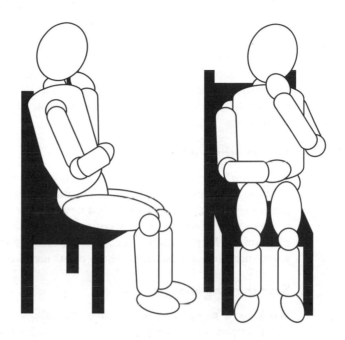

At Disney, an idea was then viewed through the lens of Realists, who applied practical reality. Here the focus was on how the idea could be implemented; people were upright and alert, and the surroundings were more conventional and office-like. This stage uses the rational, "judging" brain circuitry, plus the default system if the concept being considered involves people.

And finally the Critics took the idea and challenged it: "Why won't this work?" At Disney they worked in a small room under the stairs referred to as the Sweat Box. Critic posture is leaning forward and alert, drawing on memory, planning and decision-making functions. Adopting these different postures sends signal to the brain to encourage that style of thinking.

Apart from relocating to Hollywood, if you want to be more creative what can you do? Neuroscience suggests a variety of practical steps:

Relax and direct your gaze inwardly

Studying the neuroscience of insight, which is closely associated with creativity, Mark Beeman and John Kounios have found that just before insight occurs the brain produces a burst of alpha waves,[314] which are associated with relaxation. This allows the brain to take a momentary break so the insight can pop-up to the surface.

If your attention is directed inwardly you're more likely to solve a problem with a flash of insight, which is why they tend to occur when you're relaxed and reflective: in the shower, taking a walk, having a cup of coffee. Many of us have insights but forget them. Deliberate creative thinkers keep a notebook on themselves at all times, and expect their morning walk around the block to be productive.

Do something different

Changing your daily routine is helpful, which is why you're more likely to have fresh ideas on holiday than sitting in traffic during the morning commute. Embedded neural pathways are less likely to be in use, allowing for new connections to be made. Psychologist Simone Ritter found that even just changing the way you make your lunchtime sandwich can help boost levels of creativity.[315]

Stop thinking about it

Work on a mindless routine task that allows the frontal lobes – associated with executive functions and control – to power down and the unconscious processes to kick in. Beeman and Kounios found it's possible to trigger this temporary brain state by meditating[316] or taking a long run. That "Aha!" moment feels instantaneous, but your unconscious mind has been working behind the scenes.[317] Plan your day with regular breaks and build in creative down-time.

According to Beeman's research, inventive brains are *less* packed and organised, and nerve traffic is slower, which seems to allow opportunities for more unusual connections to be made.

Make it hard

An old friend of mine always had to make a problem harder before she solved it: analysing mountains of data, worrying about the meaning of the analysis, re-cutting the data in different ways... all this had to happen before she moved to a solution. It turns out that's a recognised part of the creative process.

Psychologist Robert Epstein says that trying to do something you're inexperienced at, or outside your range of skills, accelerates the flow of new ideas.[318] He describes a challenging situation as being like an "extinction" procedure in a behavioural laboratory. In challenging situations, a great deal of behaviour just does not work and this allows past behaviours, any that have ever worked under similar conditions, to be tried. This in turn gets many behaviours competing which greatly enhances the generative process. Feelings of frustration and confusion are a by-product of these competing behaviours.

An example: you try to turn the handle on a door that's always opened easily, but it won't budge. You apply more force to trying to turn the knob. Then you try pulling on the knob, or pushing it. Then maybe you wiggle it. What you do will depend on your history with doors. Eventually you find a brick and break the glass.

The shouting and kicking you were doing along the way is a common feature of the creative process: think of temperamental poets, composers and inventors. Frustration can be a signal that you are on the verge of a new idea. Epstein says you shouldn't expect to find a whole solution, but you'll stimulate a lot of interesting new ideas.

Just improvise

Welcome more rapper or jazz-style improvisation into your life[319] to help you shed inhibitions and improve an ability to take a risk. Musician and researcher Charles Limb says most of daily life is unscripted and improvised.

Make connections

Meet more people, have new experiences, know more; reading or experiencing life widely generates more "material" to use and create new connections. Psychologist Jessica Payne's research shows that people who have slept well also make more connections.[320] So after your busy day doing new things, get a good night's sleep.

Be in a good mood

Numerous researchers including Mark Beeman have found that people who are in a positive mood have more creative insight[321] and find the process easier. If you're feeling glum, take time out to cheer yourself up before tackling the problem. Listen to music, watch a funny programme or do something that makes you feel happy.

Creativity can be encouraged by all of these ideas. The one thing you don't want to do though is try too hard.

"'Aha!' I solved it!"

Insight: how to develop it

Work can be a challenge: so many problems to solve and so much to do that there's little time to think about the issues, let alone crunch the numbers and analyse the data. And even if you do have time, does the data really point the way to the solution?

People tend to solve problems in two different ways. Either they work logically through the evidence, or the solution pops into their mind along with a feeling that the answer is right. We call this insight, or an "Aha!" moment. Insight can save you lots of work and may even get you to be more productive, creative and effective, but it's seldom included in a job specification or reviewed at appraisal.

Why do we need insight?

Most problems at work tend to be complex and have more variables than our working memory can hold onto at one time. For example, thinking about how to improve engagement, you would need to consider some or all of the following:

- the quality and skills of your managers
- the strategy of the company
- the hot buttons and preferences of the CEO and multiple other stakeholders
- survey results
- how this fits with all the other initiatives you have going on
- the resources you have

You'll be able to add at least three more factors to your version of this list. Improving engagement is not a linear, rational problem: there's no "right" answer. This means that our conscious problem-solving resources are not very helpful when we're addressing these sorts of issues.

So how else can we solve these problems? Consultant David Rock says that over the years he has asked a few thousand people how they solve complex problems at work. He consistently finds that they don't come to the solution through analysis; the answer always arrives suddenly, usually when the issue is out of conscious awareness,[322] just as they fall asleep or wake up, during exercise, when they're in the shower, or other times when their brain is not busy.

What is insight?

We're not talking about general creativity here: that's a process, a way of thinking and perceiving. (For more about how creativity works, turn to the chapter *"What's the truth about being creative?"* in the *Leading purpose* section, and for how to develop it in yourself read *"I need to get creative. Easier said than done."* in this section.) Insight is also different from intuition, which is a nudge or a hint about the direction you need to take, rather than the whole solution.

Insight is the moment of clarity when a solution comes to you, and you know it's correct. And the whole answer tends to come at once.

How do insights work?

Mark Beeman of Northwestern University is probably the best-known and most respected neuroscientist working on insight.[323] He summarises the elements that make up insight as unconscious processing: solutions come to people when they're *not* thinking about the problem in the same way as they have before (think Archimedes in his bath). A relaxed mind: you're calm, and ideally in a good mood. And a sudden answer: when the solution comes it's a surprise but you're confident in it – you just know it works.

So here's a bit more detail on those elements, with the scientific evidence pointing to how insight happens and how you can create the optimum conditions for your own insights.

Unconscious processing

Beeman's research suggests that insight tends to involve connections between small numbers of neurons.

An insight is often a long-forgotten memory, or a combination of memories aligned in new ways. These memories don't have lots of neurons linking them together, which is why we need a quiet mind to notice the new connections and the insight they provide. A busy mind with little down-time tends to overlook the insight. We tend to notice insights when the overall activity level in the brain is low and we are not busy thinking or doing very much; we might be in the shower, walking in the country or just dropping off to sleep.

Inward-looking

Beeman has also found insight happens when we are looking "beyond the box," not *at* the problem, but inside ourselves. Our attention can be externally focused (reading this chapter) or internally focused (an image has been generated in your mind's eye by a word on the page).

We flick between these two states all the time. When people have insights they are often "mind-wandering,"[324] says psychologist Jonathon Schooler, rather than focused on the problem. Mark Beeman has recorded alpha wave activity in the visual and auditory cortex just before the moment of insight,[325] which indicates that people shut out external stimuli to save brain resources for noticing the insight.

Relaxed positive mind

Beeman can *predict* which method (logic or insight) someone will use to solve a problem[326] by the type of activity in their brain immediately before the problem is presented to them. He says mental state determines our approach, and also personal preference. Someone's resting state of brain activity also indicates which approach they may take.

In a similar study, Joydeep Bhattacharya of Goldsmiths and Bhavin Sheth of the University of Houston identified that the brain knows how it will solve a problem eight seconds before the conscious answer appears.[327] Sheth suggests this could be the brain capturing transformational thought in action (the "Aha!" moment) *before* the brain's owner is consciously aware of it

Positive mood

There's plenty of anecdotal evidence that being in a good mood helps problem-solving,[328] and it's well-supported by the science. Participants who were happy when they arrived for an experiment, or who were put into a positive mood in the lab, solved 10% more problems overall, and solved 20% more of them by insight.

A positive mood induces a broader focus of attention, allowing more creative and flexible responses which are good for tackling complex issues. Negative emotions tend to increase physiological arousal, narrow focus and restrict behaviour.[329] This happens because when people are happy their perception is wider;[330] when they're anxious they exhibit more "tunnel vision."

Sudden answer

If you want insights you need to stop trying to solve a problem.

A distinctive feature of problem-solving is that people get stuck. They go round and round the data and the issues and can't see the solution. This happens because we tend to get fixated on a small set of solutions. The more we work on this same wrong solution, the more we prime the brain for that solution and the harder it is to think of new ideas.

Insights tend to happen when people give up, at least temporarily.

Psychologist Stellan Ohlsson's "inhibition theory" indicates that we need to inhibit the *wrong* solutions for the right one to come to our attention.[331] Also, effort tends to involve a lot of electrical activity, and can reduce the likelihood of noticing the quiet signals of insight. You are more likely to get an answer to a problem if you let go of trying (remember: we have many more resources for non-conscious processing than for conscious processing).

Beeman also found that these sudden answers tend to be correct:[332] 92-94% of insight answers were correct compared with about 80% of answers produced by logical analysis.

How to have more insight

Following on from Beeman's research we've created a shorthand model to help you remember the steps to increase insight. But remember that first it's important to put your brain into the state that increases the chances of insight occurring: relax and put yourself in a good mood by watching a funny film or going for your favourite walk.

A guide to increasing insight:

Step	Activity
Awareness	Review and research the problem to be solved. At this point you may feel a little stuck if you are concerned about solving the problem, or you may feel focused. Be aware of your mood and put yourself into a positive state.
Hold back	Stop trying to actively solve the problem. "Put it on the back burner" and get engaged in a completely different type of activity: go for a walk, or tidy the office.
Answer	This is the moment of insight. Usually accompanied by energy. Within the brain a reward of dopamine is released when the answer appears.

While insight is rewarding we need to reinforce the new neural links to maintain focus and action. So *write down* the insight, *explain* it to someone else, or *visualise* yourself with the problem solved.

Creating insight in the organisation

And how do we apply all this to our wider work context?

When we're solving problems in conjunction with other people at work, we tend to do the opposite of what the science indicates will be most effective. We put pressure on ourselves with a deadline, we gather more data, we brainstorm as a group... all of which demands a lot of brain-processing and makes it hard to have insight. It also tends to reduce the range of solutions as a group conforms to consensus, collective thinking.

A better approach is to define a question as a group, then for people to individually take time off and allow their brains to process and solve the problem. The group then comes together to review and agree on the solutions.

You'll find the steps for creating insight are useful in many work situations, especially in coaching and training when you're trying to get people to change. People who gain insight for themselves, rather than being told what to do, are more likely to act on it.

"Only people who can't multi-task say it's a problem."

Multi-tasking is a myth: here's the evidence

Technology has made life easier in so many ways. I can remember being stuck on a train and having to borrow the only mobile phone in the carriage to call home: the handset was the size of a briefcase and the call must have cost a small fortune.

Nowadays we'd be texting and tweeting, and using GPS to pinpoint our exact location. But we're all aware that technology has its downside. We allow it to grab our attention. It's difficult to have a conversation without a phone call interrupting, and even when you're alone there are incoming alerts for messages and emails, a reminder for your next meeting, your child's private ring tone and so much more.

Trend consultant and writer Linda Stone says we're addicted to media:[333] "Constantly scanning for opportunities...in an effort to miss nothing" with what she calls "continuous partial attention."

Alongside the impact on our attention-span is a rise in expectations about the speed at which we should be able to get information or a response to communications.

Hyper-environment

Psychiatrist Edward Hallowell has called this the "hyperkinetic work environment,"[334] and we can all recognise its features:

- constant interruptions
- demands to always be "on duty"
- difficulty remembering things and maintaining focus
- feeling stressed most of the time

One of the ways people try to manage this work environment is through "multi-tasking," and those who think they're good at it will tell you so with pride. It's now widely believed that multi-tasking is an essential skill for survival in today's workplace. Many bosses either implicitly or explicitly expect their staff to be proficient multi-taskers. But what do we mean by it?

The term was originally used in the computer industry to describe a processor's ability to carry out more than one task at a time. And humans *can* multi-task as well: we can walk and talk, listen to music while we drive, or sit in a meeting and daydream.

The multi-tasking myth

But what's going on here is that *different* parts of the brain are working on different things at the same time. What science has shown is that it's *not* possible to ask the same brain areas to do two things at once.

You can demonstrate this by trying to rotate your left foot whilst at the same time drawing the figure eight with your right finger. It's the same with cognitive tasks: try composing an important email while talking on the phone at the same time.

Neuroscience is providing evidence that the concept of multi-tasking is a myth. What we're actually doing is *jumping between* two or more tasks. And each time we shift back and forth there's a productivity cost.

Test your multi-tasking

If you don't believe me try this quick test: with a stopwatch measure how long it takes you to count quickly from 1 to 10. Now do the same thing except saying the alphabet from A to J.

Now measure how long it takes when you put the two tasks together: alternately saying a letter and a number (A, 1, B, 2... etc).

I can guarantee it will take more than twice as long to do the combined task as you took for each single task, because the brain slows down when it has to keep switching between numbers and letters. (For most people the first two tasks might take a couple of seconds each. The mixed, switching task typically takes 15 to 20 seconds.)

Why? As well as the slower processing, your working memory gets fatigued, and that's independent of how stressed you are, or how much you've been using your brain today which might slow things down even more. You may also have forgotten where you were in the task a couple of times.

Not convinced? Here's some of the research.

Research on multi-tasking

Psychologist Katherine Moore, University of Michigan has found that irrelevant cues introduced when a person is concentrating hijack the attention system[335] and impair cognitive performance. And Glenn Wilson of Kings College has demonstrated that switching between different technologies, like emailing and answering the phone constantly, reduced IQ scores by 10 points.[336]

There is also evidence that multi-tasking has an impact on long-term memory and our ability to learn.[337] At Columbia Karin Foerde has found that those who learn a task without distraction performed much better and remembered more than the group who were distracted with noises such as a phone during learning. And it's not only immediate recall that was affected: brain scans during the test showed that the hippocampus, the area of the brain responsible for encoding long-term memory, was only active in the group who were not distracted.

So, what do we need to do?

We need to change the work patterns in our organisations if we're going to achieve the levels of productivity needed to match the economic, commercial and social changes going on around us. Our people need to be more productive – and neuroscience indicates that *putting an end* to multi-tasking is the way to improve productivity.

We need to encourage people to focus, and concentrate on one task at a time.

For HR professionals this means we've got two important tasks ahead of us: educating managers, and looking at the explicit and implicit work practices in our organisations that may be encouraging (or requiring) multi-tasking. And one way to get started is to be a role model and stop playing the multi-tasking game yourself.

Wait up: is multi-tasking always bad?

There is evidence that some of these distractions help us to focus our mental energies effectively[338] – if we work with them strategically.

Testing it out

A study at Carnegie Mellon measured the impact of electronic interruptions on mental clarity. Psychologist Eyal Peer and his colleagues assembled three test groups to complete a standard cognitive skill test:

- The control group completed the test with no interruptions.
- The second group was told they might be interrupted during the test, and did receive text messages while they were completing the exercise.
- The third group were told they might be interrupted, but were allowed to complete the test undisturbed.

The results?

- Participants who rated themselves highly as multi-taskers performed poorly in all of the tasks and also proved worse at analytical reasoning.
- The interrupted group produced the worst test scores: 20 percent lower than the uninterrupted control group.

- But the group which *thought* they were going to be interrupted (but weren't) did far better than the control group. Their average scores were 43 per cent higher.

So, what's going on?

The mere threat of interruptions seems to have kept that group focused. The researchers believe that participants marshalled extra brain-power to steel themselves against interruption, and this served as a kind of deadline that helped them focus even better.

The researchers say that further study is needed, but these results suggest that the possibility of interruption could be just the right kind of pressure we need to focus our attention.

It looks as though our *mindset* about interruptions is more significant than the interruption itself. If we allow ourselves to be distracted by technology our attention and cognitive ability will be impaired, but if we control this our performance is potentially improved.

So the good news is that we don't have to eliminate distracting technology from our lives. It appears that with the right mindset we can avoid distractions (even if we don't know when they'll happen), and harness that focus for greater productivity.

For individuals the question is: "What mindset do you bring to work?" And for HR professionals the question is how do your policies and work patterns help the mindset of employees and managers to maximise their productivity?

"What's all the hype about meditation?"

The business benefits of mindfulness

Remember when CEOs thought "workplace culture" was a soft, fluffy idea that had no relevance to what they did? It's strikingly similar to how many business-people are thinking about mindfulness meditation today.

A number of high-profile companies like Google now run in-house mindfulness courses for their employees, and we're increasingly seeing it appear in leadership development programmes. It's claimed to becoming a popular practice amongst CEOs[339] including News Corp's Rupert Murdoch, Bill Ford of Ford Motors and Marc Benioff of Salesforce.com. And then there are the individuals who turn to it because they want to feel better, manage their stress and improve work performance.

What happened with "culture" is that it became the backbone of strategy implementation; you'd now be hard-pressed to find a CEO or HR leader that isn't concerned about their company's culture. Our prediction is that the same will also be true of mindfulness as a tool for improving leadership and employee performance.

Why? Because if we look at the science, the evidence for its effectiveness is pretty compelling.

What is mindfulness?

One of the leading teachers and academics in the field is Jon Kabat-Zinn, founder of the Mindfulness-Based Stress Reduction programme at the University of Massachusetts Medical Center. His definition of the practice is:

> *"Mindfulness means paying attention in a particular way; on purpose, in the present moment, and non-judgmentally."* [340]

His description calls attention to both the results of mindfulness practice, and the practice itself. And the evidence reveals that the results are extremely relevant for businesses and business-people.

In very simple terms, mindfulness is about focusing attention on breathing, and the body. By focusing attention people learn to control their body's sensory volume – something we all do all the time, but which mindfulness can help us to have more conscious control over.

In this chapter we're specifically looking at mindfulness, not all kinds of meditation. That's partly because most of the scientific data relates to people who are using this particular technique. And partly because the meaning of the term "mindfulness" goes beyond the act of meditation and really describes the way we could interact with the world.

What's the evidence?

Scientists are naturally curious about what might be happening in the brain when people practice mindfulness meditation. Using fMRI scans (functional magnetic resonance imaging) they have been able to compare the brains of people who practice the technique with those who don't. And much of the research is showing that meditation causes the brain to undergo observable physical changes, many of which are beneficial.

The most significant difference is that the brain becomes less "busy." There's a measurable decrease in beta waves (indicators that the brain is actively processing information) after just a 20-minute meditation session.

A 2009 study compared the brains of people who meditate with those who don't, and found a number of differences in structure in the brainstem region (the part of the brain which manages the cardiorespiratory system). These differences point to benefits for breathing and heart rate, and improved immune responses.[341]

People who meditate may also be able to process information faster, according to a 2012 study from the UCLA Laboratory of Neuro Imaging which discovered that meditators have measurably more "gyrification" in their brains:[342] wrinkling caused by growth of the cerebral cortex. The researchers believe this may improve memory-formation, attention and decision-making.

Meditation focuses attention on the current moment, rather than intrusive thoughts. An earlier study by UCLA researchers found that meditation practice was linked to enlarged hippocampal and frontal areas of the brain,[343] indicating more positive emotions, more emotional stability, and more intentional behaviour – all highly desirable personal outcomes, not least for business leaders and anyone interested in improving their performance at work.

Better memory and attention

Because mindfulness involves awareness and focusing of attention, its practice improves focus in the real world. Attention is like a muscle that needs to be strengthened with regular use, and this turns out to be a long-term result of regular meditation practice.

There is also robust evidence that meditation improves rapid memory recall.[344] Catherine Kerr of Brown University has found that people who meditate are able to screen out distractions and increase their productivity more quickly than those who do not meditate. She suggests that this ability to ignore distractions could explain "their superior ability to rapidly remember and incorporate new facts."

Reduced anxiety

And the more people meditate, the less anxious they appear to be.[345] This seems to be a result of a loosening of connections to the medial prefrontal cortex, the default network responsible for how we think about ourselves. The effect is reduced reactions to fear and strong emotions, as well as a reduction in the physical sensations that go with them. There is also less self-criticism and negative self talk.

At the same time meditation appears to strengthen the connections between the part of the brain which manages reasoning, and our bodily-sensation and fear centres.[346] So when we experience upsetting sensations or emotions, we are able to stand back and view them rationally. That's a valuable ability when we encounter a significant change at work, if it means we're able to understand it more objectively, without getting caught up in concerns about what it all might mean.

More empathy and compassion

Compassion may not always be a quality publicly valued by business leaders, but it is a skill that many find need of, especially in tough economic times. Research has shown that those who practice meditation regularly score higher for empathy and compassion.[347]

An experiment at Boston University showed participants images of people that they would have good, bad, or neutral reactions to. The subjects who meditated were able to focus their attention and reduce their emotional reactions to these images, even when they weren't in a meditative state. They also experienced more compassion for others when shown disturbing images.

And a study from the University of Wisconsin found that people who meditated regularly had stronger activation in their temporal parietal junctures[348] – the part of the brain linked to empathy – compared with those who didn't meditate. The ability to put yourself in your client's or your colleague's shoes, and understand what's going on for them, is a powerful skill in business.

Less stress

Mindfulness meditation helps people perform under pressure while feeling less stressed.[349] A Washington University study of HR managers had one-third of the study group participating in mindfulness meditation training, another third taking relaxation training, and the last group given no training at all.

A stressful multi-tasking test was given to all the managers at the start and end of the eight-week period of the practice. During the concluding test, the group that had participated in meditation training experienced less stress than either of the other groups.

Stress is a significant factor in business today, which has an impact on attention, productivity and attendance. Employees and business leaders who meditate are better at seeing potentially stressful events in context. They experience less actual stress, and when it does occur they manage the impact of it better.

So... be mindful!

There's strong scientific evidence that meditation can help you perform better. The trick is to do it regularly and to build the "mindfulness muscle." If you're inspired to use meditation, UK-based company Get Some Headspace[350] is targeted at business-people and others who are looking for a secular approach, and their app is a very good way to get started.

As an HR professional, being aware of the performance benefits of mindfulness gives you an edge. And personally experiencing it gives you credibility to talk about its use in business and get ahead of the curve as it becomes the next big thing.

"I can't avoid stress in my job."

Not all stress is bad for you

"It seems that we have it backward in our society. We tend to look up to people who are under a great deal of stress."

Richard Carlson, Don't Sweat the Small Stuff[351]

We all seem to be familiar with the symptoms of stress at work: irritability, anxiety, headaches, neck and shoulder tension, back pain, loss of sleep... And that's before we get to the heavy-hitters like ulcers and heart attacks. In YouGov's 2013 Big Work Survey nearly two-thirds of UK respondents said they were stressed at work.[352]

But is stress always a bad thing? There is some interesting research that could have us thinking differently about its role in workplace performance.

Good and bad stress

Since 1908 the "inverted-U model"[353] (also known as the Yerkes-Dodson Law after its psychologist inventors) has been used to demonstrate the relationship between stress, or arousal, and performance. According to the model, peak performance is achieved when people experience a moderate level of stress, typically close to the top of an inverted U on the chart. When we experience too little or too much arousal, or stress, there's a negative impact on performance.

The inverted U model

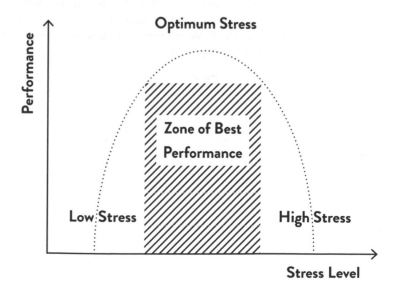

The bottom-left-hand corner of the U is where people are under challenged. It's that old adage: "If you want something done, ask a busy person." Not enough stress, and you just can't get round to writing that report, making that phone call or even just tidying the office.

At the midpoint we're in "flow",[354] a state defined by psychologist Mihaly Csikszentmihalyi in 1990 who has studied the experience for many years. He has defined a formula to help people achieve the flow state. In essence, it involves striking a balance between how difficult you believe a task to be, and how capable you think you are of carrying it out. If the challenge is too low you go into the drone zone, and never engage. If you think the task is beyond you, you go into the panic zone and go to pieces.

Once arousal passes the mid-point (the peak of the upside-down U), there is "over-arousal:" what we would describe as "being stressed." In this state we're likely to react emotionally, we may lose sleep, be forgetful, and be poor at making connections between bits of information. It's that feeling when you say something and then realise you have not made the connection with something you already knew about that person.

How stress hormones work

We have a number of different stress hormones that affect our body, and they are not all "bad" – it's an excess that causes the problems.

Adrenaline, noradrenaline and cortisol are part of the group of hormones called glucocorticoids which are essential for us to function properly in the face of danger. They trigger the stress response developed to keep us safe: it is the flight, fight, freeze response. These hormones are useful in helping us to learn and form new memories, but with extended stress we can enter a state called cortisol dominance, which negatively affects learning, attention-span and memory.

What each person may experience as stress is completely individual. It may stress you if there's a backlog of work waiting to be done, or if family disagreements aren't out in the open. But to your team it may be stressful always having you two steps ahead of them on the workload. And for your partner, being told "we need to talk" about family issues may feel like major confrontation.

In other words, what matters most is not *what* happens to you, but how you *react* to what happens to you.

What happens to brains under stress?

According to neuroendocrinologist Bruce McEwen, stress is "all in our head"[355] since our brain is responsible for recognising and responding to stressors. The areas that are mainly involved are the amygdala, the hippocampus, and the prefrontal cortex, which work with the hypothalamus to flip on or shut down the production of stress hormones and other automatic responses to over-arousal, such as increased heart rate.

But researchers are now learning how stress can physically alter the brain, which in turn may affect how we learn, form memories, and even make decisions. Stress does some nasty things to our brain, though some of the effects are reversible.

Neurobiologist Tallie Baram and colleagues looked at how short-term but acute stress (such as a very difficult board meeting) affects the adult brain. They found that the brain produces a different type of stress hormone in response to short-term stressors,[356] called corticotrophin (CRH). Just a few hours of CRH exposure was enough to destroy the delicate balance between the parts of the brain that transmit and receive messages.

Fred Helmstetter of the University of Wisconsin found that the hippocampus memory-forming region of the brain actually shrank slightly[357] in rats exposed to chronic stress. This has also been found in patients suffering from post-traumatic stress disorder. In the short-term we can overcome the impact of stress with exercise, sleep and relaxation, and by practicing meditation. But prolonged stress damages the hippocampus, and this does not seem to be completely reversible.

The effects of stress on your body

The effects of the fight-or-flight state don't only occur in the brain: our bodies are physically affected as well. Blood flow is directed away from extremities and towards the heart, lungs, legs and spine.

Historically this was to help us maximize running and fighting, but it reduces fine motor skills dramatically. And because the body wants to use all of the available energy for fighting or running away, it stops other processes like digestion – which is why we often feel sick during or after high-stress situations. It's also why we often can't remember circumstantial details after a stressful situation, only the ones related to the event.

You may have experienced how fast your heart beats during stressful situations. The fast heartbeat in turn sends a signal to the brain's prefrontal cortex, the "executive" brain that handles planning, analytical thinking and decision-making, and tells it to shut down temporarily. This allows the limbic "kill or be killed" reaction of the brain to take over. When we're in this state, instinct and ingrained training take over from rational thought and reasoning. This is useful if you are running from a tiger but less helpful during a performance review or a board meeting.

Stress has been implicated in various health issues, particularly chronic stress that continues over long periods of time. It can lower immune system functioning, making us more susceptible to illness, high blood pressure and heart disease, as well as causing everyday aches and pains, weigh-gain, sleep-loss, a reduced sex drive and skin conditions such as hives or eczema.

Believing in stress is unhealthy

In recent research some of the beliefs about stress are being called into doubt. Scientists at the University of Wisconsin-Madison say that believing stress is bad for you is... really bad for you.[358]

An eight-year study found that 182,000 people died prematurely from the *belief* that stress was bad for them. Health psychologist Kelly McGonigal estimates that would make stress the 15th largest cause of death in the United States.[359]

Other research has looked at what might happen if we change the way we think about stress:[360] if we re-reappraised the feelings associated with stress and thought of them as helpful. For example, we might think of butterflies in the stomach as a signal that we're *ready* to make a presentation, or translate that feeling of "nervousness" as excitement.

The benefits of re-appraising stress

Re-appraisal teaches us to think of stress as a tool that helps maximise performance. Re-framing the meaning of the physiological signals that go with stress can break the link between negative experiences and poor physiological responses, with benefits for physiological reactions, attention-span and performance.

In other research it's been found that spending time socialising and caring for other people can also create resilience to stress,[361] and actually reduces death rates amongst those who experience stress. Michael Poulin of the University of Buffalo and his team interviewed almost 850 people, who were asked to report stressful events they had experienced in the past year and also how much they had supported other people. Deaths that occurred within the group in the next five years were tracked using obituaries and public death records.

Every major stress event increased an individual's risk of death by 30%. But this increased risk was erased for those who reported helping others, even if they dealt with additional stress.

"The harmful effects of stress on health are not inevitable"[362] McGonigal says. "How you think and how you act can transform your experience of stress. When you choose to view your stress response as helpful, you create the biology of courage. And when you choose to connect with others under stress, you can create resilience."

There are important implications for HR. On a personal level, what are your beliefs about stress? For your organisation, how are you talking about stress and responding to it? And from the view point of people's performance at work: how are you helping people re-frame their experience?

"Life's tough: what's the key to thriving?

Mental toughness: you need it, and it's a skill you can learn

This is a story about one of our clients, considered to be one of the rising stars of her firm. She was in line for a key overseas promotion when family tragedy struck: her mother was diagnosed with a terminal illness. She was torn between spending time with her family and taking on the challenging new role. Both her boss and her mentor counselled her against taking time out at a crucial stage of her career. But she knew her own mind and shifted her focus for a time to her family, later returning to her career with renewed motivation.

What she had was mental toughness. She knew what she wanted, what was right and had the self-belief to follow her heart.

Mental strength is about emotional regulation, managing our reactions and staying positive in the face of setbacks or when we're under stress. It takes commitment and discipline. It's easy to feel mentally strong when life is good; it's when things are going pear-shaped that mental strength is tested.

In our research on *HR Leaders*, mental strength emerged as one of the defining characteristics of the successful leaders we interviewed. For them it included managing their sense of purpose, such as, "Be visionary, spot opportunities and think differently." A clear purpose helped to provide their motivation to keep going despite obstructions. It also included discipline around managing energy and taking care of themselves – most had some form of meditation or fitness regime. And they consciously managed their self-belief when they hit stumbling blocks. "I believe in my own resilience and robustness," one of them told us.

What you need is "grit"

Psychologist Angela Duckworth at the University of Pennsylvania has shown that the most successful are not those with the highest IQs, or even EI, but the ones who possess a set of skills she calls "grit."[363] (We might assume they're embodied by Mattie Ross, gutsy heroine of the John Wayne film *True Grit*.)

Duckworth describes grit as passion and purpose, sticking with goals over time, and having the stamina and determination to keep working to make a sense of purpose a reality. "Part of what it means to be gritty is to be resilient in the face of failure or adversity," she says. You can test your own grit by taking Duckworth's online survey[364] on the University of Pennsylvania website.

Duckworth has determined that natural talent is not the answer, and may even be inversely related to success. And a number of studies suggest that grit is not something people have or don't have:[365] it's not an innate character trait but a way of approaching the world and the challenges it throws up. And it can be learned.

When we're working with leaders we include a number of elements in our model of tough-mindedness, including self-belief, purpose, meaning and motivation, and attention. So if you want to get a bit grittier, and develop your tough-mindedness in order to reach your full potential, practise the following skills.

Self-belief

Self-belief or self-esteem appears to be made up of three elements: your level of commitment, confidence in your ability to carry out the goal or purpose, and the amount of control you have over what you want to do. None of these are fixed, and your beliefs will change how you feel about each of them at any one time.

Understanding your core beliefs and how they colour your experience of the world is a crucial element in developing strong self-belief. How are they helping or hindering you? How do your beliefs influence your thoughts, and "self-talk" such as "I was a real idiot not to win the argument about project funding?"

Do your beliefs tend to be black-and-white, based on absolutes? ("Engineers are the only people who can solve these sorts of problems.") These are often beliefs that can propel you forward... or hold you back. If you can see, with reflection, that they're holding you back, can you recognise circumstances when they haven't held true? Few things in life are absolute unless we choose them to be.

Noticing success, and reinterpreting

Notice what you're doing that works. It's easy to always focus on our failures and the things that need fixing, and to miss how much progress we've made. What new skills are you using, and how do you think differently? Keep some kind of journal to track your progress. Success builds self-belief and further commitment to our goals.

Our confidence can be undermined by how we feel in the moment. Think about the language you use: do you find yourself saying, "They made me feel..." or, "They won't agree...?" Would it be more useful if you were saying "I don't agree with him but..." or, "I won't know unless I have the conversation?"

What is the most helpful way you could be viewing a situation? Research by neuroscientist Kevin Ochsner and psychologist James Gross has found that reappraising a situation is a highly effective skill that harnesses our power to interpret things differently, or change the meaning of a situation. And it can be taught.

Studies show that when we change the meaning of a situation, the threat response in our brain and the level of arousal is significantly reduced,[366] giving us the opportunity to activate control and change our emotional response to the problem or challenge. It gives us a chance to engage the higher-order thinking resources of the logical, executive brain: the prefrontal cortex.

Ochsner vividly demonstrated this effect in an experiment where participants were shown a picture of people crying outside a church.[367] Most people assumed it was a photograph of a funeral scene, but they were then told it was a wedding, with people shedding tears of joy for a newly-married couple. The new "meaning" of the event resulted in reduced activity in the "emotional" limbic region of the brain and reactivation of the prefrontal cortex.

What situation would it be useful for you to give a different meaning to? How would this change your emotional response and your future behaviour?

Meaning and motivation

A sense of purpose creates energy and motivation which goes beyond the immediate rewards of the job. Behavioural economist Dan Ariely says, "When we think about labour we usually think about motivation and payment as the same thing,[368] but the reality is that we should probably add all kinds of things into it – meaning, creation, challenges, ownership, identity, pride." Knowing that no-one wants or recognises your work is highly demotivating, he proposed.

Ariely asked people to build Lego models for money. When the models were finished they were kept, and participants were offered less money to build another Lego model. Most people continued building for less and less money (Ariely calls this the Meaningful condition). In the second part of the experiment, the completed Lego models were dismantled in front of the participants. Ariely called this the Sisyphic condition, after Sisyphus, the king in Greek mythology condemned for eternity to push a rock up a hill, only to see it roll down again.

Even though there was very little meaning attached to this exercise (after all, they were only building Lego models) it made a difference: many more Lego models were built under Meaningful conditions, even though participants were being paid the same in both situations, and even if people in the Sisyphic situation loved building with Lego.

It turned out that participants in the experiment could predict the different result when it was explained to them what was going on, but they underestimated the size of the effect. And in a variation of the test, it turned out that just ignoring the efforts of participants reduced their willingness to build the models. Meaning and recognition creates motivation even when it's small or about relatively insignificant things, says Ariely. A small amount of recognition, sharing learning or passing on expertise can add meaning to what we do.

Energy and emotion

One of the features of our successful leaders was their management of mental energy. Few believed that a traditional work/life pattern was feasible for their role; they couldn't just leave work at six and switch off. They knew there would be times when they needed to give their all, and other times when they could sit back a little.

Managing mental energy is even more important than managing time: we waste brain-power by ruminating and worrying. Teach yourself to put things aside or deal with the issue. Look at what you can and cannot control, and focus on what's within your control rather than what's not. The more you practise this the more it becomes the way you use energy.

Practise noticing your emotions and just being with them. Being mentally strong doesn't mean you *don't* have concerns or episodes of self-doubt, but it is about how you use them to learn and take a different course of action, or to check your intuition before you act. Practise noticing body signals and gut reactions that alert you to take a different path or decision. (There's more on understanding gut feelings in our chapter in the *Leading purpose* section.)

Re-focus your attention

What are you giving your attention to? We get HR leaders to complete an exercise which helps them to see where their own focus is: on themself or others? On innovation, or process? Where is your focus: on your problems or possibilities? Focusing on problems is comfortable for our brain; it's predictable – we've probably encountered a similar problem before. But it's probably not helping you believe in yourself, or move forward. Successful leaders take the lessons learned from problems and setbacks and move on.

Shifting focus is about the goals and the plan you put in place, and also about the language you use. Think more about outcomes: *what* you will do, rather than *why* something happened. Direct your attention towards the future rather than the past.

Change is typically experienced as a threat response in the brain, but by adopting a different mindset it can be an opportunity. Adopting a growth mindset reframes or reappraises change[369] as a learning opportunity: a chance to develop new skills. Tough-minded people take well-thought-through risks, where the pros and cons have been calculated. Stretching yourself builds self-belief, and so does overcoming obstacles. The brain sees a new you, one who is better than the "you" prior to the challenge. And that's a reward.

Tough-mindedness is a skill you can learn and a practice you can adopt for success.

"I'm lucky: I don't need much sleep"

The evidence on how sleep affects your work

It's surprising how you hear senior leaders referring to how little sleep they need. It would be the rare CEO who would confess: "Seven hours a night, or I'm a zombie."

Margaret Thatcher claimed to need only four hours sleep a night, and a 2012 article in Business Insider referred to a "sleepless elite" who can get by with a few hours and still function well.[370] Marissa Mayer (Yahoo): four to six hours a night. Donald Trump: three to four hours a night. Indra Nooyi (PepsiCo): four hours.

There's a slightly macho quality to the justification (even from women) that they "just have too much to do to spend time on sleeping." It all sounds a little like the CEO sprinting ahead of the team going out for a morning jog on a weekend retreat, calling: "Keep up, keep up!"

Is this culture of minimal sleep peculiar to the business world? You wouldn't hear a top tennis-player saying how little sleep they survive on. It would seem... foolish, a flaw in their training regime – as though they're denying themselves a potential added advantage.

Leaving aside all the issues of team support and a leader's ability to delegate rather than doing it all yourself, what is the impact of limited sleep on performance? Neuroscience research is showing that limited sleep *does* have an impact, and usually one that should concern anyone who wants to perform well. People who sacrifice sleep, from CEOs to forklift drivers, may be doing themselves and their company harm.

The physical effects of sleep-deprivation

Recent research in Sweden tested a number of men who were deprived of sleep for one night. They found increases in blood concentrates similar to those associated with brain damage.[371] There were only a small number of participants in the study, so further research is needed, but researcher Christian Benedict says, "The findings of our trial indicate that a good night's sleep may be critical for maintaining brain health."

Other studies try to give a measure of the impact of lack of sleep. Harvard Medical School researchers found that a week of sleeping four or five hours a night has an impact on performance equivalent to someone with a blood alcohol level of 0.1%.[372] (That's twice the legal alcohol limit in many western countries.) The researchers say that it's clear that the effects of moderate sleep loss on performance are similar to moderate alcohol intoxication.

This is ironic, considering that the workplace drinking culture has changed so drastically over the past two decades. Few people drink at lunch anymore, the Friday drink-up is largely a thing of the past, and in many organisations being drunk at work is grounds for immediate dismissal.

"If you're not getting enough sleep before work, research shows you might as well be working drunk,"[373] says a leading researcher in the field, Jessica Payne of Notre Dame University. She was not speaking metaphorically. Yet operating with inadequate sleep is still regarded as acceptable, and even as a positive trait in leaders, similar to an ability to cope well under stress.

How not-enough sleep affects memory

Payne's research into the impact of sleep on performance[374] has focused on memory and the ability to make connections.

Many of us have an idea that our brain is like a computer and is inactive during "sleep mode." In fact the brain is very busy, regulating and processing emotions, making decisions and accessing implicit knowledge, processing memories and learning. In an fMRI scanner researchers can see that the limbic areas of the brain which manage these activities are active. An area which is largely dormant is the dorsal lateral prefrontal cortex, mainly responsible for executive functioning (planning, organising, strategising, and managing time and space). It's thought this is to free up processing power for the limbic system.

Researchers believe that the sleeping brain is smart, and is making decisions about what to remember and what to forget, and sorting emotional information from background detail.

Research participants studying a story with both neutral and emotionally-significant information and pictures were found to have less memory of the background details of the story whether awake or after sleep, but much more memory for emotional data after sleeping. The negative emotional data was remembered the most.

It seems the brain does not care so much about the neutral data, but in sleep sorts and retains the emotional content. As a survival adaptation this would have helped us to remember things that are important for us to learn – even if they were negative.

If you can only remember the negative emotional impact of what happened yesterday, how are you going to make good judgements today? And if you only remember certain types of information your decisions are likely to be biased.

Sleep and cognitive performance

Payne's research has also shown the impact on cognitive ability. People who lack sleep make fewer neural connections and have fewer insights.[375]

One researcher calls this sleeping process "creative cognition," and it enhances the ability to make inferences. In an experiment aimed at getting people to form associations, it was found that if participants were given a break but remained awake they showed some improvement in performing the task. However if they slept during the break a huge increase in ability was recorded. Sleep helps us make inferential jumps.

In another experiment the researchers tested insightful problem solving. A massive increase in insight was found after a night's sleep compared with wakeful rest.

Sleep and emotions

Sleep is also helping to regulate emotional response. Evidence from an fMRI study shows that after sleep there is a more refined activation of the brain's "braking system" which helps to manage our emotions, and also reduced activity in the amygdala, which is responsible for emotional activity. If we have limited or disturbed sleep there is hyper-activity in the amygdala, with none of the regulatory circuits working well.

Science is also showing that if we improve the length and quality of our sleep we reduce our stress levels. Levels of cortisol, the stress hormone, are higher in someone who is not sleeping well.[376]

Does any of this matter?

Many senior leaders believe it's the responsibility of their team to make life a bit easier for them, and that they should pick up the slack (or steer clear!) when they're performing under pressure.

Even if that is the accepted corporate culture, Payne's research demonstrates that lack of sleep affects leadership performance in more significant ways. Sleep plays an important role in emotional regulation, and this is about more than avoiding Grumpy Boss Syndrome.

The quality of decision-making is affected: there will be a tendency to focus on negative data and it's likely that decisions will be influenced by mood and the level of emotional arousal. Making the decision to sack someone, or to restructure the company, may not be a very rational judgement after a poor night's sleep.

Impact on focus

Everyone loses focus at times, but this is where someone who is sleep-deprived falls into a trap. If we start to lose focus but have had enough sleep, our brain is able to compensate and increase attention. If we are sleep-deprived, our brain can't refocus.[377] "The main finding is that the brain of the sleep-deprived individual is working normally sometimes, but intermittently suffers from something akin to power failure," says Harvard neuroscientist Clifford Saper.

Sleep-deprived people have limited brainpower to steer themselves back to focus once they lose attention. But even more significantly, they don't notice their decrease in performance and may have a false sense of competency.

How much sleep is enough?

Research findings show that the formula for optimum performance is mild stress, good sleep and a good mood. But how much sleep is enough to ensure that we'll rise to the challenge of a reasonable amount of pressure with equanimity (if not enthusiasm!), ready to exercise our best cognitive abilities?

The answer is no one really knows. What is right for one person may not be enough for another, or excessive for someone else. People need to monitor their own sleep needs and performance. But for those who really want an objective measure, Daniel Kripke of the UC San Diego School of Medicine has found that "People who sleep between six-and-a-half and seven-and-a-half hours a night live the longest,[378] are happier and most productive."

Introduce exercise or a meditative practice into your daily regime; there's evidence that it not only works to boost your performance, but also encourages deeper, more restful sleep. And look at your daily habits. How late do you work? Do you always put the TV on for an hour or so before going to bed? Is your tablet or phone always on the bedside table, ready to interrupt your sleep?

Organisations demand a lot from their leaders and the neuroscience research clearly demonstrates that macho all-nighters cannot deliver best performance. We owe it not only to ourselves to get adequate sleep for our health and wellbeing, but also to the company's bottom line.

"A 'power pose' will make me better at my job?"

How your body affects your performance

There is a growing body of evidence – no pun intended – that you can improve the performance of your brain by using your body more effectively. The research shows that the way you hold your body is directly communicated to your brain, and affects your mood and your cognitive performance.

Of course, we're all aware that how we use our bodies affects how other people see us. Actors use these skills on stage to project a character, and improvisation coach Keith Johnstone teaches the same stagecraft skills.[379] We're quick to pick up visual cues about who is high confidence or high status, and who is low status, and Johnstone teaches classes on "status postures."

Interestingly, he also explores how our own perceived relative status directs our internal dialogue, and how that in turn impacts on our posture. It's a circular communication: our internal dialogue directs our body posture, which is communicated to the brain, which in turn creates physiological changes in the body.

This isn't a new idea, nineteenth-century philosopher and psychologist William James caused a storm of controversy when he published his 1884 treatise on the nature of emotion, which posed the question: do we run from a bear because we are afraid,[380] or are we afraid *because* we run? Does the reaction of running away stimulate physical responses – including increased heart rate and raised blood pressure – which we read as fear?

Smiling makes you happier

If you're not sure you agree with James, consider the old adage: "Smile and you'll feel better." Fritz Strack's often-replicated "pencil experiment"[381] tested this two-way connection between the physiology and emotion of smiling back in 1988. Participants were made to hold a pencil in a way that forced them to naturally activate the smile muscles. The pencil can be lengthwise between the teeth, or hanging down from the tip between your teeth. Either way, you get the smile. Other participants were asked to hold the pencil between their lips without touching the pencil with their teeth, and this activated a frown. Both groups then rated the "funniness" of cartoons. Those who were simulating smiling rated the cartoons as funnier. Try it, you'll see.

As soon as we are born, we begin developing rich neural pathways between the behaviour of smiling and positive emotion[382] and memories of positive emotion, says Dana Carney from UC Berkeley's Haas School of Business. Over time, the brain associates the use of certain facial muscles – those that create a smile – with happiness.

Psychologists Tara Kraft and Sarah Pressman have looked at the potential benefits of smiling in helping us to recover from stress. They reviewed how different types of smiling, and the awareness of smiling, could affect an individual's recovery from a stressful situation. Their findings suggest that smiling during brief periods of stress can help reduce the impact on the body,[383] regardless of whether the person actually feels happy or not. But only Duchenne smiles – the most genuine smiles which engage the muscles in the cheeks and around the eyes, as well as the muscles around the mouth – stimulate these positive effects.

Better posture for positive thinking

You probably have a sense that the person sitting up straight at their desk is in a more productive mental state than someone who is slumped.

A study by Erik Peper, a leading psychophysiologist and biofeedback researcher, has found this is another two-way connection: participants who sat up straight found it easier to generate positive thoughts and memories.[384] Other work has demonstrated that bad posture can result in feelings of helplessness and stress.

Power poses

Harvard Business School's Amy Cuddy is a leading researcher on how people judge and influence each other. Her TEDTalk "Your body language shapes who you are" is one of the top-15 most-viewed.[385] At the start she asks her audience to check how they are sitting and take note of their posture. It's a very useful exercise for us all to do regularly. We all develop habits of standing or sitting in particular ways, which may be sending signals to our brain which have an impact on our performance.

Cuddy says that adopting high-status or "power poses" changes the chemicals in the body.[386] She has found that holding a power pose for as little as two minutes is enough to create a 20% increase in testosterone and a 25% decrease in the stress hormone cortisol. Not surprisingly, power posers of both sexes have reported greater feelings of being powerful and in charge.

Increased confidence is also perceived by others. Previous research has established that changes in situation, like becoming the leader of a group, can alter hormone levels. In primates, for example, after an alpha male dies, the testosterone levels of the replacement leader increase. Stock market traders who are on a winning streak have increased testosterone levels.[387] The hormonal shifts measured in Amy Cuddy's experiment show that changes can be influenced independent of role and situation. The physical poses are enough.

Cuddy has found that people who persist with adopting a more assertive stance feel differently about themselves. They become the person who is confident enough to ask questions in class: faking it works.

When we act as if we are confident, strong and powerful, our body and our brain believe it. If we keep doing it, we eventually become it. Cuddy says, "We tend to forget the other audience that's influenced by our non-verbals: ourselves." [388]

Fitness and focus

It's not only using our bodies to project power and status that is effective; it seems that yoga practice can be used to enhance focus and awareness.[389] Researchers from the University of Illinois studied people who did a 20-minute yoga session involving seated, standing and floor postures, as well as a deep-breathing and meditative pose at the end. Immediately afterwards participants showed significant improvement on cognitive tests evaluating their reaction times, accuracy, and memory.

And general fitness is also associated with better performance, especially for memory: many studies have found that exercisers performed significantly better on memory and cognitive tests.

Recent research at Boston University looking at the mental activities governed by the hippocampus found that people with a medium level of fitness – not athletes or people who undertake endurance training – remembered 73% of the pictures they were shown,[390] compared with the 67% recalled by the more sedentary trial subjects. And in a test matching pictures of faces with names, again, the fitter people made fewer mistakes.

Researchers suggest that fitness strengthens memory by neurogenesis: the growth of new neurons in the hippocampus.

What should we do?

Apart from smiling and getting fit, taking regular breaks and moving will definitely improve your performance. Movement reduces anxiety and generates energy that you probably didn't realise was missing. There are plenty of handy apps that will remind you to keep moving.

And if you have a big meeting coming up, remember to take a mo-

ment to collect yourself and adopt the power pose just before you
enter the room.

"Moving up the career ladder via the gym?"

Physical fitness: it really does give you the edge

Lunchtime running clubs, subsidised gym membership, the after-work squash league... if you're not a fitness enthusiast it can feel as though those people have unfairly gained the higher moral ground. Isn't it enough that you contribute to the charity cake bakes at work?

Does physical fitness make any difference to your ability to do the job? The short answer is yes: it most certainly does. Or rather, there is a clear relationship between physical exercise and mental alertness. So let's examine the scientific evidence.

Brains perform better with physical activity

One thing that evolutionary historians are sure about is that our brains developed while we were on the move.[391] Our prehistoric ancestors would travel around 10 miles a day and as a result the brain evolved under conditions of constant motion. In recent times, we have become much more sedentary, spending up to eight hours a day deskbound – but is it possible that motion still influences our cognitive skills?

Research has consistently shown that exercisers outperform couch potatoes[392] in tests that measure long-term memory, reasoning, attention and problem-solving. Researchers found a group of non-exercisers, measured their mental abilities, exercised them for a period of time and then re-examined their brain performance. They consistently found that when non-exercisers are enrolled in an aerobic exercise programme all kinds of mental abilities are enhanced.

Similar results have been found with school-age children.[393] In one study, children jogged for 30 minutes two or three times a week. After 12 weeks, their cognitive performance had improved significantly compared with pre-exercise levels. When the exercise programme was withdrawn, their scores plummeted back to their pre-study levels.

There is also evidence that exercise helps prevent the harmful results of stress.[394] Researchers have found that in animals running prevents the activation of new neurons in response to stress. In sedentary mice, stress activated new neurons in the hippocampus, but after six weeks of running exercise, the stress-induced activation of both new and mature neurons disappeared.

What kind of activity, and how much?

Different studies have focused on different types of exercise, but the general consensus is that two 30-minute aerobic activities a week and some strength training will make a difference. The American Heart Association recommends 30 minutes of moderate exercise five days a week.[395]

Why does it work?

Oxygen is carried in the blood with the purpose of taking away toxic waste from the cells. When you exercise, you increase blood flow across the tissues of your body and this stimulates the blood vessels to create a powerful flow-regulating molecule called nitric oxide. As the flow improves, the body makes new blood vessels, which penetrate deeper into the body tissues. This allows more access and more efficient waste-disposal of the toxins that build up in the body's cells. Brain tissues are included in this process. Imaging studies have shown that exercise increases blood volume in a region of the brain called the dentate gyrus,[396] part of the hippocampus – a region intricately involved in memory formation.

Another brain-specific effect of exercise has been identified at the molecular level. Early studies have indicated that exercise also encourages one of the brain's most powerful growth stimulants,[397] BDNF (Brain Derived Neurotrophic Factor) which aids the development of healthy tissue. This exerts a fertiliser-like growth effect on neurons in the brain, and keeps existing neurons young and healthy, making them much more willing to connect with one another. It also encourages neurogenesis, the formation of new cells in the brain. Exercise increases the level of usable BDNF in the cells.

Take your fitness regime to work

Are treadmill desks the solution for sedentary workers? Microsoft, Evernote, and the Hyatt and Marriott hotel chains are reported to be using them, and Google installed two-dozen treadmill desks between its New York City and San Francisco offices. There have been a number of foot and ankle injuries reported where workers have fallen off, so the jury is still out on their effectiveness.

Beyond such headline-catching installations, what are some of the things that you could do to improve your fitness at work?

Manage by walking about: leave the executive office and drop by the company coffee shop, the production floor, or the loading docks. This could put you in unfamiliar territory, which is a good thing for broadening your perspective, and the very act of walking and moving about invigorates your brain. That's why when you have a mental block on some problem, getting up and changing your environment can lead to an "Aha!" moment.

Coaching on the go: in our development programmes we've introduced the notion of coaching pairs coaching each other while they're out walking. Participants have told us they've found it very beneficial, helping with reflection and perspective.

Role model good exercise habits: take up that corporate gym membership deal, and build it into your weekly routine. Be visible in your exercise habits: it will help to strengthen your resolve and also encourage your team to do likewise. There's a reason Google have bicycles to get around the Google campus!

Build exercise into leadership development programmes: if you're organising the venue, choose somewhere that's exercise-friendly and build time into the timetable for you and your colleagues to get out for a vigorous walk or a run, or use the pool or the gym.

Fit employees are capable of mobilising their cognitive abilities better than sedentary employees.[398] You'll not only feel better yourself, but exercise will also boost the collective brain power of your organisation. For companies whose competitive edge rests on creative intellectual horsepower (and that's pretty much every organisation), a fit workforce makes a strategic difference.

"How can I cope better with setbacks?"

Developing the power of resilience

You and a colleague have been working on a new project proposal which gets rejected by the board. You're gutted, and finding it hard to get past the sense of disappointment, the feeling that your career has stalled. But your colleague seems to be much more philosophical about the decision. She's shrugged it off and seems to be getting on with things. Didn't she have as much invested in getting the project off the ground – didn't it matter as much to her? Or is she just coping better?

The difference is resilience.

It's the art of adapting well in the face of adversity: when a proposal is rejected, when a valued colleague moves to another company, or if you lose your job in a downsizing. Some people describe it as the ability to bend without breaking.

Biologically, resilience is the ability to manage the physical and neurological impact of the stress response. Stress can have a significant impact on the immune system, and makes us physically ill, but the effects are entirely dependent on how we, individually, react to it. (Read more about that in the chapter in this section *"I can't avoid stress in my job."*

What makes us resilient?

Studies of twins suggest that at least some of our response to stress, and our ability to cope with it, is inherited. Having a sociable personality that embraces novel tasks and interests, and being accepting of yourself and your faults makes someone more resilient.

But our environment also comes into play: the patterns of behaviour we've learned, our education, support from our family, our income and security. But research also shows that we can build resilience with some discipline and consistent practice.

Resilience in the brain develops through repeated experience.[399] Any experience, whether positive or negative, causes neurons in the brain to activate. The strengthened connections between them create neural circuits and pathways that make it likely we will respond to the same or a similar situation in the same way that we reacted before.

This is the brain's natural way of encoding patterns that become the automatic, unconscious habits that drive our behaviours. It relies upon the neuroplasticity of the brain: its capacity to grow new neurons and, more importantly, new connections among the neurons. When we choose to act in particular ways, repeatedly, to the extent we form new habits and ways of behaving, we are engaging in self-directed neuroplasticity.

How can we become more resilient?

Some of the effective strategies that are well-supported by scientific evidence for developing resilience include:

Learn "emotional regulation"

Two approaches to self-regulation that have been extensively studied are reappraisal and mindfulness meditation. You can read more about both of these in our chapters *"Would I pass the marshmallow test?"* and *"What's all the hype about meditation?"*

Reappraisal is a technique for reinterpreting the cause of a negative emotion or stress. So instead of seeing your rejection for promotion as a failure, you reappraise it as an opportunity to build mastery and deepen expertise in your current role.

Columbia University's Kevin Ochsner has found that reappraisal results in changes in the brain,[400] particularly in the prefrontal cortex: the centre for planning, directing and inhibiting. It also *decreases* the activity of the amygdala, responsible for emotion. The result is that an experience is less emotionally charged and it's possible for the person to interpret it more positively. People who practise this technique report greater psychological wellbeing than those who suppress their emotions.

So when you're faced with a negative experience you may find it useful to ask yourself: "Is there a different way to look at this?" Be like the optimistic friend who would put a different spin on it for you.

Our experience of using this strategy with clients, especially in very tough circumstances, is that it can be challenging and it takes practice. Ochsner has found that training in reappraisal, especially using the technique of distancing from the problem,[401] is successful.

Another method for increasing resilience and managing emotions is mindfulness meditation, which has been found to improve focus and wellbeing, and encourage more flexible thinking.[402] Brain scans have shown increases in activity in the left prefrontal cortex (which is associated with emotional control), a boost in positive emotions, and faster recovery from feelings of disgust, anger and fear.

Adopt a positive outlook on life

Optimism is associated with good mental and physical health, which probably stems from a better ability to regulate the stress response. Psychologist Barbara Frederickson has found that negative emotions tend to increase physiological arousal, narrow focus and restrict behaviours[403] to those which are essential for survival, like just getting your report done in the usual way, and avoiding social interaction and helping anyone else.

Positive emotions, by contrast, reduce stress and broaden focus, leading to more creative and flexible responses. In this frame of mind you'd be more likely to come up with a new report format which works better, get input from colleagues, or help your junior by coaching them to do the data analysis.

Do you believe you're in control?

Psychologist Julian Rotter has developed the concept of "locus of control."[404] Some people, he says, view themselves as essentially in control of the good and bad things they experience: they have an internal locus of control. Others believe that things are done *to* them by outside forces, or happen by chance (an external locus).

These viewpoints are not absolutes, says Laurence Gonzales, author of *Surviving Survival: The Art and Science of Resilience*. "Most people combine the two," he says, "But research shows that those with a strong internal locus are better off.[405] In general, they're less likely to find everyday activities distressing. They don't often complain, whine, or blame. And they take compliments and criticism in their stride."

Developing an internal locus takes discipline and self- awareness, but it enables you to envisage options and scenarios based on intuition and foresight, which means you can create plans in anticipation, or in the midst of a challenge.

And what about optimism?

Resilience is associated with a type of realistic optimism. If you're too optimistic you may miss negative information or ignore it rather than deal with it. Over-optimism results in risks, which may actually increase stress. The most resilient people seem to be able to tune out negative words and events and develop the habit of interpreting situations in a more positive manner. Oxford psychologist Elaine Fox says we can train ourselves to do this.[406]

What this means for us in business is that we should take a positive outlook whilst carefully assessing and acknowledging risks using techniques like pre-mortems[407] and appreciative enquiry.[408]

Get fit

Aerobic exercise has been shown to reduce symptoms of depression and anxiety[409] and improve attention, planning, decision-making and memory. And exercise appears to aid resilience by boosting levels of endorphins as well as the neurotransmitters dopamine and serotonin which may elevate mood. It also suppresses the release of the stress hormone cortisol.

Develop your resilience muscle

Researchers recommend "workouts," or tasks that get gradually more challenging. This idea of "stress inoculation" is based on the theory that increasing the degree of difficulty teaches us to handle higher levels of challenge and stress.

If you dread giving presentations then offering to give the after-dinner toast at an annual dinner, and signing-up for a speaking club, can be part of a process gradually training yourself out of the fear.

The same approach as training for a marathon also works for mental challenges,[410] according to the authors of *Resilience: the science of mastering life's greatest challenges*. However, just as with an athlete's training and competition programme, it's important to build-in recovery time: extended periods of stress without a recovery period can be damaging. One of the skills of resilient people, according to performance psychologist[411] Jim Loehr, is knowing when they need a break.

Maintain your support networks

Developing your network of supportive friends, family and colleagues is another important way to enhance your resilience. Don't be too busy to do lunch, help someone or stop and talk to a colleague: it reduces your stress response and bolsters your courage and self-confidence, and creates a safety net.

Social ties make us feel good about ourselves: they activate the reward response in our brain. Objectively evaluate your network and analyse its strengths. You may have support in your home life, but do you also have it at work? Who do you know who could help you with different types of challenges? Who understands you, and has the skills you could call on in a crisis?

Follow good role models

We're familiar with the idea of role models in business and leadership development. But thinking about who your models are for resilience may be a new idea for you. Consider who you know who has been through tough times in the business and has come through. What are the characteristics of their strength and how did they manage the challenge?

Psychologist Albert Bandura believes modelling is most effective when the observer analyses what they want to imitate[412] by dissecting different aspects and creating rules that can guide their own action.

It's all about belief

Psychologist Edith Grotberg believes that everyone needs to remind themselves regularly of their strengths.[413] She suggests we cultivate resilience by thinking about three areas:

- Strong relationships, structure, rules at home, role models: these are external supports.
- Self-belief, caring about other people, being proud of ourselves: these are inner strengths that can be developed.
- Communicating, solving problems, gauging the temperament of others, seeking out good relationships: these are the interpersonal and problem-solving skills that can be acquired.

At the heart of resilience is a belief in ourselves. Resilient people don't let adversity define them: they move towards a goal beyond themselves and see tough times as just a temporary state of affairs.

"What's that X-factor... the power of connection that some people have?"

The neuroscience of presence, and how you can learn it

You know that feeling you get from someone who establishes a sense of connection with you that is almost palpable? It could be a charismatic leader in your organisation, or a close friend, or a shop assistant. But for that period of time they are completely focused on you and your needs.

They are *present*, and their ability to be present with us invites us to be present as well: it draws us into more meaningful communication. You can identify these people across the room at those after-conference cocktail parties. They're not the ones regaling a group with war-stories of business success. They're the ones who are listening closely, who are engaged in thoughtful conversations that look more like a real exchange of views than performances.

This kind of presence shouldn't be confused with power and status. There are glamorous people who will turn heads as they come into the room, but they may not have this capacity for personal connection – they could always seem rather aloof or more interested in their story rather than the story of the other person. It's possible that their fame and status makes it *harder* for them to connect.

"I see you"

The type of connection we're talking about is summed up in the traditional style of greeting among the tribespeople of northern Natal, in South Africa: "Sawa bona" means literally "I see you." To which the response is, *"Sikhona,"* "I am here." It's an exchange that suggests that until you're "seen" you don't exist, and when you're seen you are brought into existence. This is the skill of deeply connecting to other people and giving them attention, and many believe it speaks to a basic human need to be validated.

For many of us this power of being-present is the X-factor in business. It's an invaluable skill for anyone, but especially for HR leaders and business partners.

Everyone is capable of this level of connection. When we achieve it we understand more of what's going on in the business, we're more influential and can increase engagement and productivity within a team.

Presence is a feeling state and one of its characteristics is that the experience feels spontaneous to both of the people involved in the conversation. There's no power play, posturing or self-consciousness, and past experience is not interfering with the interaction. There's also an element of energy.

The power of presence

Psychology has for many years emphasised the importance of not just words in communication, but also the power of body language and tone of voice. People watch and make judgements on what is real and relevant to them,[414] and what is for show. This is largely intuitive, but research from Sandy Pentland at MIT has been able to verify and even put numbers on these factors. (We've referred to this research in the chapter *"Emotional Intelligence: our leaders aren't convinced"* in the *Leading talent, engagement and learning* section.)

Pentland has found that we act on and are influenced by the "honest signals" people send – the unconscious and non-verbal language that includes tone and energy. These signals contrast with "dishonest" signals that may be employed, for example, when people are pretending to be interested. The MIT team have developed an electronic badge which can measure "honest signals".

Pentland says that the ability to communicate "honest signals" is a significant factor in the success of individuals and teams,[415] and can account for as much as 50% of the success of a group when working together and getting results.

As he points out, we all know this at some level. We know when a leader or a team is being effective and productive and can notice the difference when they are not. Pentland has found that a particular type of person is most effective in teams; he calls them "charismatic connectors" and they have many of the characteristics we associate with presence. They mainly work to connect people and information, talking to everybody and driving the conversation around a team.

Pentland found that people can be trained to amplify their honest signals by putting in more energy, or to communicate more effectively using non-verbal cues. His research indicates that when people are communicating honestly there is better understanding, motivation and productivity in a team: changes like these can improve productivity by as much as eight per cent in call-centre teams.[416]

What inhibits our ability to be present?

It seems that the ability to connect should be a learnable skill. But what gets in the way of our achieving it? In discussions with clients we find these are the main issues:

Distractions: everything from automatically checking our mobile phones to having a discussion standing at the desk rather than walking to a meeting area.

Internal dialogue: all that noise in our heads, which might be self-consciousness, planning what to say next, or wondering what the other person thinks of us.

Threat response: we may start by being closely engaged but lose it when we feel "threatened" by what the person is saying, or how they're saying it. We need to be comfortable to stay present. The CORE model which we describe in *Brain basics* can help you identify what's triggering your disconnection.

Judgement: we make them all the time. Is this person being honest? Have they said what they really feel? Judgements can block our ability to listen, close down curiosity and reduce empathy. We need to catch ourselves doing it, and make a conscious effort to "suspend judgement."

Habit: we can just get into the habit of not fully connecting, and it often happens when we try to do two things at once so our attention is split. We need to practise to make paying attention our new habit.

Learning the skills

Research by social psychologist Amy Cuddy has shown that when people adopt new postures, such as appearing more powerful, or appearing to be more interested[417] in other people, the brain starts to change and the adopted approach can be integrated into everyday behaviour. This suggests that people can be coached to acquire the essential skills of presence, and not just the most visible behaviours.

In our Head Heart + Brain training we conduct an exercise where people rehearse an upcoming meeting. We don't worry about content but instead focus on body posture, tone of voice, speed of speaking and the energy of the speaker.

Observers then coach the speaker to make very small adjustments, one at a time, to posture, tone, speed or energy. The observers repeat their adjustment coaching until they believe the speaker is confident and is achieving the best possible impact.

We've had numerous reports back from participants who have achieved remarkable results. One particularly sceptical HR professional needed to attend a meeting with his CEO in the middle of the workshop, presenting a radical new approach. He rehearsed the meeting with the group and returned to the workshop beaming. He'd put the coaching to effect and the pitch went flawlessly:

proposal accepted. He was a lot less sceptical about the rest of the workshop content, and so were his colleagues.

Presence requires practice

The *experience* of presence may feel spontaneous and unpractised, but if you've got out of the habit of connecting with people in this way, or you have never learnt the skills, you will need to apply some conscious effort in order to exercise the art of being present yourself:

> **Develop personal awareness:** being present for others depends on your mood at any given time, and being able to change it. Practise noticing your state and naming it, and be aware of "What do I do, how do I do it, and why do I do it."

> **Develop physical awareness:** you speak through your body, and as Pentland's research has shown, people pick up on this and respond to it. Everyone needs the quotation from Ralph Waldo Emerson somewhere close at hand: *"Who you are speaks so loudly I can't hear what you are saying."* Until these skills become second nature, don't go into an interaction without re-tuning for the right degree of energy and relaxation.

> **Exercise emotional control:** you need to be able to step outside the immediate interaction, sense what is working and what is not, and make the required adjustments. Being curious is a great help: it's nearly impossible to be judgemental or listen to your own internal dialogue if you are deeply curious about the other person.

Presence calls for practice and intention. You need to believe that it's a worthwhile skill to acquire, and compare how it feels when you are present with someone rather than when you're distracted. Notice the difference in your understanding and influence and it will help you to practise "seeing" other people.

References

Introduction

Brain basics
Understanding how the brain works

1   **Maslow got it wrong with his hierarchy of human needs...**
Abraham Maslow (1943). Hierarchy of needs.
A theory of human motivation. Psychology Review 50.

2   **the brain networks for physical pain are also used
for social pain...**
Naomi Eisenberger, Matthew Lieberman and Kipling Williams
(2003). Does rejection hurt? An fMRI study of social exclusion.
Science 302.

3   **our minds are less like hermetically sealed vaults that
separate each of us from one another, and more like
"Trojan horses"...**
Matthew Lieberman (2013). Social: Why our brains
are wired to connect. Oxford University Press.

4   **70% of what we do is governed by habit...**
Kevin Ochsner (2010). The Formation of Habit.
Presentation at the NeuroLeadership Summit, Boston.

5   **all decisions have an emotional element...**
Antonio Damasio (1994). Descartes' Error: Emotion, Reason,
and the Human Brain. Putnam Adult.

6   **using simple language to "name" emotions *lowers*
the arousal...**
Matthew Lieberman, Naomi Eisenberger, Molly Crockett,
Sabrina Tom, Jennifer Pfeifer and Baldwin Way (2007).
Putting feelings into words: Affect labeling disrupts amygdala
activity to affective stimuli. Psychological Science 18.

CORE principles
A brain-savvy model for relationships

7   **Certainty: our confidence that we know what
the future holds...**
Trey Hedden and John Gabrieli (2006). The ebb and flow
of attention in the Human Brain. Natural Neuroscience 9.

8   **Options: the extent to which we feel we have choices...**
Susan Mineka and Robert Hendersen (1985). Controllability
and Predictability in Acquiring Motivation. Annual Review
of Psychology 36.

9   **Reputation: our relative importance to others
(our social ranking)...**
Caroline Zink, Yunxia Tong, Qiang Chen, Danielle Bassett,
Jason Stein and Andreas Meyer-Lindenberg (2008).
Know Your Place: Neural Processing of Social Hierarchy
in Humans. Neuron 58(2).

10   **Equity: our sense of fairness...**
Golnaz Tabibnia and Matthew Lieberman (2007).
Fairness and Cooperation Are Rewarding: Evidence from
Social Cognitive Neuroscience. Annals of the New York
Academy of Sciences 1118.

Neuroscience at work in HR

Our study
The background and numbers

11   **a theory that explains how, why, and at what rate
new ideas spread...**
Everett Rogers (1962). Diffusion of Innovations.
Glencoe Free Press.

12   **We anticipate that the CIPD's recent endorsement
of neuroscience...**
David Rock and Peter Cheese (2013). Neuroscience and
its impact on people development. CIPD.co.uk podcast.

13   **a survey to measure the awareness and application
of a number of new methodologies...**
John McGurk (2012). From steady state to ready state: A need
for fresh thinking in learning and talent development? CIPD.

14   **"Flow" state and the work of Mihaly Csikszentmihalyi...**
Mihaly Csikszentmihalyi (2008). Flow: The Psychology
of Optimal Experience. Harper Perennial.

Case studies
Organisations using neuroscience to solve business issues

15   **The other examples of applying neuroscience to change
mainly used the SCARF model...**
David Rock (2009). Your Brain at Work: Strategies for
Overcoming Distraction, Regaining Focus, and Working
Smarter All Day Long. HarperBusiness.

16   **For example, positive psychology guru Martin Seligman...**
Martin Seligman (2003). Authentic Happiness: Using the
New Positive Psychology to Realise Your Potential for Lasting
Fulfilment. Nicholas Brealey Publishing.

17   **appreciative inquiry expert David Cooperrider...**
David Cooperrider and Suresh Srivastva (2000). Appreciative
Inquiry in Organizational Life. Research in Organizational
Change and Development 1.

18   **Tal Ben-Shahar was engaged to teach positive principles
including "re-framing" questions...**
Tal Ben-Shahar (2007). Happier: Learn the Secrets to Daily
Joy and Lasting Fulfillment. McGraw-Hill.

19   **the NeuroPower model developed by Peter Burow...**

Peter Burow (2013). NeuroPower: Leading with
NeuroIntelligence. Copernicus Publishing.

20 **drawing on the work of neuroscientist Matt Lieberman...**
Matthew Lieberman (2013). Social: Why our brains are wired
to connect. Oxford University Press.

21 **The team also used the principles of "nudge"...**
Richard Thaler and Cass Sunstein (2009). Nudge: Improving
Decisions About Health, Wealth and Happiness. Yale University
Press.

22 **work was done to create a 'growth mindset'...**
Carol Dweck (2006). Mindset: The New Psychology of Success.
Random House.

Leading purpose

"Why are we doing this?"
Having a clear purpose and direction

23 **great companies and leaders talk about *why* they're doing
something...**
Simon Sinek (2009). How great leaders inspire action.
TEDxPuget Sound.

24 **the role of mirror neurons...**
Robert Spunt, Emily Falk and Matthew Lieberman (2010).
Dissociable Neural Systems Support Retrieval of How and Why
Action Knowledge. Psychological Science 20(10).

25 **differences in how the two brain systems react when we
see and think about the actions of other people...**
Emily Falk, Sylvia Morelli, Locke Welborn, Karl Dambacher
and Matthew Lieberman (2013). Creating Buzz: The Neural
Correlates of Effective Message Propagation. Psychological
Science.

26 **the default system is activated when people hear
information that they're going to relay to other people...**
Emily Falk, Sylvia Morelli, Locke Welborn, Karl Dambacher
and Matthew Lieberman (2013). Creating Buzz: The Neural
Correlates of Effective Message Propagation. Psychological
Science.

"Where should I be focusing my attention?"
Choosing where your attention should be

27 **Attention is not one brain process...**
Seth Horowitz (2012). The Universal Sense: How Hearing
Shapes the Mind. Bloomsbury.

28 **How well people can sense their heartbeats is a way
of measuring their self-awareness**
William O'Brian, Graham Reid and Kenneth Jones (1989).

Differences in heart beat awareness among males and higher and lower levels of systolic blood pressure. International Journal Of Psychophysiology 29.

And also:

Hugo Critchly, Stefan Wiens, Pia Rotshtein, Arne Ohman and Raymond Dolan (2004). Neural Systems supporting interoceptive awareness. Nature Neuroscience 7.

29 **signals from the insula and the amygdala...**
Antonio Damasio (1994). Descartes' Error: Emotion, Reason, and the Human Brain. Putnam Adult.

30 **interviews carried out by Cambridge neuroscientist John Coates with traders...**
John Coates (2012). The Hour Between Dog and Wolf: Risk Taking, Gut Feelings and the Biology of Boom and Bust. HarperCollins.

31 **a longitudinal study tracking 1,037 children...**
Terrie Moffitt, Louise Arseneault, Daniel Belsky, Nigel Dickson, Robert Hancox, HonaLee Harrington, Renate Houts, Richie Poulton, Brent Roberts, Stephen Ross, Malcolm Sears, Murray Thomson and Avshalom Caspi (2011). A gradient of childhood self-control predicts health, wealth, and public safety. Proceedings of the National Academy of Sciences 108(7).

32 **In the original experiment...**
Walter Mischel, Ebbe Ebbesen and Antonette Raskoff Zeiss (1972). Cognitive and attentional mechanisms in delay of gratification. Journal of Personality and Social Psychology 21(2).

33 **we need to understand our own feelings in order to understand the feelings of others...**
Haakon Engen and Tania Singer (2013). Empathy circuits. Current Opinion in Neurobiology 23(2).

34 **people who are most alert to social situations exhibit stronger activity...**
Allison Jahn, Andrew Fox, Heather Abercrombie, Steven Shelton, Terrence Oakes, Richard Davidson and Ned Kalin (2010). Subgenual PFC Activity Predicts Individual Differences in HPA Activity Across Different Contexts. Biological Psychiatry 67.

35 **Brain scans of seasoned business decision-makers...**
Daniella Laureiro-Martínez, Stefano Brusoni and Maurizio Zollo (2010). The neuroscientific foundations of the exploration–exploitation dilemma. Journal of Neuroscience, Psychology, and Economics 3(2).

"Empathy is the answer... or is it?"

Empathy and perspective, which you need when

36 **Adam Grant tells a story...**
Adam Grant (2013). Give and Take: A Revolutionary Approach to Success. Weidenfeld & Nicolson.

37 **people with damage to the brain areas associated with empathy...**
Antonio Damasio (1994). Descartes' Error: Emotion, Reason, and the Human Brain. Putnam Adult.

38 **those who were empathetic ended up with worse deals...**
Adam Galinsky (2001). First offers as Anchors: The role of perspective-taking and negotiator focus. Journal of Personality and Social Psychology 81(4).

39 **an increased ability to discover hidden agreements...**
Adam Galinsky (2001). First offers as Anchors: The role of perspective-taking and negotiator focus. Journal of Personality and Social Psychology 81(4).

40 **empathy can be learned...**
Helen Riess, John Kelley, Robert Bailey, Emily Dunn and Margot Phillips (2011). Empathy training for resident physicians: a randomized controlled trial of a neuroscience-informed curriculum. Journal of General Internal Medicine, 26(1).

41 **putting yourself physically into a state can generate changes...**
Amy Cuddy, Caroline Wilmuth and Dana Carney (2012). The Benefit of Power Posing Before a High-Stakes Social Evaluation. Harvard Business School Working Paper 13(027).

"What's the truth about being creative?"

4 myths about creativity, and how it actually works

42 **people can indeed enhance their ability to solve problems creatively, by developing four core competencies...**
Robert Epstein, Steven Schmidt and Regina Warfel (2008). Measuring and Training Creativity Competencies: Validation of a New Test. Creativity Research Journal 20(1).

43 **researchers have examined the fMRI... scans of over 1,000 people...**
Jared Nielsen, Brandon Zielinski, Michael Ferguson, Janet Lainhart and Jeffrey Anderson (2013). An Evaluation of the Left-Brain vs. Right-Brain Hypothesis with Resting State Functional Connectivity Magnetic Resonance Imaging. PLOS One.

44 **"Creativity is the production of something both novel and useful"...**
Rex Jung (2011). Creativity and the Brain. TEDx.

45 **the main brain areas which are important at different stages of the creative process...**
Scott Barry Kaufman (2013). The real neuroscience of creativity. Beautiful Minds blog for Scientific America.

46 **the "salience network"...**
Valerie Bonnelle, Timothy Ham, Robert Leech, Kirsi Kinnunen, Mitul Mehta, Richard Greenwood and David Sharp (2012).

Salience network integrity predicts default mode network function after traumatic brain injury. Proceedings of the National Academy of Sciences of the United States of America.

47 **a "first approximation" about how creativity maps on to the human brain...**
Rex Jung, Brittany Mead, Jessica Carrasco and Ranee Flores (2013). The structure of creative cognition in the human brain. Frontiers in Human Neuroscience 7(13).

"Gut feeling: Is it a useful guide in business?"
What is it, and is it reliable

48 **Studying the effects of behaviour on economics...**
Daniel Kahneman and Amos Tversky (1979). Prospect Theory: An Analysis of Decision under Risk. Econometrica 47(2).

49 **the impact that our body can have on our thinking...**
John Coates (2012). The Hour Between Dog and Wolf: Risk Taking, Gut Feelings and the Biology of Boom and Bust. HarperCollins.

50 **The human vagus nerve system has an estimated 500 million neurons...**
John Coates (2012). The Hour Between Dog and Wolf: Risk Taking, Gut Feelings and the Biology of Boom and Bust. HarperCollins.

51 **It's so complex it has been called our second brain...**
Michael Gershon (1998). The Second Brain. HarperCollins.

52 **Kahneman has called them fast and slow decisions...**
Daniel Kahneman (2011). Thinking Fast and Slow. Farrar, Straus and Giroux.

53 **A useful study summarising the link between body signals and decision-making...**
Colin Camerer, George Loewenstein and Drazen Prelec (2005). Neuroeconomics: How Neuroscience Can Inform Economics. Journal of Economic Literature 43.

54 **Most of our thinking is automatic...**
Pawel Lewicki, Thomas Hill and Maria Czyzewska (1992). Nonconscious Acquisition of Information. American Psychologist 47(6).

55 **intuition is a skill that can be developed...**
Gary Klein (1998). Sources of Power: How people make decisions. MIT Press.

56 **emotional tags, or markers the brain attaches to data...**
Antonio Damasio (1994). Descartes' Error: Emotion, Reason, and the Human Brain. Putnam Adult.

57 **rationality does not help us without these emotional markers...**
Antoine Bechara, Hanna Damasio and Antonio Damasio (2000). Emotion, decision making and the orbitofrontal cortex. Cerebral Cortex 10 (3).

58   **"Everyone knows how panic is increased by flight"...**
William James (1884). What is an Emotion? Mind 9(34).

59   **their pre-conscious quickly picked up the patterns...**
Antoine Bechara, Hanna Damasio and Antonio Damasio
(2000). Emotion, decision making and the orbitofrontal cortex.
Cerebral Cortex 10 (3).

60   **it's been shown that patients with severe brain damage...**
Michael Gazzaniga and Joseph LeDoux (1978). The Integrated
Mind. Plenum Press.

61   **people frequently trick themselves into thinking they
understand the true reasons for their actions...**
Joseph LeDoux, Donald Wilson and Michael Gazzaniga (1977).
A Divided Mind: Observations on the Conscious Properties
of the Separated Hemispheres. Annals of Neurology 2.

62   **Similar "story telling" has been identified when traders
have responded to a questionnaire...**
John Coates (2012). The Hour Between Dog and Wolf: Risk
Taking, Gut Feelings and the Biology of Boom and Bust.
HarperCollins.

63   **Gut reactions, it turns out, may have a *higher* rate of
accuracy...**
Gerd Gigerenzer (2007). Gut Feelings: The Intelligence of the
Unconscious. Viking Adult.

64   **heartbeat awareness is linked to body sensitivity...**
William O'Brian, Graham Reid and Kenneth Jones (1989).
Differences in heart beat awareness among males and higher
and lower levels of systolic blood pressure. International Journal
Of Psychophysiology 29.
And also:
Hugo Critchly, Stefan Wiens, Pia Rotshtein, Arne Ohman
and Raymond Dolan (2004). Neural Systems supporting
interoceptive awareness. Nature Neuroscience 7.

"Is there a science to making better decisions?"
Logic, emotions, and whether you've had lunch:
the science of decision-making

65   **gave a group of people $20 each, and asked them to bet
on the toss of a coin...**
Antonio Damasio (1994). Descartes' Error: Emotion, Reason,
and the Human Brain. Putnam Adult.

66   **"A good decision is one in which the decision-maker is
happy with the decision...**
Marina Krakovsky (2010). How Do We Decide? Inside the
'Frinky' Science of the Mind. Stanford Business.

67   **decision-making and emotions are physically linked
in the brain...**
Antonio Damasio (1994). Descartes' Error: Emotion, Reason,

and the Human Brain. Putnam Adult.

68   **emotions provides a tag that helps us in the process
of choice...**
Antonio Damasio (1994). Descartes' Error: Emotion, Reason,
and the Human Brain. Putnam Adult.

69   **the unconscious brain is far more dominant in decision-
making than we might previously have believed...**
David Jetson (2013). Finding Emotional Freedom: Access
the Truth Your Brain Already Knows. CreateSpace.

70   **"The belief in the academic field is that emotions are
essential to decision making...**
Baba Shiv, George Loewenstein and Antoine Bechara (2005).
The Dark Side of Emotion in Decision-Making: When
Individuals with Decreased Emotional Reactions Make More
Advantageous Decisions. Cognitive Brain Research 23.

71   **Prospect Theory proposes that we are risk averse...**
Daniel Kahneman and Amos Tversky (1984). Choices, Values
and Frames. American Psychologist 39(4).

72   **brain-damaged patients who felt no loss aversion earned...**
Baba Shiv, George Loewenstein and Antoine Bechara (2005).
The Dark Side of Emotion in Decision-Making: When
Individuals with Decreased Emotional Reactions Make More
Advantageous Decisions. Cognitive Brain Research 23.

73   **we all have two ways of thinking...**
Daniel Kahneman (2011). Thinking Fast and Slow. Farrar,
Straus and Giroux.

74   **we often accept the quick-and-dirty assessments
of the intuitive, largely unconscious System 1...**
Daniel Kahneman (2011). Thinking Fast and Slow. Farrar,
Straus and Giroux.

75   **in the morning when our hormones are most likely
to favour decision-making...**
Marina Krakovsky (2010). How Do We Decide? Inside the
'Frinky' Science of the Mind. Stanford Business.

76   **people who had eaten a satisfying meal took less risk...**
Mkael Symmonds, Julian Emmanuel, Megan Drew, Rachel
Batterham and Raymond Dolan (2010). Metabolic State Alters
Economic Decision Making under Risk in Humans. PLOS One.

77   **sleep deprivation can change the way the brain assesses
economic value...**
Vinod Venkatraman, Scott Huettel, Lisa Chuah, John Payne
and Michael Chee (2011). Sleep Deprivation Biases the Neural
Mechanisms Underlying Economic Preferences. The Journal
of Neuroscience 31(10).

78   **"sleep on it" is backed up by neuroscience research...**
John Creswell, James Bursley and Ajay Satpute (2013). Neural
reactivation links unconscious thought to improved decision
making. Social, Cognitive, and Affective Neuroscience.

"Biased decisions? Not me."

A bias check for your decisions

79 **psychologist Daniel Kahneman has described two human thought systems...**
Daniel Kahneman (2011). Thinking Fast and Slow. Farrar, Straus and Giroux.

80 **The tendency to use reference points can lead us astray...**
Douglas Kenrick, Vladas Griskevicius, Jill Sundie, Norman Li, Yexin Li and Steven Neuberg (2009). Deep Rationality: The Evolutionary Economics of Decision Making. Social Cognition 27(5).

81 **There is evidence in salary negotiations...**
Todd Thorsteinson (2011). Initiating Salary Discussions With an Extreme Request: Anchoring Effects on Initial Salary Offers. Journal of Applied Social Psychology 41(7).

82 **helping others is the root to success at work...**
Adam Grant (2013). Give and Take: A Revolutionary Approach to Success. Weidenfeld & Nicolson.

83 **The term loss aversion, coined by Amos Tversky and Daniel Kahneman...**
Daniel Kahneman and Amos Tversky (1984). Choices, Values and Frames. American Psychologist 39(4).

84 **A version of this is the IKEA effect...**
Dan Ariely (2008). Predictably Irrational: The Hidden Forces that Shape Our Decisions. HarperCollins.

85 **intuition is the brain putting together knowledge and experience in new ways...**
Gary Klein (1998). Sources of Power: How people make decisions. MIT Press.

86 **certainty bias fools us into placing too much store on intuition...**
Robert Burton (2008). On Being Certain: Believing You Are Right Even When You're Not. St Martin's Press.

"I'm just doing what I'm good at – or am I stuck in a rut?"

Understanding habits

87 **as they continued to press the lever the rats developed an ingrained habit...**
Anthony Dickinson (1985). Actions and Habits: The Development of Behavioural Autonomy. Philosophical Transactions of the Royal Society of London B308(1135).

88 **as much as 70% of what we do is habit...**
Kevin Ochsner (2010). The Formation of Habit. Presentation at the NeuroLeadership Summit, Boston.

89 **two neural "loops" in the brain that code for actions and habits...**
Bernard Balleine and John O'Doherty (2010).

Human and Rodent Homologies in Action Control: Corticostriatal Determinants of Goal-Directed and Habitual Action. Neuropsychopharmacology 35.

90 **glucose levels may determine the amount of willpower you have to resist habitual behaviour...**
EJ Masicampo and Roy Baumeister (2008). Toward a Physiology of Dual-Process Reasoning and Judgment: Lemonade, Willpower, and Expensive Rule-Based Analysis. Psychological Science 19(3).

91 **it isn't glucose levels that determine our willpower but our mindset...**
Veronika Job, Gregory Walton, Katharina Bernecker and Carol Dweck (2013). Beliefs about willpower determine the impact of glucose on self-control. Proceedings of the National Academy of Sciences 7.

92 **willpower is not about what you *do*, but how you *think* about a situation...**
Roy Baumeister and John Tierney (2012). Willpower: Why Self-Control is the Secret of Success. Penguin.

"So, I need to think about my thinking?"
Introspection: the essential skill

93 **this ability to think about thinking is rooted in the brain and that we may be able to improve our ability to do it...**
Stephen Fleming, Rimona Weil, Zoltan Nagy, Raymond Dolan and Geraint Rees (2010). Relating introspective accuracy to individual differences in brain structure. University College London, Science 329.

94 **the brain is designed to recognise patterns...**
Robert Burton (2008). On Being Certain: Believing You Are Right Even When You're Not. St Martin's Press.

95 **Studies have shown that even short periods of practising being mindful provide significant health benefits...**
Catherine Kerr (2012). Mindfulness Starts With the Body: A View from the Brain. TEDxCollegeHill.

96 **learning how our brain works also creates new abilities to think about thinking...**
David Rock (2009). Why Learning About the Brain Can Be a (Positive) Addiction, in Your Brain at Work. HarperBusiness.

97 **the close link between self-regulation and personal productivity...**
Yuichi Shoda, Walter Mischel and Philip Peake (1990). Predicting Adolescent Cognitive and Self-Regulatory Competencies from Preschool Delay of Gratification: Identifying Diagnostic Conditions. Developmental Psychology 26 (6).

"Goals... how do I set them up right?"

6 steps for success in setting up your goals

98 **personal beliefs make all the difference...**
Carol Dweck (2006). Mindset: The New Psychology of Success.
Random House.

99 **you can only really work on one or two goals at once...**
Quoted by David Rock (2011). NeuroLeadership Summit,
San Francisco.

100 **the *how* and the *why* are processed by different parts
of the brain...**
Robert Spunt, Emily Falk and Matthew Lieberman (2010).
Dissociable Neural Systems Support Retrieval of How and Why
Action Knowledge. Psychological Science 20(10).

101 **trying to avoid a thought makes it even more active in your
mind...**
Daniel Wegner, David Schneider, Samuel Carter and Teri White
(1987). Paradoxical Effects of Thought Suppression. Journal of
Personality and Social Psychology 53(1).

102 **people need to have a vision of the future to resist
impulsive behaviour...**
Jan Peters and Christian Buchel (2010). Episodic Future
Thinking Reduces Reward Delay Discounting through an
Enhancement of Prefrontal-Mediotemporal Interactions.
Neuron 66(1).

103 **those who thought it would be hard to lose weight proved
to be more successful...**
Amy Wysoker (2002). A study of beliefs relating to weight
loss and weight gain. Newsletter of the Long Island University
School of Health Professionals and Nursing.

104 **Believing in success is also essential for creating and
sustaining motivation...**
Jason Mitchell, Jessica Schirmer, Daniel Ames and Daniel
Gilbert (2011). Medial Prefrontal Cortex Predicts Intertemporal
Choice. Journal of Cognitive Neuroscience 23(4).

"How do I get my HR initiative agreed?"

The neuroscience of being influential

105 **Neuroscience sheds new light on how people react in social
situations...**
Matthew Lieberman and Naomi Eisenberger (2008). The pains
and pleasures of social life: A social cognitive neuroscience
approach. NeuroLeadership Journal 1.

106 **What counts as a threat?...**
Evian Gordon (2008). NeuroLeadership and integrative
Neuroscience: "It's about validation stupid!" NeuroLeadership
Journal 1.

107 **This happens because, from an evolutionary perspective...**
Matthew Lieberman (2013). Social: Why our brains are wired
to connect. Oxford University Press.

"Is there a better way to have a difficult conversation?"
The right way to have the conversations we dread

108 **This is known as *"emotional* empathy"...**
Daniel Goleman (2011). The Brain and Emotional Intelligence:
New Insights. More Than Sound e-book.

109 **this type of empathy depends on our tuning in to our *own*
body's emotional signals...**
Matthew Lieberman (2013). Social: Why our brains are wired
to connect. Oxford University Press.

110 **the "we" circuitry...**
Daniel Goleman (2012). Leadership: A Master Class with
Daniel Goleman (DVD set). More Than Sound.

111 **"cognitive empathy," or perspective-taking...**
Daniel Goleman (2013). Focus: The Hidden Driver
of Excellence. Bloomsbury Publishing.

112 **"Empathic concern" taps into the brain's circuitry
for parental love...**
Daniel Goleman (2013). Focus: The Hidden Driver
of Excellence. Bloomsbury Publishing.

113 **Managers with a fixed mindset, who basically believe
"someone can either do it, or they can't"...**
Carol Dweck (2006). Mindset: The New Psychology of Success.
Random House.

"Is it really possible to make change happen easily?"
5 discoveries that will save your change programme

114 **they need to believe what you believe...**
Simon Sinek (2009). Start with Why: How Great Leaders
Inspire Everyone to Take Action. Portfolio Hardcover.

115 **more likely to stick to their goal, if they have a clear
picture of what the future will be like...**
Jan Peters and Christian Buchel (2010). Episodic Future
Thinking Reduces Reward Delay Discounting through an
Enhancement of Prefrontal-Mediotemporal Interactions.
Neuron 66(1).

116 **computer modelling to measure when a minority belief
becomes the prevailing belief...**
Jierui Xie, Sameet Sreenivasan, Gyorgy Korniss, Weituo Zhang,
Chjan Lim and Boleslaw Szymanski (2011). Social consensus
through the influence of committed minorities. Physical Review
84(1).

117 **People are warmer and friendlier when they're holding
a hot cup of coffee...**

Ruud Custers and Henk Aarts (2010). The unconscious will: How the pursuit of goals operates outside of conscious awareness. Science 329.

118 **it makes more sense to work to reduce their arousal ...**
Jessica Cohen and Matthew Lieberman (2010). The common neural basis of exerting self-control in multiple domains. Self Control and Society, Oxford University Press.

Leading the function

"We don't have in-groups – we just have the right kind of people."
Why our brains love to categorise, and how to limit the damage of in-groups and out-groups

119 **Neuroscience is now beginning to break down the sequence of processes...**
Pascal Molenberghs (2013). The neuroscience of in-group bias. Neuroscience and Biobehavioral Reviews 37(8).

120 **"The human mind must think with the aid of categories...**
Gordon Allport (1979). The Nature of Prejudice. Perseus Books.

121 **We store broad representations for our different categories...**
David Amodio (2008). The social neuroscience of intergroup relations. European Review of Social Psychology 19.

122 **That first categorisation affects our subsequent processing...**
David Amodio (2012). Why Culture Matters. NeuroLeadership Summit, New York.

123 **which all serves to build trust within the group...**
Pascal Molenberghs (2013). The neuroscience of in-group bias. Neuroscience and Biobehavioral Reviews 37(8).

124 **the effect of in-group identification becomes even more intense when people are threatened...**
Walter Stephan, Kurt Boniecki, Oscar Ybarra, Ann Bettencourt, Kelly Ervin, Linda Jackson, Penny McNatt and Lausanne Renfro (2002). The Role of Threats in the Racial Attitudes of Blacks and Whites. Personality and Social Psychology Bulletin 28.

125 **you will be more able to understand the perspective of your in-group colleagues...**
Mirre Stallen, Ale Smidts and Alan Sanfey (2013). Peer influence: neural mechanisms underlying in-group conformity. Frontiers in Human Neuroscience.

126 **She divided her class of eight year-olds into two groups on the basis of eye colour...**
Jane Elliott (1968). As profiled in A Class Divided. PBS Frontline, 1985.

127 **teams of black and white participants were scanned using fMRI...**
Kyle Ratner and David Amodio (2013). Seeing "'us vs. them'": Minimal group effects on the neural encoding of faces. Journal of Experimental Social Psychology 49(2).

"So, are male and female brains different?"
Gender differences in the brain, and whether it matters

128 **distinctive differences between male and female brains can be seen in the womb...**
Reuwen Achiron, Shlomo Lipitz and Anat Achiron (2001). Sex-related differences in the development of the human fetal corpus callosum: in utero ultrasonographic study. Prenatal Diagnosis 21.

129 **A recent study that received a lot of popular press coverage mapped the connections in male and female brains...**
Madhura Ingalhalikar, Alex Smith, Drew Parker, Theodore D. Satterthwaite, Mark Elliott, Kosha Ruparel, Hakon Hakonarsond, Raquel Gurb, Ruben Gurb and Ragini Verma (2013). Sex differences in the structural connectome of the human brain. Proceedings of the National Academy of Sciences.

130 **The brain in human males is on average about 10% larger than female brains...**
Lise Eliot (2009). Girl Brain, Boy Brain? Scientific American.

131 **men have 6.5 times more grey matter than women...**
Richard Haier, Ronald Yeo, Kevin Head and Michael Alkired (2005). Quoted in
Intelligence In Men And Women Is A Gray And White Matter. ScienceDaily.

132 **"Female brains might be more efficient,"...**
Richard Haier, Rex Jung, Ronald Yeo, Kevin Head and Michael Alkired (2005). The neuroanatomy of general intelligence: sex matters. Neuroimage 25(1).

133 **Men tend to process more in the left side of their brain...**
Jennifer Larson, Stewart Mostofsky, Melissa Goldberg, Laurie Cutting, Martha Denckla and Mark Mahone (2007). Effects of gender and age on motor exam in typically developing children. Developmental neuropsychology 32(1).

134 **if there is a greater brain area dedicated to a set of skills, it follows that the skills will be more refined...**
David Geary (1998). Male, female: The evolution of human sex differences. American Psychological Association 12.

135 **the areas of the brain activated while participants of both genders listened to an audio-book...**
Michael Phillips, Mark Lowe, Joseph T. Lurito, Mario Dzemidzic and Vincent Matthews (2001). Temporal lobe activation demonstrates sex-based differences during passive listening. Radiology 220.

136 **this behaviour, referred to as "relational aggression," may have given females a survival advantage...**
David Geary (1998). Male, female: The evolution of human sex differences. American Psychological Association 12.

137 **Women, it transpires, are more likely to rely on landmark cues...**
Georg Gron, Arthur Wunderlich, Manfred Spitzer, Reinhard Tomczak and Matthias Riepe (2000). Brain activation during human navigation: gender-different neural networks as substrate of performance. Nature neuroscience 3(4).
And also:
Noah Sandstrom, Jordy Kaufman and Scott Huettel (1998). Males and females use different distal cues in a virtual environment navigation task. Brain Research: Cognitive Brain Research 6(4).

138 **An alternative view is that nurture develops these differences in children...**
Jennifer Larson, Stewart Mostofsky, Melissa Goldberg, Laurie Cutting, Martha Denckla and Mark Mahone (2007). Effects of gender and age on motor exam in typically developing children. Developmental neuropsychology 32(1).

139 **fMRI scanning to study how emotion is processed in the brains of children...**
William Killgore, Mika Oki and Deborah Yurgelun-Todd (2001). Sex-specific developmental changes in amygdala responses to affective faces. NeuroReport.

140 **sections of the brain used to control aggression and anger responses are larger in women...**
Raquel Gur and Ruben Gur (2002). Gender differences in aging: cognition, emotions, and neuroimaging studies. Dialogues in Clinical Neuroscience 4(2).

141 **men and women tend to be stressed by different issues...**
John Coates (2012). The Hour Between Dog and Wolf: Risk Taking, Gut Feelings and the Biology of Boom and Bust. HarperCollins.

"My 'feedback' is your 'criticism.' How can I get it right?"
How brains process feedback: what does and doesn't work

142 **A helpful definition of feedback...**
John Hattie and Helen Timperley (2007). The Power of Feedback. Review of Educational Research 77(1).

143 **The most comprehensive study of performance feedback...**
Avraham Kluger and Angelo DeNisi (1998). Feedback interventions: Toward the understanding of a double-edged sword. Current Directions in Psychological Science 7(3).

144 **Continual feedback may improve performance through improved motivation.**
Judi Komaki, Arlene Heinzmann and Loralie Lawson (1980).

Effect of training and feedback: Component analysis of a behavioural safety program. Journal of Applied Psychology 65(3).

145 **Fixed and Growth mindsets...**
Carol Dweck (2006). Mindset: The New Psychology of Success. Random House.

146 **Feedback which fosters self-esteem can boost performance...**
Avraham Kluger and Angelo DeNisi (1998). Feedback interventions: Toward the understanding of a double-edged sword. Current Directions in Psychological Science 7(3).

147 **approval also reduces intrinsic motivation to gain mastery...**
Avraham Kluger and Angelo DeNisi (1998). Feedback interventions: Toward the understanding of a double-edged sword. Current Directions in Psychological Science 7(3).

148 **Our brain pays a lot of attention to assessing our social position...**
Matthew Lieberman and Naomi Eisenberger (2008). The pains and pleasures of social life: A social cognitive neuroscience approach. NeuroLeadership Journal 1.

149 **other people's success or failure can trigger envy...**
Hidehiko Takahashi, Motoichiro Kato, Masato Matsuura, Dean Mobbs, Tetsuya Suhara and Yoshiro Okubo (2009). When Your Gain Is My Pain and Your Pain Is My Gain: Neural Correlates of Envy and Schadenfreude. Science 323(5916).

150 **supporting a sense of competence makes people feel good...**
Edward Deci and Richard Ryan (2008). Facilitating optimal motivation and psychological well-being across life's domains. Canadian Psychology 49.

151 **UK leaders, on the whole, are failing to maximise feelings of reward in their workforces...**
Head Heart + Brain (2013). Brain-savvy Leaders.

152 **how organisations sustain effective performance and high employee satisfaction...**
Teresa Amabile, Steven Kramer and Sharon Williams (2011). The Progress Principle: Using Small Wins to Ignite Joy, Engagement, and Creativity at Work. Harvard Business Review Press.

"I dream about performance management that works."
Brain-savvy performance management

153 **vividly imagining the future activates the hippocampus...**
Jan Peters and Christian Buchel (2010). Episodic Future Thinking Reduces Reward Delay Discounting through an Enhancement of Prefrontal-Mediotemporal Interactions. Neuron 66(1).

154   **38% of feedback made performance worse...**
Avraham Kluger and Angelo DeNisi (1996). The Effects
of Feedback Interventions on Performance: A Historical Review,
a Meta-Analysis, and a Preliminary Feedback Intervention
Theory. Psychological Bulletin II9(2).

155   **we think about our future self in the same way as we think
about another person...**
Jason Mitchell, Jessica Schirmer, Daniel Ames and Daniel
Gilbert (2011). Medial Prefrontal Cortex Predicts Intertemporal
Choice. Journal of Cognitive Neuroscience 23(4).

156   **performance actually decreases with higher levels
of reward...**
Dan Ariely (2008). Predictably Irrational: The Hidden Forces
that Shape Our Decisions. HarperCollins.

157   **the neuroscience of reward...**
Daniel Pink (2009). Drive: the surprising truth about what
motivates us. Riverhead.

"Are we missing out on free rewards?"
Brain-savvy reward strategies

158   **the most widely-read articles he publishes are about the
workings of the brain...**
Art Kleiner and Matthew Lieberman (2012). Memes and
buzz: The neuroscience of changing minds. NeuroLeadership
Summit, New York.

159   **financial *incentives* inhibit rather than promote creative
problem solving and motivation...**
Daniel Pink (2009). Drive: the surprising truth about what
motivates us. Riverhead.

160   **the most satisfied people are those with the strongest
social connections rather than the most money...**
Bruno Frey and Alois Stutzer (2002). What Can Economists
Learn From Happiness Research? Journal of Economic
Literature 40.

161   **financial incentives actually reduce motivation and
pleasure at work...**
Samuel Bowles and Sandra Colania-Reyes (2009). Economic
Incentives and Social Preferences: A Preference-Based Lucas
Critique of Public Policy. Economics Department Working
Paper University of Massachusetts, Amherst, Economics
Department Working Paper.

162   **those offered low and medium-level rewards perform
better or just as well as each other...**
Dan Ariely (2008). Predictably Irrational: The Hidden Forces
that Shape Our Decisions. HarperCollins.

163   **when people were asked to perform in public, their
performance diminished...**
Dan Ariely (2008). Predictably Irrational: The Hidden Forces

that Shape Our Decisions. HarperCollins.

164   **a state of "flow"...**
Mihaly Csikszentmihalyi (2008). Flow: The Psychology
of Optimal Experience. Harper Perennial.

165   **those employees who are highly engaged and able
to sustain their performance over time...**
Gretchen Spreitzer and Christine Porath (2012). Creating
Sustainable Performance. Harvard Business Review.

166   **They make their companies more money...**
Alex Edmans (2012). The Link Between Job Satisfaction
and Firm Value, With Implications for Corporate Social
Responsibility. Academy of Management Perspectives.

167   **when people or their efforts are ignored,
they need *more* money...**
Dan Ariely (2012). What makes us feel good about our work?
TEDxRiodelaPlata.

168   **"Social is not one of our programmes – it is our basic
operating system"...**
Matthew Lieberman (2012). Memes and buzz:
The neuroscience of changing minds. NeuroLeadership
Summit, New York.

169   **we are motivated more by social rewards than
by monetary rewards...**
Naomi Eisenberger and Matthew Lieberman (2004).
Why rejection hurts: a common neural alarm system for physical
and social pain. Trends in Cognitive Sciences, UCLA.

170   **Being treated fairly by others, for example, increases
activity in the ventral striatum and ventromedial
prefrontal cortex...**
Golnaz Tabibnia and Matthew Lieberman (2007). Fairness and
Cooperation Are Rewarding: Evidence from Social Cognitive
Neuroscience. Annals of the New York Academy of Sciences
1118.

171   **increased satisfaction is associated with three factors...**
Daniel Pink (2009). Drive: the surprising truth about what
motivates us. Riverhead.

172   **self-directed decision-making encourages employees
to thrive...**
Gretchen Spreitzer and Christine Porath (2012). Creating
Sustainable Performance. Harvard Business Review.

173   **Enhancing social contact in the workplace can also
be very rewarding...**
Matthew Lieberman (2013). Social: Why our brains are wired
to connect. Oxford University Press.

174   **strategies like encouraging employees in close proximity
to make eye contact...**
Shawn Achor (January 2012). Positive Intelligence.
Harvard Business Review.

175   **we feel envious if someone we relate to receives greater reward and recognition...**
Hidehiko Takahashi, Motoichiro Kato, Masato Matsuura, Dean Mobbs, Tetsuya Suhara and Yoshiro Okubo (2009). When Your Gain Is My Pain and Your Pain Is My Gain: Neural Correlates of Envy and Schadenfreude. Science 323(5916).

176   **additional money will not motivate discretionary effort...**
Daniel Pink (2009). Drive: the surprising truth about what motivates us. Riverhead.

"Thanks for coming in to meet us: please tell us about..."
First-round interviews: how being brain-savvy can help

177   **mindset: your outlook, the frame of mind you bring to a task...**
Carol Dweck (2006). Mindset: The New Psychology of Success. Random House.

178   **we perform at our best when we're mildly stressed...**
Jessica Payne (2011). Learning, memory and sleep in humans. Sleep Medicine Clinics 6(1).

"Welcome back: it's good to meet with you again..."
Second-round interviews: avoiding bias in selection

179   **we have two thought systems....**
Daniel Kahneman (2011). Thinking Fast and Slow. Farrar, Straus and Giroux.

180   **our own opinions, beliefs, preferences, values and habits are "normal" and that other people share them...**
John Darley and Paget Gross (2000). A Hypothesis-Confirming Bias in Labelling Effects. In Stereotypes and prejudice: essential readings, edited by Charles Stangor, Psychology Press.

181   **we pay more attention to negative rather than positive experiences or information...**
Roy Baumeister, Ellen Bratslavsky, Catrin Finkenauer and Kathleen Vohs (2001). Bad is stronger than good. Review of General Psychology 5.

182   **we're biased to believe that physically attractive people also possess many other socially desirable personality traits...**
Anthony Little, Michael Burt and David Perrett (2006). What is good is beautiful: face preference reflects desired personality. Science Direct: Personality and Individual Differences 41.
Harvard-sponsored Project Implicit online tests...
Project Implicit. https://www.projectimplicit.net

183   **Harvard-sponsored Project Implicit online tests...**
Project Implicit. https://www.projectimplicit.net

"Why are people so resistant to change?"
The threat response and change – how to make it more rewarding

184 **around 70% of change initiatives fail or only partially succeed...**
Economist Intelligence Unit (2011). Leaders of change: Companies prepare for a stronger future. The Economist.

185 **change creates the same sort of painful experience in the brain...**
Matthew Lieberman and Naomi Eisenberger (2008). The pains and pleasures of social life: A social cognitive neuroscience approach. NeuroLeadership Journal 1.

186 **our brain responds to patterns, and likes to create them...**
Trey Hedden and John Gabrieli (2006). The ebb and flow of attention in the Human Brain. Natural Neuroscience 9.

187 **Doing something different to the norm sends an "error" message to brain...**
Evian Gordon (2000). Integrative neuroscience: Bringing together biological, psychological and clinical models of the human brain. Singapore Harwood Academic Publications.

"Once upon a time there was an HR leader..."
The neuro-power of stories

188 **similar brain regions are activated in both listener and the storyteller...**
Greg Stephens, Lauren Silbert and Uri Hasson (2010). Speaker–listener neural coupling underlies successful communication. Proceedings of the National Academy of Sciences 107(32).

189 **when we hear inspirational stories, more blood flows to the brain stem...**
Darby Saxbe, Xiao-Fei Yang, Larissa Borofsky and Mary Helen Immordino-Yang (2012). The Embodiment of Emotion: Language use during the feeling of social emotions predicts cortical somatosensory activity. Social Cognitive and Affective Neuroscience 8(7).

190 **we think in narrative all the time...**
Norman Farb, Zindel Segal, Helen Mayberg, Jim Bean, Deborah McKeon, Zainab Fatima and Adam Anderson (2007). Attending to the present: mindfulness meditation reveals distinct neural modes of self-reference. Oxford Journals: Social Cognitive and Affective Neuroscience 2(4).

191 **They are 65% personal stories and gossip...**
Robin Dunbar (1998). Grooming, Gossip and the Evolution of Language. Harvard University Press.

192 **what happens in the brain when people hear an idea that is destined to spread successfully...**
Emily Falk, Sylvia Morelli, Locke Welborn, Karl Dambacher

and Matthew Lieberman (2013). Creating Buzz: The Neural Correlates of Effective Message Propagation. Psychological Science.

193   **we bring our social concerns into play when we assimilate new information...**
Emily Falk, Sylvia Morelli, Locke Welborn, Karl Dambacher and Matthew Lieberman (2013). Creating Buzz: The Neural Correlates of Effective Message Propagation. Psychological Science.

194   **substantial overlap in the brain networks we use to understand stories and the networks we use to understand other people...**
Raymond Mar (2011). The Neural Bases of Social Cognition and Story Comprehension. Annual Review of Psychology 62.

195   **when a listener's brain activity in the default network mirrors the speaker's brain activity...**
Greg Stephens, Lauren Silbert and Uri Hasson (2010). Speaker–listener neural coupling underlies successful communication. Proceedings of the National Academy of Sciences 107(32).

196   **implications for the dissemination of ideas, values, and culture...**
Emily Falk, Sylvia Morelli, Locke Welborn, Karl Dambacher and Matthew Lieberman (2013). Creating Buzz: The Neural Correlates of Effective Message Propagation. Psychological Science.

Leading talent, engagement and learning

"Emotional Intelligence: our leaders aren't convinced."
The persuasive science of EI

197   **groundbreaking work in developing the theory of multiple intelligence...**
David Wechsler (1939). The Measurement of Adult Intelligence. Williams & Witkins.
And also:
Howard Gardner (1993). Frames of Mind: The theory of multiple intelligences. Basic Books.

198   **Peter Salovey and John Mayer defined EI...**
Peter Salovey and John Mayer (1990). Emotional Intelligence. Baywood Publishing.

199   **Daniel Goleman's influential article What Makes a Leader?...**
Daniel Goleman (1998). What Makes a Leader? Harvard Business Review.

200   **The brain areas which help people to understand other people are largely the same ones...**
Matthew Lieberman (2013). Social: Why our brains are wired

to connect. Oxford University Press.

201 **So it's not possible to be doing a task or thinking about ...**
Anthony Jack, Abigail Dawson, Katelyn Begany, Regina Leckie,
Kevin Barry, Angela Ciccia and Abraham Snyder (2013).
fMRI reveals reciprocal inhibition between social and physical
cognitive domains. NeuroImage 66.

202 **The mentalizing system is quick to switch on...**
Matthew Lieberman (2013). Social: Why our brains are wired
to connect. Oxford University Press.

203 **2.5% of people accurately predict what others will know...**
Matthew Lieberman (2011). Importance of the social brain for
leaders. NeuroLeadership Summit, San Francisco.

204 **the release of cortisol into the bloodstream has a
widespread impact on the body...**
Bruce McEwan (2013). The Brain on Stress: Toward an
Integrative Approach to Brain, Body, and Behavior. Perspectives
on Psychological Science 8(6).

205 **a wearable electronic sensor to measure exactly what good
communication involves...**
Daniel Olgu'ınOlgu'ın and Alex Pentland (2007). Sociometric
Badges: State of the Art and Future Applications. IEEE 11th
International Symposium on Wearable Computers, Boston 2007.
And also:
Anne Eisenberg (2008). Understanding conversations: You May
Soon Know if You're Hogging the Discussion. New York Times,
October 25 2008.

"We're spending enough money – why isn't our training and development working?"

A different type of audit: make connections, anticipate
resistance and allow time for learning

206 **the brain learns best when it is mildly stressed, has a good
mood, and has had a good sleep...**
Jessica Payne (2011). Learning, memory and sleep in humans.
Sleep Medicine Clinics 6(1).

207 **ideal conditions for work and learning are a balance
between the level of challenge in a situation and the
participant's perceived ability...**
Mihaly Csikzentmihalyi (1997). Finding Flow: The psychology
of engagement with everyday life. Basic Books.

208 **in the short-term synapses get even stronger than
previously thought, but then quickly go through a
transitional phase where they weaken...**
Brett Benedetti, Yoshio Takashima, Jing Wen, Joanna Urban-
Ciecko and Alison Barth (2012). Differential Wiring of
Layer 2/3 Neurons Drives Sparse and Reliable Firing During
Neocortical Development. Cerebral Cortex 23 (11).

209 **giving them time to reflect, if only for a few minutes, makes their decisions much better...**
John Creswell, James Bursley and Ajay Satpute (2013). Neural reactivation links unconscious thought to improved decision making. Social, Cognitive, and Affective Neuroscience.

210 **The mood of the programme also has a significant impact...**
Jessica Payne (2011). Learning, memory and sleep in humans. Sleep Medicine Clinics 6(1).

211 **people need to identify new cues, and create routines and rewards for themselves...**
Charles Duhigg (2012). The Power of Habit. Random House.

"Why do we put training into buckets?"
Training for the role rather than core skills

212 **the "flexible hub" theory of the brain in relation to transferring skills...**
Michael Cole, Patryk Laurent and Andrea Stocco (2013). Rapid instructed task learning: A new window into the human brain's unique capacity for flexible cognitive control. Cognitive, Affective, and Behavioral Neuroscience 13(1).

"Will our training produce the kind of leaders we want?"
It's about the design: a quick fix won't change behaviour

213 **companies have been spending well on leadership development...**
Richard McBain, Abby Ghobadian, Jackie Switzer, Petra Wilton, Patrick Woodman and Gemma Pearson (2012). The Business Benefits of Management and Leadership Development. Chartered Management Institute.

214 **companies globally expected to increase their spend by 39%...**
The Conference Board and Right Management (2013). Strategic Leadership Development: Global Trends and Approaches. Right Management.

215 **the Brain-savvy *leaders* study of more than 2,000 UK workers...**
Head Heart + Brain (2013). Brain-savvy leaders.

216 **70% of what we do is habitual...**
Kevin Ochsner (2010). The Formation of Habit. Presentation at the NeuroLeadership Summit, Boston.

217 **"neurons that wire together fire together"...**
Donald Hebb (1949). The Organization of Behavior. Wiley & Sons.

218 **Eighty-five per cent of the areas of the brain that are used to think about ourselves are also used to think about others...**

Matthew Lieberman (2013). Social: Why our brains are wired to connect. Oxford University Press.

219 **learning something so that we can teach others makes it stickier still...**
Matthew Lieberman (2013). The social brain and its superpowers. TEDxStLouis.

220 **reflection may be reducing learning, not increasing it...**
Brett Benedetti, Yoshio Takashima, Jing Wen, Joanna Urban-Ciecko and Alison Barth (2012). Differential Wiring of Layer 2/3 Neurons Drives Sparse and Reliable Firing During Neocortical Development. Cerebral Cortex 23 (11).

221 **giving them time to reflect, if only a few minutes, makes their use of the information more effective...**
John Creswell, James Bursley and Ajay Satpute (2013). Neural reactivation links unconscious thought to improved decision making. Social, Cognitive, and Affective Neuroscience.

222 **To establish a new habit people must create a cue...**
Charles Duhigg (2012). The Power of Habit. Random House.

"Is the future of learning programmes virtual?"
Beyond faceless cost-saving: the real advantages of virtual learning

223 **the Khan University (which provides free online tutorials...**
Salman Khan (2011). Let's use video to reinvent education. TED2011.

"I keep telling them they should be using coaching..."
Coaching vs telling: here's the evidence of what works

224 **The brain likes order, and tries to connect new information to what is already known...**
Gerald Edelman (1987). Neural Darwinism: The Theory of Neuronal Group Selection. Basic Books.

225 **our ability to make predictions, based on the connections our brain makes, is what differentiates us from other animals...**
Jeffrey Hawkins, Sandra Blakeslee (2004). On Intelligence. Times Books.

226 **only 30% of what we do is under our conscious control...**
Kevin Ochsner (2010). The Formation of Habit. Presentation at the NeuroLeadership Summit, Boston.

227 **we must go beyond the conscious "reflective" systems where goals are created...**
Matthew Lieberman (2007). The X- and C-systems: The neural basis of automatic and controlled social cognition. In Fundamentals of Social Neuroscience, edited by Eddie Harmon-Jones and Piotr Winkielman, Guilford Press.

228　**there's a necessary sequence for creating new habits of behaviour...**
Matthew Lieberman and Elliot Berkman (2009).
The neuroscience of goal pursuit. In The Psychology of Goals, edited by Gordon Moskowitz and Heidi Grant, Guilford Press.

"They just need to copy the role model?"
It's not just about showing how, but understanding why

229　**Work by Matt Lieberman at UCLA has focused on...**
Robert Spunt, Emily Falk and Matthew Lieberman (2010).
Dissociable Neural Systems Support Retrieval of How and Why Action Knowledge. Psychological Science 20(10).

"A nice hotel, plenty of coffee, role-play exercises... what have we missed?"
5 ways to make your Development Centre work

230　**our brain needs just the right amount of two important neurochemicals: dopamine and norepinephrine...**
Amy Arnsten and Trevor Robbins (2002). Neurochemical modulation of prefrontal cortical function in humans and animals. In The Frontal Lobes, edited by Donald Stuss and Robert Knight, Oxford University Press.

231　**We know that memory is located in different centres of the brain...**
Xu Liu, Steve Ramirez, Petti Pang, Corey Puryear, Arvind Govindarajan, Karl Deisseroth and Susumu Tonegawa (2012).
Optogenetic stimulation of a hippocampal engram activates fear memory recall. Nature 484.

232　**the key to optimising learning and building long-term memory is to create "ownership" of learning content...**
Povl Jensen (2005). A contextual theory of learning and the learning organization. Knowledge and Process Management 12(1).

"If talent is our number-one priority, why don't we have a queue for our top jobs?"
Change your talent culture and develop the pipeline

233　**Research by Peter Heslin, who frequently collaborates with Carol Dweck, measured managers' mindsets...**
Peter Heslin, Don VandeWalle and Gary Latham (2006).
Keen to help? Managers' implicit person theories and their subsequent employee coaching. Personnel Psychology 59.

234　**this doesn't work in high-change, high-challenge environments...**
Carol Dweck. How Your Mindset Impacts Your Success in Business and in Life: Carol Dweck Talking

to Karen Elmhirst. HR.com

235 **we need to praise the effort and struggle undertaken...**
Carol Dweck. How Your Mindset Impacts Your Success in
Business and in Life: Carol Dweck Talking to Karen Elmhirst.
HR.com

236 **experimented with changing fixed-mindset beliefs
to growth-mindset beliefs with some success...**
Carol Dweck (2006). Mindset: The New Psychology of Success.
Random House.

237 **workshops can turn managers' beliefs from fixed to
growth, and the evidence seems to be that the change
persists...**
Peter Heslin, Don VandeWalle and Gary Latham (2006).
Keen to help? Managers' implicit person theories and their
subsequent employee coaching. Personnel Psychology 59.

"Not another staff survey..."

4 steps for creating effective engagement

238 **a poll of more than 2,000 UK employees to ask them about
their leaders...**
Head Heart + Brain (2013). Brain-savvy Leaders.

239 **it leads to a real improvement on the bottom line...**
John Gibbons (2006). Employee Engagement: A Review of
Current Research and Its Implications. The Conference Board.

240 **the relationship with the immediate line manager is the
strongest of all drivers...**
John Gibbons (2006). Employee Engagement: A Review of
Current Research and Its Implications. The Conference Board.

241 **the superpowers identified by neuroscientist Matt
Lieberman...**
Matthew Lieberman (2013). The social brain and its
superpowers. TEDxStLouis.

"Can we make work more fulfilling?"

Understanding the see-saw between task and people focus

242 **Alain de Botton believes we shouldn't expect too much,
based on his observations of the professionals he got to
know...**
Alain de Botton (2009). The Pleasures and Sorrows of Work.
Pantheon.

243 **fulfilment is a sought-after but unattainable aspiration
for many employees...**
Fulfilment@work. Ranstad UK, 2013.

244 **asked managers to consider strategic and tactical
workplace dilemmas while they were in the scanner...**
Roderick Gilkey, Ricardo Caceda and Clinton Kilts (2010).
When Emotional Reasoning Trumps IQ. HBR Magazine.

245 **leaders who are poor at managing and understanding social interactions are missing important opportunities...**
Matthew Lieberman (2013). Social: Why our brains are wired to connect. Oxford University Press.

246 **When we are thinking about ourselves, or others, and activating the mentalizing circuits we close down...**
Matthew Lieberman (2013). Social: Why our brains are wired to connect. Oxford University Press.

247 **Engaging people in problem solving or creating insight...**
Karuna Subramaniam, John Kounios, Todd Parrish and Mark Jung-Beeman (2009). A Brain Mechanism for Facilitation of Insight by Positive Affect. Journal of Cognitive Neuroscience 21(3).

248 **telling is likely to set up a threat response...**
Woogul Lee and Johnmarshall Reeve (2012). Self determined, but not non-self determined, motivation predicts activation in the anterior insular cortex: An fMRI study of personal agency. Social Cognitive and Affective Neuroscience.

249 **social needs are primary in the brain...**
Matthew Lieberman (2013). Social: Why our brains are wired to connect. Oxford University Press.

250 **Social pain activates the same regions as physical pain...**
Naomi Eisenberger, Johanna Jarcho, Matthew Lieberman and Bruce Naliboff (2006). An experimental study of shared sensitivity to physical pain and social rejection. Pain 126.

"How trusting should we be as an organisation?"
The science of trusting your people, and why it matters

251 **Trust has been shown to be a core component of employee engagement...**
Trust In Institutions. 2012 Edelman Trust Barometer.

252 **countries characterised by high levels of trust amongst citizens are also the most economically successful...**
Stephen Knack and Paul Zak (2002). Building trust: public policy, interpersonal trust, and economic development. Supreme Court Economic Review 10.

253 **when participants felt they were trusted, their brains responded by producing oxytocin...**
Paul Zak (2007). The neuroeconomics of trust. In Renaissance in Behavioral Economics, edited by Roger Frantz, Routledge.

254 **the rise in oxytocin levels resulted in participants behaving in a more trustworthy way...**
Paul Zak (2007). The neuroeconomics of trust. In Renaissance in Behavioral Economics, edited by Roger Frantz, Routledge.

255 **qualified trust operates quite differently to unconditional trust...**
Frank Krueger, Kevin McCabe, Jorge Moll, Nikolaus Kriegeskorte, Roland Zahn, Maren Strenziok, Armin Heinecke

and Jordan Grafman (2007). Neural correlates of trust. Proceedings of the National Academy of Sciences 104(50).

256 **changes in oxytocin were related to levels of empathy, and could be used to predict people's feelings of empathy...**
Jorge Barraza and Paul Zak (2009). Empathy towards strangers triggers oxytocin release and subsequent generosity. Annals of the New York Academy of Sciences 1167.

257 **when male participants are distrusted it results in a rise in levels of a hormone called dihydrotestosterone...**
Paul Zak, Robert Kurzban, Sheila Ahmadi, Ronald Swerdloff, Jang Park, Levan Efremidze, Karen Redwine, Karla Morgan and William Matzner (2009). Testosterone administration decreases generosity in the ultimatum game. PLOS One 4(12).

258 **the hormone can *increase* emotional pain...**
Yomayra Guzman, Natalie Tronson, Vladimir Jovasevic, Keisuke Sato, Anita Guedea, Hiroaki Mizukami, Katsuhiko Nishimori and Jelena Radulovic (2013). Fear-enhancing effects of septal oxytocin receptors. Nature Neuroscience 16.

259 **Netflix having no requirement for employees to have holiday-time signed off...**
Patty McCord (2014). How Netflix Reinvented HR. Harvard Business Review.

Leading yourself

"I know I'm smart..."
Talent mindset: what do you believe about your abilities?

260 **people tend to have one of two sets of beliefs that create their mindset about work, learning and their own abilities...**
Carol Dweck (2006). Mindset: The New Psychology of Success. Random House.

261 **people with a growth mindset work harder, learn from experience and are willing to take more risks...**
Carol Dweck (2006). Mindset: The New Psychology of Success. Random House.

"I'm great! Why do I need self-awareness?"
Self-knowledge makes for better performance

262 **leaders who have high levels of self-awareness are able to build teams that are high-performing...**
J P Flaum (2010). When it comes to business leadership, nice guys finish first. Green Peak Partners.

263 **thinking about ourselves, recognising images of ourselves and reflecting on our thoughts and feelings are all forms of self-awareness...**

Bud Craig (2009). How do you feel — now? The anterior insula and human awareness. Nature Reviews Neuroscience 10.

264 **recognition and *thinking about* ourselves happens in different brain regions...**
William Kelley, Todd Heatherton and Neil Macrae (2002). Finding self? An event-related fMRI study. Journal of cognitive Neuroscience 14 (5).

265 **Ninety-four per cent of all studies of self reflection have identified activity in the medial prefrontal cortex...**
Matthew Lieberman (2010). Social cognitive neuroscience. Handbook of social psychology 5th edition. John Wiley & Sons.

266 **Other similar theories include the "social construction of reality"...**
The Social Construction of Reality: A Treatise in the Sociology of Knowledge. 1991. Thomas Luckmann & Peter L. Berger. Penguin; New Ed edition.

267 **Having our beliefs and values unconsciously influenced by those around us...**
Matthew Lieberman (2013). Social: Why our brains are wired to connect. Oxford University Press.

268 **"reflective appraisal generation" approach...**
George Herbert Mead (1934). Mind, self and society from the stand point of a social behaviourist (edited by Charles Morris). Scribner.

269 **adolescents would have more need to actively think about the views of others...**
Jennifer Pfeifer, Carrie Masten, Larissa Borofsky, Mirella Dapretto, Andrew Fuligni and Matt Lieberman (2009). Neural correlates of direct and reflected self-appraisals in adolescents and adults: When social perspective-taking informs self-perception. Child Development 80.

270 **"Living for others is such a relief...**
Alain de Botton (2012). @alaindebotton.

271 **Steve Jobs advised graduates...**
Steve Jobs (2005). Stanford Commencement speech.

"Am I good enough?"

Self-esteem or self-compassion: how to develop a high-status mindset

272 **Researchers have used fMRI...**
Debra Gusnard, Erbil Akbudak, Gordon Shulman and Marcus Raichle (2001). Medial prefrontal cortex and self-referential mental activity: relation to a default mode of brain function. Proceedings of the National Academy of Sciences 98(7).

273 **the brain's "default mode" network, first identified by Marcus Raichle...**
Debra Gusnard, Erbil Akbudak, Gordon Shulman and Marcus

Raichle (2001). Medial prefrontal cortex and self-referential mental activity: relation to a default mode of brain function. Proceedings of the National Academy of Sciences 98(7).

274 **we create a representation of our own and someone else's status in our brain when we communicate...**
Caroline Zink, Yunxia Tong, Qiang Chen, Danielle Bassett, Jason Stein and Andreas Meyer-Lindenberg (2008). Know Your Place: Neural Processing of Social Hierarchy in Humans. Neuron 58(2).

275 **the low self-esteem "involuntary defeat response"...**
Leon Sloman, Paul Gilbert and Gary Hasey (2003). Evolved mechanisms in depression: the role and interaction of attachment and social rank in depression. Journal of Affective Disorders 74(2).

276 **changes in the levels of the neurotransmitter serotonin, linked to feelings of wellbeing and happiness...**
Ray Fuller (1995). Neural Functions of Serotonin. Scientific American Science and Medicine 2(4).

277 **Research indicates that high serotonin levels in the brain produce a sense of high self-esteem...**
Roger Masters and Michael McGuire (editors) (1993). The Neurotransmitter Revolution: Serotonin, Social Behavior, and the Law. Southern Illinois University Press.

278 **Serotonin fluctuations help us to negotiate social hierarchies...**
Ray Fuller (1995). Neural Functions of Serotonin. Scientific American Science and Medicine 2(4).

279 **an increase in self- esteem or status is one of the greatest feelings...**
John Coates (2012). The Hour Between Dog and Wolf: Risk Taking, Gut Feelings and the Biology of Boom and Bust. HarperCollins.

280 **You can elevate your self-esteem and status through winning against others...**
Keise Izuma, Daisuke Saito and Norihiro Sadato (2008). Processing of Social and Monetary Rewards in the Human Striatum. Neuron 58(2).

281 **thinking about others largely use the same circuits...**
Michael Lombardo, Bhismadev Chakrabarti, Edward Bullmore, Sally Wheelwright, Susan Sadek, John Suckling, Simon Baron-Cohen and MRC AIMS Consortium (2009). Shared Neural Circuits for Mentalizing about the Self and Others. Journal of Cognitive Neuroscience.

282 **self-compassion, rather than self-esteem, may be the key to managing the impact of setbacks...**
Juliana Breines and Serena Chen (2012). Self-compassion increases self-improvement motivation. Personality and Social Psychology Bulletin 38(9).

283 **self-compassion leads to higher levels of personal wellbeing, optimism and happiness...**
Kristin Neff, Stephanie Rude and Kristin Kirkpatrick (2007). An examination of self-compassion in relation to positive psychological functioning and personality traits. Journal of Research in Personality 41(4).

284 **Those who were directed to take a self-compassionate view of their earlier failure studied 25% longer...**
Juliana Breines and Serena Chen (2012). Self-compassion increases self-improvement motivation. Personality and Social Psychology Bulletin 38(9).

"How can my memory of the event be completely different to everyone else's?"

How memory works, and what you can do to get around its limitations

285 **there are *four* components to how it works...**
Peter Doolittle (2013). How your "working memory" makes sense of the world. TEDGlobal.

286 **the average is just four completely independent pieces of information...**
Peter Doolittle (2013). How your "working memory" makes sense of the world. TEDGlobal.

287 **Researchers in Japan tested whether training could increase the working memory...**
Tracy Alloway and Ross Alloway (2009). The efficacy of working memory training in improving crystallized intelligence. Nature Precedings.

288 **performing working memory tasks increases the release of the neurotransmitter dopamine...**
Fiona McNab, Andrea Varrone, Lars Farde, Aurelija Jucaite, Paulina Bystritsky, Hans Forssberg and Torkel Klingberg (2009). Changes in cortical dopamine D1 receptor binding associated with cognitive training. Science 323(5915).

289 **memory as more like a Wikipedia page that you can go in and re-write...**
Charles Morgan, Steven Southwick, George Steffian, Gary Hazlett and Elizabeth Loftus (2013). Misinformation can influence memory for recently experienced, highly stressful events. International Journal of Law and Psychiatry 36(1).

290 **the "experiencing self" and as the "remembering self"...**
Daniel Kahneman (2010). The riddle of experience vs memory. TED2010.

"Would I pass the marshmallow test?"
The success factors of self-control

291 **Walter Mischel's "Marshmallow Test"...**
Walter Mischel, Ebbe Ebbesen and Antonette Raskoff Zeiss
(1972). Cognitive and attentional mechanisms in delay of
gratification. Journal of Personality and Social Psychology 21(2).

292 **Following up with the participants years later...**
Walter Mischel, Yuichi Shoda and Philip Peake (1988).
The nature of adolescent competencies predicted by preschool
delay of gratification. Journal of Personality and Social
Psychology 54(4).

293 **the ability to control and wait does not predict anything
on its own...**
Angela Duckworth, Eli Tsukayama and Teri Kirby (2013).
Is It Really Self-Control? Examining the Predictive Power of the
Delay of Gratification Task. Personality and Social Psychology
Bulletin 39(7).

294 **people who have the greatest self-regulation...**
Megan O'Connor, Nicholas Cooper, Leanne Williams,
Savannah DeVarney and Evian Gordon (2010).
NeuroLeadership and the productive brain. NeuroLeadership
Journal 3.

295 **the prefrontal cortex is taken over by the limbic system...**
Matthew Lieberman, Naomi Eisenberger, Molly Crockett,
Sabrina Tom, Jennifer Pfeifer and Baldwin Way (2007). Putting
feelings into words: Affect labeling disrupts amygdala activity to
affective stimuli. Psychological Science 18.

296 **stress permeates out through our skin and "infects"
the people sitting close to us...**
Elaine Hatfield, John Cacioppo and Richard Rapson (1993).
Emotional contagion. Current Directions in Psychological
Science 2.

297 **a model for emotional regulation, assessing the pros
and cons...**
James Gross (1998). The Emerging Field of Emotion
Regulation: An Integrative Review. Review of General
Psychology 2(5).

"I set goals, but making progress is hard."
6 ways to keep going with your goals

298 **this kind of planning will help your brain to detect and
seize the opportunity when it arises...**
Peter Gollwitzer and Gabriele Oettingen (2011). Planning
promotes goal striving. In Handbook of self-regulation:
Research, theory, and applications (2nd edition),
edited by Kathleen Vohs and Roy Baumeister, Guilford.

299 **"if-then" statements, or implementation intentions work well for many people...**
Peter Gollwitzer, Frank Wieber, Andrea Meyers and Sean McCrea (2010). How to maximize implementation intention effects. In Then a miracle occurs: Focusing on behavior in social psychological theory and research, edited by Christopher Agnew, Donal Carlston, William Graziano and Janice Kelly, Oxford Press.

300 **People have one or other of two broad motivation preferences...**
Katrina Koslov, Wendy Berry Mendes, Petra Pajtas and Diego Pizzagalli (2011). Asymmetry in Resting Intracortical Activity as a Buffer to Social Threat. Psychological Science.

301 **Dopamine is a powerful part of the brain's reward system...**
Mark Howe, Patrick Tierney, Ann Graybiel, Stefan Sandberg and Paul Phillip (2013). Prolonged dopamine signalling in striatum signals proximity and value of distant rewards. Nature 500.

302 **Harnessing the power of belief is also effective...**
Shelley Taylor and Peter Gollwitzer (1995). Effects of mindset on positive illusions. Journal of Personality and Social Psychology 69.

303 **a habit is like a folded piece of paper...**
William James and Robert Richardson (2010). Heart of William James. Harvard University Press.

304 **Another useful technique is known as mental contrasting...**
Paschal Sheeran, Peter Harris, Jennifer Vaughan, Gabriele Oettinger and Peter Gollwitzer (2013). Gone exercising: Mental contrasting promotes physical activity among overweight, middle-aged, low-SES fishermen. Health Psychology 32.

305 **link the progress you need to make to any significant dates...**
Johanna Peetz and Anne Wilson (2013). Marking Time: Selective Use of Temporal Landmarks as Barriers Between Current and Future Selves. Social Psychology Bulletin.

306 **Psychologist Angela Duckworth calls this quality "grit"...**
Angela Duckworth (2013). The key to success? Grit. TEDx.

307 **Studies show that people with grit stay in education longer and achieve higher results...**
Angela Duckworth (2013). The key to success? Grit. TEDx.

308 **One study has demonstrated that parole judges' decisions...**
Roy Baumeister and John Tierney (2011). Willpower: Rediscovering the greatest human strength. Penguin.

"How can I get out of this rut?"
How behaviours become habits, and how you can make new ones

309 **a three-stage process for creating, or changing habits...**
Charles Duhigg (2012). The Power of Habit. Random House.

310 **"For a habit to stay changed, people must believe that change is possible"...**
Charles Duhigg (2012). The Power of Habit. Random House.

311 **The "What-the-Hell" Effect...**
Dan Ariely (2012). The (Honest) Truth About Dishonesty: How We Lie to Everyone – Especially Ourselves. Harper.

"I need to get creative. Easier said than done."
Brain savvy techniques to boost creativity

312 **The Disney process had three distinct stages...**
Michael Michalko (2011). Walt Disney's Creative Thinking Technique. Creativethinking.net

313 **when rappers are in full creative flow...**
Allen Braun and Siyuan Liu (2012). Neural Correlates of Lyrical Improvisation: An fMRI Study of Freestyle Rap. Nature.

314 **just before insight occurs the brain produces a burst of alpha waves...**
Mark Jung-Beeman, Azurii Collier and John Kounios (2008). How insight happens: learning from the brain. NeuroLeadership Journal 1.

315 **changing the way you make your lunchtime sandwich can help boost levels of creativity...**
Simone Ritter, Rodica Ioana Damian, Dean Keith Simonton, Rick van Baaren, Madelijn Strick, Jeroen Derks and Ap Dijksterhuis (2012). Diversifying experiences enhance cognitive flexibility. Journal of Experimental Social Psychology 48.

316 **it's possible to trigger this temporary brain state by meditating...**
Mark Jung-Beeman, Azurii Collier and John Kounios (2008). How insight happens: learning from the brain. NeuroLeadership Journal 1.

317 **That "Aha!" moment feels instantaneous, but your unconscious mind has been working behind the scenes...**
John Kounios and Mark Beeman (2009). The Aha! Moment: The Cognitive Neuroscience of Insight. Current Directions in Psychological Science 18.

318 **trying to do something you're inexperienced at, or outside your range of skills, accelerates the flow of new ideas...**
Robert Epstein (1996). Capturing Creativity: How to enhance the creativity of a person and figuring out the mysteries of the creative process. Psychology Today.

319 **Welcome more rapper or jazz-style improvisation into your life...**
Charles Limb (2011). Your brain on improv. TEDxMidAtlantic.

320 **people who have slept well also make more connections...**
Jessica Payne (2011). Learning, memory and sleep in humans. Sleep Medicine Clinics 6(1).

321 **people who are in a positive mood have more creative insight...**
Karuna Subramaniam, John Kounios, Todd Parrish and Mark Jung-Beeman (2009). A Brain Mechanism for Facilitation of Insight by Positive Affect. Journal of Cognitive Neuroscience 21(3).

"Aha!' I solved it!"
Insight: how to develop it

322 **the answer always arrives suddenly, usually when the issue is out of conscious awareness...**
David Rock (2011). The Aha Moment. www.davidrock.net.

323 **Mark Beeman of Northwestern University is probably the best-known and most respected neuroscientist working on insight...**
Mark Jung-Beeman, Azurii Collier and John Kounios (2008). How insight happens: learning from the brain. NeuroLeadership Journal 1.

324 **When people have insights they are often "mind-wandering"...**
Benjamin Baird, Jonathan Smallwood, Michael Mrazek, Julia Kam, Michael Franklin and Jonathan Schooler (2012). Inspired by distraction: Mind-wandering facilitates creative incubation. Psychological Science 23(10).

325 **alpha wave activity in the visual and auditory cortex just before someone has an insight...**
Mark Jung-Beeman, Azurii Collier and John Kounios (2008). How insight happens: learning from the brain. NeuroLeadership Journal 1.

326 **Beeman can *predict* which method (logic or insight) someone will use to solve a problem...**
John Kounios, Jennifer Frymiare, Edward Bowden, Jessica Fleck, Karuna Subramaniam, Todd Parrish and Mark Jung-Beeman (2006). The prepared mind: Neural activity prior to problem presentation predicts solution by sudden insight. Psychological Science 17.

327 **the brain knows how it will solve a problem eight seconds before the conscious answer appears...**
Bhavin Sheth, Simone Sandkühler and Joydeep Bhattacharya (2008). Posterior beta and anterior gamma predict cognitive insight. Journal of Cognitive Neuroscience 21(7).

328 **being in a good mood helps problem-solving...**
Karuna Subramaniam, John Kounios, Todd Parrish and Mark
Jung-Beeman (2009). A Brain Mechanism for Facilitation of
Insight by Positive Affect. Journal of Cognitive Neuroscience
21(3).

329 **Negative emotions tend to increase physiological arousal,
narrow focus and restrict behaviour...**
Barbara Frederickson (2013). Positive emotions broaden and
build. In Advances on Experimental Social Psychology 47,
edited by Patricia Devine and Ashby Plant, Academic Press.

330 **when people are happy their perception is wider...**
Karuna Subramaniam, John Kounios, Todd Parrish and Mark
Jung-Beeman (2009). A Brain Mechanism for Facilitation of
Insight by Positive Affect. Journal of Cognitive Neuroscience
21(3).

331 **we need to inhibit the *wrong* solutions for the right one
to come to our attention...**
Stellan Ohlsson (2011). Deep Learning: How the Mind
Overrides Experience. Cambridge University Press.

332 **sudden answers tend to be correct...**
Karuna Subramaniam, John Kounios, Todd Parrish and Mark
Jung-Beeman (2009). A Brain Mechanism for Facilitation of
Insight by Positive Affect. Journal of Cognitive Neuroscience
21(3).

"Only people who can't multi-task say it's a problem."
Multi-tasking is a myth: here's the evidence

333 **we're addicted to media...**
Linda Stone. lindastone.net

334 **the "hyperkinetic work environment"...**
Edward Hallowell (2007). CrazyBusy: Overstretched,
Overbooked, and About to Snap! Strategies for Handling Your
Fast-Paced Life. Ballantine Books.

335 **irrelevant cues introduced when a person is concentrating
hijack the attention system...**
Katherine Sledge Moore, Clare Porter and Daniel Weissman
(2005). Made you look! Consciously perceived, irrelevant
instructional cues can hijack the attentional network.
Neuroimage.

336 **emailing and answering the phone constantly, reduced IQ
scores by 10 points...**
Glenn Wilson (2005). Quoted in Emails "pose threat to IQ."
Martin Wainwright, The Guardian.

337 **multi-tasking impact on long-term memory and our
ability to learn...**
Karin Foerde, Barbara Knowlton and Russell Poldrack (2006).
Modulation of competing memory systems by distraction.
Proceedings of the National Academy of Sciences 103(31).

338   **distractions help focus mental energies effectively...**
Linda Ray and Adair Jones (2013). Attention Matters:
Is there an upside to interruption? Brainwaves For Leaders,
neurocapability.wordpress.com/

"What's all the hype about meditation?"
The business benefits of mindfulness

339   **It's claimed to be becoming a popular practice amongst CEOs...**
Zoe Kinias, Andrew Hafenbrack and Jane Williams (2013).
Meditate for More Profitable Decisions. Knowledge newsletter,
INSEAD.

340   **"Mindfulness means paying attention in a particular way...**
Jon Kabat-Zinn (1994). Wherever You Go, There You Are:
Mindfulness Meditation in Everyday Life. Hyperion.

341   **benefits for breathing and heart rate, and improved immune responses...**
Peter Vestergaard-Poulsen, Martijn van Beek, Joshua Skewes,
Carsten Bjarkam, Michael Stubberup, Jes Bertelsen and Andreas
Roepstorff (2009). Long-term meditation is associated with
increased gray matter density in the brain stem. Neuroreport
20(2).

342   **measurably more "gyrification" in their brains...**
Eileen Luders, Florian Kurth, Emeran Mayer, Arthur Toga,
Katherine Narr and Christian Gaser (2012). The Unique Brain
Anatomy of Meditation Practitioners: Alterations in Cortical
Gyrification. Frontiers in Human Neuroscience.

343   **meditation practice was linked to enlarged hippocampal and frontal areas of the brain...**
Eileen Luders, Arthur Toga, Natasha Lepore and Christian
Gaser (2009). The underlying anatomical correlates of long-
term meditation: Larger hippocampal and frontal volumes
of gray matter. Neuroimage 45(3).

344   **meditation improves rapid memory recall...**
Catherine Kerr, Matthew Sacchet, Sara Lazar, Christopher
Moore and Stephanie Jones (2013). Mindfulness starts with
the body: somatosensory attention and top-down modulation
of cortical alpha rhythms in mindfulness meditation. Frontiers
in Human Neuroscience.

345   **the more people meditate, the less anxious they appear to be...**
Catherine Kerr, Matthew Sacchet, Sara Lazar, Christopher
Moore and Stephanie Jones (2013). Mindfulness starts with
the body: somatosensory attention and top-down modulation
of cortical alpha rhythms in mindfulness meditation. Frontiers
in Human Neuroscience.

346 **meditation appears to strengthen the connections between the part of the brain which manages reasoning, and our bodily-sensation and fear centres...**
David Vago and David Silbersweig (2012). Self-awareness, self-regulation, and self-transcendence (S-ART): a framework for understanding the neurobiological mechanisms of mindfulness. Frontiers in Human Neuroscience.

347 **those who practice meditation regularly score higher for empathy and compassion...**
Gaelle Desbordes, Lobsang Negi, Thaddeus Pace, Alan Wallace, Charles Raison and Eric Schwartz (2012). Effects of mindful-attention and compassion meditation training on amygdala response to emotional stimuli in an ordinary, non-meditative state. Frontiers in Human Neuroscience.

348 **people who meditated regularly had stronger activation in their temporal parietal junctures...**
Antoine Lutz, Julie Brefczynski-Lewis, Tom Johnstone and Richard Davidson (2008). Regulation of the neural circuitry of emotion by compassion meditation: effects of meditative expertise. PLOS One.

349 **mindfulness meditation helps people perform under pressure while feeling less stressed...**
David Levy, Jacob Wobbrock, Alfred Kaszniak and Marilyn Ostergren (2012). The Effects of Mindfulness Meditation Training on Multitasking in a High-Stress Information Environment. Proceedings of Graphics Interface.

350 **UK-based social enterprise Get Some Headspace...**
www.getsomeheadspace.com

"I can't avoid stress in my job."
Not all stress is bad for you

351 **Richard Carlson, Don't Sweat the Small Stuff...**
Richard Carlson (1997). Don't Sweat the Small Stuff... and it's all small stuff: Simple Ways to Keep the Little Things from Taking Over Your Life. Hyperion.

352 **nearly two-thirds of UK respondents said they were stressed at work...**
YouGov (2013). The Big Work Survey. yougov.co.uk.

353 **the "inverted-U model"...**
Robert Yerkes and John Dodson (1908). The relation of strength of stimulus to rapidity of habit-formation. Journal of Comparative Neurology and Psychology 18.

354 **At the midpoint we're in "flow"...**
Mihaly Csikzentmihalyi (1997). Finding Flow: The psychology of engagement with everyday life. Basic Books.

355 **stress is "all in our head"...**
Bruce McEwan (2013). The Brain on Stress: Toward an Integrative Approach to Brain, Body, and Behavior.

Perspectives on Psychological Science 8(6).

356 **the brain produces a different type of stress hormone in response to short-term stressors...**
Pamela Maras and Tallie Baram (2012). Sculpting the Hippocampus from within: Stress, Spines, and CRH. Trends in Neurosciences 35.

357 **the hippocampus memory-forming region of the brain actually shrank slightly...**
Doug Schultz, Nicholas Balderston and Fred Helmstetter (2012). Resting-state connectivity of the amygdala is altered following Pavlovian fear conditioning. Frontiers in Human Neuroscience.

358 **believing stress is bad for you is... really bad for you...**
Abiola Keller, Kristin Litzelman, Lauren Wisk, Torsheika Maddox, Erika Cheng, Paul Creswell and Whitney Witt (2012). Does the perception that stress affects health matter? The association with health and mortality. Health Psychology 31(5).

359 **that would make stress the 15th largest cause of death in the United States....**
Kelly McGonigal (2013). How to make stress your friend. TEDGlobal.

360 **what might happen if we change the way we think about stress...**
Jeremy Jamieson, Wendy Berry Mendes and Matthew Nock (2012). Improving Acute Stress Responses: The Power of Reappraisal. Association for Psychological Science 20(10).

361 **spending time socialising and caring for other people can also create resilience to stress...**
Michael Poulin, Stephanie Brown, Amanda Dillard and Dylan Smith (2013). Giving to others and the association between stress and mortality. American Journal of Public Health 103(9).

362 **"The harmful effects of stress on health are not inevitable"...**
Kelly McGonigal (2013). How to make stress your friend. TEDGlobal.

"Life's tough: what's the key to thriving?

Mental toughness: you need it, and it's a skill you can learn

363 **who possess a set of skills she calls "grit"...**
Angela Duckworth (2013). The key to success? Grit. TEDx.

364 **test your own grit by taking Duckworth's online survey...**
https://sasupenn.qualtrics.com/SE/?SID=SV

365 **a number of studies suggest that grit is not something people have or don't have ...**
Angela Duckworth, Christopher Peterson, Michael Matthews and Dennis Kelly (2007). Grit: Perseverance and passion for long-term goals. Journal of Personality and Social Psychology 92(6).

366 **when we change the meaning of a situation, the threat response in our brain and the level of arousal is significantly reduced...**
Kevin Ochsner and James Gross (2005). The cognitive control of emotion. Trends in Cognitive Sciences 9(5).

367 **participants were shown a picture of people crying outside a church...**
Kevin Ochsner, Rebecca Ray, Jeffrey Cooper, Elaine Robertson, Sita Chopra, John Gabrieli and James Gross (2004). For better or for worse: Neural Systems Supporting the Cognitive Down- and Up-regulation of Negative Emotion. Neuroimage 23(2).

368 **we usually think about motivation and payment as the same thing...**
Dan Ariely (2012). What makes us feel good about our work? TEDxRiodelaPlata.

369 **Adopting a growth mindset reframes or reappraises change...**
Carol Dweck (2006). Mindset: The New Psychology of Success. Random House.

"I'm lucky: I don't need much sleep."
The evidence on how sleep affects your work

370 **a "sleepless elite" who can get by with a few hours and still function well...**
Carolyn Cutrone and Max Nisen (2012). 19 Successful People Who Barely Sleep. www.businessinsider.com.

371 **increases in blood concentrates similar to those associated with brain damage...**
Christian Benedict (2013). Acute sleep deprivation increases serum levels of neuron-specific enolase (NSE) and S100 calcium binding protein B (S-100B) in healthy young men. Sleep.

372 **sleeping four or five hours a night has an impact on performance equivalent to someone with a blood alcohol level of 0.1%...**
Drew Dawson and Kathryn Reid (1997). Fatigue, alcohol and performance impairment. Nature 388.

373 **you might as well be working drunk...**
Jessica Payne (2013). Leadership Stamina. Neuroleadership Summit, London.

374 **Payne's research into the impact of sleep on performance...**
Jessica Payne, Robert Stickgold, Kelly Swanberg and Elizabeth Kensinger (2008). Sleep Preferentially Enhances Memory for Emotional Components of Scenes. Psychological Science 19(8).
And also:
Jessica Payne (2011). Sleep on it: Stabilizing and transforming memories during sleep. Nature Neuroscience 14(3).

375 **People who lack sleep make fewer neural connections and have fewer insights...**
Jakke Tamminen, Jessica Payne, Robert Stickgold, Erin Wamsley and Gareth Gaskell (2010). Sleep spindle activity is associated with the integration of new memories and existing knowledge. Journal of Neuroscience 30(43).

376 **Levels of cortisol, the stress hormone, are higher in someone who is not sleeping well...**
Jessica Payne and Lynn Nadel (2004). Sleep, dreams and memory consolidation: The role of the stress hormone cortisol. Learning & Memory 11.

377 **If we are sleep deprived, our brain can't refocus...**
Clifford Saper and Thomas Scammell (2013). Emerging therapeutics in sleep. Annals of Neurology 74(3).

378 **"People who sleep between six-and-a-half and seven-and-a-half hours a night live the longest...**
Daniel Kripke, Lawrence Garfinkel, Deborah Wingard, Melville Klauber and Matthew Marler (2002). Mortality associated with sleep duration and insomnia. Archive of General Psychiatry 59.

"A 'power pose' will make me better at my job?"
How your body affects your performance

379 **improvisation coach Keith Johnstone teaches the same stagecraft skills...**
Keith Johnstone (2013). Interview No.3: Status. Youtube.com.

380 **do we run from a bear because we are afraid...**
William James (1884). What is an Emotion? Mind 9(34).

381 **Fritz Strack's often-replicated "pencil experiment"...**
Fritz Strack, Leonard Martin and Sabine Stepper (1988). Inhibiting and facilitating conditions of the human smile: a nonobtrusive test of the facial feedback hypothesis. Journal of Personality and Social Psychology 54(5).

382 **we begin developing rich neural pathways between the behaviour of smiling and positive emotion...**
Dana Carney and Randall Colvin (2010). The circumplex structure of affective social behavior. Social Psychological and Personality Science 1.

383 **smiling during brief periods of stress can help reduce the impact on the body...**
Tara Kraft and Sarah Pressman (2012). Grin and bear it: The influence of manipulated facial expression on the stress response. Psychological Science 23(11).

384 **participants who sat up straight found it easier to generate positive thoughts and memories...**
Erik Peper, Katherine Gibney and Catherine Holt (2013). Make Health Happen: Training Yourself to Create Wellness. Kendall Hunt.

385 **Her TEDTalk "Your body language shapes who you are" is one of the top-15 most-viewed...**
Amy Cuddy (2012). Your body language shapes who you are. TEDGlobal.

386 **adopting high-status or "power poses" changes the chemicals in the body...**
Amy Cuddy (2012). Your body language shapes who you are. TEDGlobal.

387 **Stock market traders who are on a winning streak have increased testosterone levels...**
John Coates (2012). The Hour Between Dog and Wolf: Risk Taking, Gut Feelings and the Biology of Boom and Bust. HarperCollins.

388 **"We tend to forget the other audience that's influenced by our non-verbals...**
Amy Cuddy (2012). Your body language shapes who you are. TEDGlobal.

389 **yoga practice can be used to enhance focus and awareness...**
Neha Gothe, Matthew Pontifex, Charles Hillman and Edward McAuley (2013). The Acute Effects of Yoga on Executive Function. Journal of Physical Activity and Health 10.

390 **people with a medium level of fitness – not athletes or people who undertake endurance training – remembered 73% of the pictures they were shown...**
Rich Barlow (April 2012). Inquiring Minds: Exercise and Mental Recall. BU Today.

"Moving up the career ladder via the gym?"
Physical fitness: it really does give you the edge

391 **our brains developed while we were on the move...**
John Medina (2008). Brain Rules: 12 principles for surviving and Thriving at Work, Home, and School. Pear Press.

392 **exercisers outperform couch potatoes...**
John Medina (2008). Brain Rules: 12 principles for surviving and Thriving at Work, Home, and School. Pear Press.

393 **Similar results have been found with school-age children...**
Darla Castelli, Charles Hillman, Sarah Buck and Heather Erwin (2007). Physical Fitness and Academic Achievement in Third- and Fifth-Grade Students. Journal of Sport and Exercise Psychology 29.

394 **There is also evidence that exercise helps prevent the harmful results of stress...**
Timothy Schoenfeld, Pedro Rada, Pedro Pieruzzini, Brian Hsueh and Elizabeth Gould (2013). Physical Exercise Prevents Stress-Induced Activation of Granule Neurons and Enhances Local Inhibitory Mechanisms in the Dentate Gyrus. The Journal

of Neuroscience 33(18).

395 **The American Heart Association recommends 30 minutes of moderate exercise five days a week...**
Physical Activity Guidelines for Americans: Recommendation statement (2008). US Department of Health and Human Services.

396 **exercise increases blood volume in a region of the brain called the dentate gyrus...**
John Medina (2008). Brain Rules: 12 principles for surviving and Thriving at Work, Home, and School. Pear Press.

397 **exercise also encourages one of the brain's most powerful growth stimulants...**
John Medina (2008). Brain Rules: 12 principles for surviving and Thriving at Work, Home, and School. Pear Press.

398 **Fit employees are capable of mobilising their cognitive abilities better than sedentary employees...**
Gerd Kempermann, Klaus Fabel, Dan Ehninger, Harish Babu, Perla Leal-Galicia, Alexander Garthe and Susanne Wolf (2010). Why and how physical activity promotes experience-induced brain plasticity. Frontiers in Neuroscience 4.

"How can I cope better with setbacks?
Developing the power of resilience

399 **Resilience in the brain develops through repeated experience...**
Jordan Nechvatal and David Lyons (2013). Coping changes the brain. Frontiers in Behavioural Neuroscience 7(13).

400 **reappraisal results in changes in the brain...**
Kevin Ochsner and James Gross (2005). The cognitive control of emotion. Trends in Cognitive Sciences 9(5).

401 **training in reappraisal, especially using the technique of distancing from the problem...**
Bryan Denny and Kevin Ochsner (2013). Behavioral effects of longitudinal training in cognitive reappraisal. Emotion.

402 **mindfulness meditation, which has been found to improve focus and wellbeing, and encourage more flexible thinking...**
Catherine Kerr (2012). Mindfulness Starts With the Body: A View from the Brain. TEDxCollegeHill.

403 **negative emotions tend to increase physiological arousal, narrow focus and restrict behaviours...**
Barbara Frederickson (2009). Positivity: Groundbreaking Research Reveals How to Embrace the Hidden Strength of Positive Emotions, Overcome Negativity, and Thrive. Crown Archetype.

404 **the concept of "locus of control"...**
Julian Rotter (1966). Generalized expectancies for internal versus external control of reinforcement. Psychological

Monographs: General and Applied 80(1).

405 **those with a strong internal locus are better off....**
Laurence Gonzales (2012). Surviving Survival:
The Art and Science of Resilience. WW Norton.

406 **we can train ourselves to do this...**
Helen Standage, Chris Ashwin and Elaine Fox (2010).
Is manipulation of mood a critical component of cognitive bias
modification procedures? Behaviour Research and Therapy
48(1).

407 **acknowledging risks using techniques like pre-mortems...**
Gary Klein (2007). Performing a Project Premortem. Harvard
Business Review.

408 **appreciative inquiry...**
Frank Barrett and Ronald Fry (2005). Appreciative Inquiry:
A Positive Approach to Building Cooperative Capacity. Taos
Institute Publications.

409 **Aerobic exercise has been shown to reduce symptoms
of depression and anxiety...**
John Medina (2008). Brain Rules: 12 principles for surviving
and Thriving at Work, Home, and School. Pear Press.

410 **The same approach as training for a marathon also works
for mental challenges...**
Steven Southwick and Dennis Charney (2012). Resilience:
the science of mastering life's greatest challenges. Cambridge
University Press.

411 **One of the skills of resilient people, according to
performance psychologist...**
Jim Loehr (2010). Building Resilience: The new Business
imperative. The Human Performance Institute.

412 **modelling is most effective when the observer analyses
what they want to imitate...**
Albert Bandura (editor) (1971). Analysis of Modeling
Processes, in Psychological Modeling: Conflicting Theories.
Transaction Publishers.

413 **everyone needs to remind themselves regularly of their
strengths...**
Edith Grotberg (editor) (2003). Resilience for Today: Gaining
Strength from Adversity. Praeger.

"What's that X-factor... the power of connection that some people have?"

The neuroscience of presence, and how you can learn it

414 **People watch and make judgements on what is real
and relevant to them...**
Alex Pentland (2012). The New Science of Building Great
Teams. Harvard Business Review Magazine.

417 **the ability to communicate "honest signals" is a significant factor in the success of individuals and teams...**
Alex Pentland (2012). The New Science of Building Great Teams. Harvard Business Review Magazine.
changes like these can improve productivity by as much as eight per cent in call-centre teams...
Alex Pentland (2012). The New Science of Building Great Teams. Harvard Business Review Magazine.
when people adopt new postures, such as appearing more powerful, or appearing to be more interested...
Amy Cuddy, Caroline Wilmuth and Dana Carney (2012). The Benefit of Power Posing Before a High-Stakes Social Evaluation. Harvard Business School Working Paper 13(027).

Further reading

If you have enjoyed some of the chapters in the book and want to delve a bit deeper here are a list of books. There are hundreds of books being published on neuroscience and related topics but these are some that I personally found readable and that added to my understanding.

Dan Ariely (2009). Predictably Irrational: The Hidden Forces that Shape Our Decisions. HarperCollins.

Dan Ariely (2012). The (Honest) Truth About Dishonesty: How We Lie to Everyone – Especially Ourselves. Harper.

Roy Baumeister and John Tierney (2011). Willpower: Rediscovering the greatest human strength. Penguin.

Bechara A, Damasio H, Damasio AR (March 2000). Emotion, decision making and the orbitofrontal cortex. Cerebral Cortex 10(3).

Tal Ben-Shahar (2007). Happier: Learn the Secrets to Daily Joy and Lasting Fulfillment. McGraw-Hill.

Peter Burow (2013). NeuroPower: Leading with NeuroIntelligence. Copernicus Publishing.

Robert Burton (2008). On Being Certain: Believing You Are Right Even When You're Not. St Martin's Press.

Doc Lew Childre Howard Martin Donna Beech (2000). The HeartMath Solution: The Institute of HeartMath's Revolutionary Program for Engaging the Power of the Heart's Intelligence HarperOne; 1 Reprint edition.

Mihaly Csikszentmihalyi (2008). Flow: The Psychology of Optimal Experience. Harper Perennial.

Mihaly Csikszentmihalyi (1997). Finding Flow: The psychology of engagement with everyday life. Basic Books.

John Coates (2012). The Hour Between Dog and Wolf: Risk Taking, Gut Feelings and the Biology of Boom and Bust. Random House.

Guy Claxton (2006). The Wayward Mind: An Intimate History of the Unconscious. Little, Brown Book Group.

Guy Claxton (1999). Hare Brain, Tortoise Mind: How Intelligence Increases When You Think Less Harper Perennial.

Antonio Damasio (1994). Descartes' Error: Emotion, Reason, and the Human Brain. Putnam Adult.

Antonio Damasio (2012). Self Comes to Mind: Constructing the Conscious Brain. Vintage; Reprint edition.

Carol Dweck (2006). Mindset: The New Psychology of Success. Random House.

Charles Duhigg (2012). The Power of Habit. Random House.

Barbara Frederickson (2009). Positivity: Groundbreaking Research Reveals How to Embrace the Hidden Strength of Positive Emotions, Overcome Negativity, and Thrive. Crown Archetype.

Adam Grant (2013). Give and Take: A Revolutionary Approach to Success. Weidenfeld & Nicolson.

Jon Kabat-Zinn (1994). Wherever You Go, There You Are: Mindfulness Meditation in Everyday Life. Hyperion.

Daniel Kahneman (2011). Thinking Fast and Slow. Farrar, Straus and Giroux.

Gary Klein (1998). Sources of Power: How people make decisions. The MIT Press.

Matthew Lieberman (2013). Social: Why our brains are wired to connect. Oxford University Press.

John Medina (2008). Brain Rules: 12 principles for surviving and Thriving at Work, Home, and School. Pear Press.

Daniel Pink (2009). Drive: the surprising truth about what motivates us. Riverhead.

John J. Ratey (2002). A User's Guide to the Brain: Perception, Attention, and the Four Theaters of the Brain. Vintage.

David Rock (2009). Your Brain at Work: Strategies for Overcoming Distraction, Regaining Focus, and Working Smarter All Day Long. HarperBusiness.

David Rock (2006). Quiet Leadership: Six Steps to Transforming Performance at Work. HarperBusiness.

Martin Seligman (2003). Authentic Happiness: Using the New Positive Psychology to Realise Your Potential for Lasting Fulfilment. Nicholas Brealey Publishing.

Simon Sinek (2009). Start with Why: How Great Leaders Inspire Everyone to Take Action. Portfolio.

Index

adopters, categories of, 29

Allport, Gordon, quote, 114

anxiety, reduction through meditation, 257

Ariely, Daniel, 132
      Predictably Irrational, 135
      quote, 265
      'What-the-Hell' effect, 238

Aristotle, quote, 86

assessment centres, 185-6

attention
      brain processes, 56-7
      focussing, 56-60, 266-7

attention control network, 67
      see also brains; creativity

attractiveness stereotyping, 145
      see also decision-bias

Beeman, Mark, 242-4, 245-9

behavioural change
      creating through training, 166, 170-72
      embedding of learning, 175, 179

behavioural economics, 82

behaviours, *see* habits

beliefs
      sharing of, 106-7
      training programmes, 170

Benedict, Christian, quote, 268

bias, *see* decision-bias

bonuses, effect on performance, 135

book sections, description, 6-7

Botton, Alain de
      Pleasures and Sorrows of Work, The, 199
      quote, 214

brains
      attention processes, 55-6
      categorisation of data, 114
      creative process, 67-8
      development, 8
      diagrams, 7, 10, 14, 16
      efficiency, 12

empathy response, activation, 61
exercise, effect on, 277-8
flexible hubs, 166
gender differences, 119-23
habitual v. intentional behaviour, 86-89
left brain/right brain myth, 66
pain networks, 7-8
priming for positive situations, 228-30
processing stories, 149
responses to different types of questions, 52-4
reward pathways, 8
self-awareness, 211-15
sleep-deprivation, effect on, 268
stress, effect on, 258-62
studying how brains work, 91-2

Burton, Robert, 85, 91

businesses
case studies using neuroscience, *see* case studies
issues facing, 22-4

Carlson, Richard, quote, 258

case studies
bias in decision-making, 42-3
change programmes, 36-39
general, 36
leadership, 39-42
learning programmes, 39, 42
performance management, 46-7
stress management, 45
talent strategy, 43-4

certainty
see also CORE model
general, 16, 99-101
in interview situations, 140-1
threat/reward response, 127, 131

change management
general, 106-10
Head Heart + Brain study, 25-7
neuroscience case studies, 36-47
resistance to change, 146-8

Chartered Institute of Professional Development (CIPD)
endorsement of neuroscience, 30
report, *From steady state to ready state*, 31

Chartered Management Institute (CMI), 2012 report, 168

children, study of willpower in, 58, 92, 227-8

CIPD, 30-1

CMI, 168

coaching
        comparison with telling, 177-80
        Head Heart + Brain presentation coaching, 286
        self-coaching, 187-8

Coates, John, 57, 69, 80, 123, 218

cognitive empathy
        see also empathy
        benefits, 61-4
        difficult conversations, 104
        general, 58-9
        learning, 63
        organisation culture, 63-4

communication, 152-3, 159
        see also story-telling

compassion, 257
        self-compassion, 219-220

confirmation bias, 144
        see also decision-bias

conversations, see difficult conversations

CORE model
        case studies, use in, 37-8, 46
        change process, 147
        examples, 17, 100
        general, 15-17, 99-100, 126, 130
        interview process, 140-1
        reinforcing habits, 237-8
        use, 15-17, 46, 99-100
        value, 17

creativity
        brain process, 66-7
        definition, 66
        Disney process, 240-2
        enhancing, 66-8, 242-4
        myths surrounding, 65-6

Cuddy, Amy, 273-4, 286

Damasio, Antonio
        Descartes' Error: Emotion, Reason and the Human Brain, 61
        research, 13, 57, 73, 78

decision-bias
        definition, 84

in interviews, 143-4
types, 83-5, 144

decision-making
see also decisions; gut feelings
checklist, 81
emotional involvement, 77-80
hormones, effect on, 80
hunger/thirst, effect on, 80
impact of body on, 70-71, 72-3
neuroscience case study, 43-4
physical process, 78
rationality, 69
reflection time, 80-1
tiredness, effect on, 80

decisions, 76-7
see also decision-making

Deming, William Edwards, quote, 157

Denckla, Martha Bridge, 120, 124

Descartes' Error: Emotion, Reason and the Human Brain
(Damasio, A.), 61

development centres, 161-166
see also leaders; training programmes

difficult conversations, 102-5, 192

Diffusion of Innovations (Rogers, E.), 29-30

Disney, Walt, quote, 241

distrust, 202-4
see also trust

Duckworth, Angela, 227, 233, 263-4

Duhigg, Charles, quote, 238

Dweck, Carol, mindset research

early adopters
definition, 30
difficulties experienced by, 34-5

early majority, definition, 30

Emerson, Ralph Waldo, quote, 287

emotional intelligence, 157-60

emotional tags, 72

emotions
controlling, 159, 229-30, 266, 280

difficult conversations, 102-5
general, 14
involvement in decision-making process, 76-81
processing, 122-3
sharing with others, 203
sleep deprivation, effect on, 270

empathy
benefits, 66
definition, 61
difficult conversations, 102-5
disadvantages, 66
general, 61
learning empathy, 63
meditation, effect on, 256
organisational culture, 63-4
relationship trust, 203

employees
engagement, 195-8
praising, 193

Epstein, Robert, 65, 243

equity
see also CORE model
general, 15, 99-101
in interview situations, 141
threat/reward response, 130

exercise, 276-7, 282
see also fitness

experiences, comparison with memories, 224-5

false conscious effect, 93, 144
see also decision-bias

feedback, 124-8, 131-2, 213

financial incentives, 134-7
see also rewards

fitness
at work, 276-7
effect on stress, 276
enhancing focus through, 274

fixed mindset
see also mindset
feedback, 126-7
general, 189, 207-10
interview candidates, 139
interviewers, 139

'flow'
>creating in workplace, 135-6, 163
>state in stress levels, 259

From steady state to ready state (CIPD report), 31

fulfilment, 199-201

gender difference in male/female brains, 119-23

Gigerenzer, Gerd, *Gut Feeling:*
The Intelligence of the Unconscious, 74

Give and Take:
A Revolutionary Approach to Success (Grant, A.), 61, 84

goals
>achieving, 231-4
>general, 131
>setting, 94-7

'golden circle', 51-2

Gonzales, Laurence, *Surviving Survival:*
The Art and Science of Resilience, 281

Grant, Adam, *Give and Take:*
A Revolutionary Approach to Success, 61, 84

'grit', 233-4, 263-4

Gross, James, 265, 299

group identity, 115-17
>*see also* in-groups; out-groups

group influence, 212-13, 238

growth mindset
>*see also* mindset
>feedback, 126-7
>general, 189-91, 208-9
>interview candidates, 139
>interviewers, 139

Gut Feeling: The Intelligence of the Unconscious
(Gigerenzer, G.), 74

gut feelings
>checking through introspection, 91
>decision-bias, 84-5
>development, 72
>effect on decision-making, 71-2
>general, 57
>reliability, 74
>training oneself to notice, 74

vagus nerve, 70-1

habits, 12, 86-89, 165, 170-1, 177-79
creating/changing, 235-39

Head Heart + Brain
2013 research on knowledge of neuroscience, 21-4
2013 study of leaders, 168-69, 195, 263
presentation coaching, 286

Heller, Robert, quote, 69

hormones
effect on decision-making, 80
effect on self-esteem, 217-18
power poses, effect on hormones, 273-75
stress hormones, 259-60

'how' questions, brain's response to, 52-4, 181-4

HR function
application of neuroscience in, 3-4, 31-2, 46-7
challenges facing, 23-4
educating professionals about neuroscience, 34-5
focussing attention, 56-60
professional development, 34
repositioning within business, 21-2
resistance to new ideas, 33-4
structure, 113

hunger, effect on decision-making, 80

imagination (default) network, 9, 67, 152, 197, 256
see also brains; creativity

in-groups
creation, 113-15
general, 12, 42-3
identifying/addressing problems, 116-18
training programmes, 162

influence, 9-11, 98-101
see also CORE model

information-processing, 151-2

innovations, adoption by HR profession, 29-30

innovators, 29

insight
see also training programmes
comparison with telling, 178-9
creating, 245-49
development through training, 170

effect of sleep deprivation, 270
self-coaching, 187-8

interpersonal intelligence, 158
see also emotional intelligence

interviews
first-round, mindset, 138-42
second-round, avoiding bias, 143-45

introspection, 90-3

intuition, *see* gut feelings

James, William, 74, 232, 272

Jung, Rex, quote, 65

Kabat-Zim, Jon, quote, 254

Kahneman, Daniel, 69, 71-2, 82, 84, 143, 224-5
Thinking Fast and Slow, 79-80

laggards, definition, 29

language, importance in change management, 107-8

language processing, 120-1

late majority, definition, 29

leaders
see also development centres; training programmes
change management, 110
development, 22-4
Head Heart + Brain 2013 study, 168-69, 195
introspection training, 92-3
neuroscience case studies, 39-42
role models, 181-4
servant leaders, 215
training programmes, 168-72, 278

Leaders Change Charter, 37, 148

learning programmes
see also training programmes; unconscious learning
general, 161, 163
neuroscience case studies, 39, 42
social learning, 171
virtual learning, 173-6
Lieberman, Matt, 10, 12-13, 41, 52-3, 151-2, 171, 179,
182-3, 197-8, 200, 213
quote, 136

limbic brain, 7, 12-13, 52, 78, 228
see also brains

locus of control, 281
>> *see also* self-control

managers, 104-5, 133, 192

Marshmallow Test, 58, 92, 227-8

Maslow's hierarchy of needs, 7

memory, 221-6

mental toughness, 263-7

mentalizing system
>> diagram, 10
>> use, 9-11, 182-3

Microsoft Corporation ranking system, 129

mindfulness, 91, 196-7, 229, 254-7, 280

mindset
>> as factor in success, 94
>> changing, 194, 209-10
>> importance, 193-4
>> measuring manager's mindset, 192
>> recruitment issues, 138
>> research on, 126-7, 207
>> technological distractions, 252-3
>> training programmes, 170
>> within organisations, 189-92

mirror neurons, 52-3, 182-3

Mischel, Walter, 58, 92, 227

motivation, 231-2, 265-6
>> *see also* goals

multi-tasking, 12, 250-3

negativity bias, 144
>> *see also* decision-bias
neocortex, 7
>> *see also* brains

Neuro-linguistic programming (NLP), 30-1

NeuroLeadership Institute, 3

NeuroPower model, 41

neuroscience
>> case studies of organisations using, *see* case studies
>> difference from NLP, 31
>> educating HR professionals, 34-5
>> effect on business policy decisions, 134

endorsement by CIPD, 30
historical background, 3
knowledge of in HR practitioners, 28
resistance to, 33-4
results of use, 46-7
use in HR, 3-4, 31-2, 117-18

new ideas, resistance to, 33-4

non-monetary rewards, 136
        see also rewards

Ochsner, Kevin, 12, 88, 170, 265, 280

options
        see also CORE model
        employee autonomy, 197
        general, 15, 99-101
        in interview process, 140-1
        threat/reward response, 128, 130

optimism, 281

out-groups
        creation, 115-16
        general, 12, 42-3
        identifying/addressing problems, 116-18

pain, *see* social pain

Payne, Jessica, 139, 163, 244, 269-70

Pentland, Sandy, 159, 285

performance
        effect of feedback on, 124-8
        link with attention, 60

performance management, 56, 129-33
        neuroscience case study, 45-6

personal change, 132
        see also goals

personal development 23

perspective-taking
        benefits, 62-3
        difficult conversations, 104
        general, 58-59
        learning, 63
        organisational culture, 63-4
        out-groups, 117

Peters, Tom, quote, 98

physiology
>physiological types, 240-2
>training to acknowledge, 167

Pink, Daniel, 134, 136

Pleasures and Sorrows of Work, The (Botton, A. de), 199

posture, 273

'power poses', 272-5

praise, importance of, 193-4

Predictably Irrational (Ariely, D.), 135

prefrontal cortex network, 7, 9, 52
>*see also* brains

presence, 284-7

professional development, 34

Progress Principle Study, 128

Prospect Theory, 79

rating/ranking scales, 132

recruitment, *see* interviews

reflection time, effect on decision-making, 80-1

remote teams, inclusion, 12

reptilian brain, 7
>*see also* brains

reputation
>*see also* CORE model
>general, 15, 99-101
>in interview situations, 141
>threat/reward response, 126, 130
>rewards of, 137

research study into neuroscience
>experience of respondents, 27
>general, 21
>industry of respondents, 26
>knowledge of neuroscience, 28
>location of respondents, 25
>responses, 22-4, 31-5
>roles of respondents, 37

resilience, 279-83

reward response
>change management trigger, 147, 162-3

general, 11-12, 15, 99
performance management trigger, 130

rewards
see also feedback; social rewards
case studies using neuroscience, 39-40, 43-6
CORE model, 15-18, 101
creating new habits with, 237
non-monetary, 136
performance management, 132-3
reputation as, 137
sleep deprivation, 80
system, advantages/disadvantages, 134-7

Rock, David, 91-2, 94, 246

Rogers, Everett, *Diffusion of Innovations*, 29-30

role models, 181-4, 282-3

salience network, 67
see also brains; creativity

Saper, Clifford, quote, 271

SCARF model, 39, 46

self-awareness, 211-15

self-coaching, 187-8
see also coaching

self-compassion, 219-20
see also compassion

self-control, 227-30, 234
see also locus of control

self-esteem, 216-20, 264

self-reflection, 9, 211-12

self-regulation techniques, 92, 280
see also self-control

servant leaders, 214-15
see also leaders

serotonin
see also hormones
effect on decision-making, 80
effect on self-esteem, 217-18

Seuss, Dr, quote, 65

Shiv, Baba, 77, 79-80

Sinek, Simon, 51-2, 106

sleep deprivation
>   effect on decision-making, 80
>   effect on learning, 163
>   mental effects, 269-70
>   physical effects, 268-69

smiling, 272-3

Smith, Adam, *Theory of Moral Sentiments*, 203

social context, 59

social control, 57

social networks, 60, 136

social pain, 7-8, 180, 201

social rewards, 8, 198, 200-1, 238
>   *see also* rewards

social status, 217-20

soft skills, 61
>   *see also* empathy

somatic markers, 57

spatial skills, 121-2

staff surveys, 195-6

story-telling, 149-53
>   *see also* telling

stress
>   effect of fitness on, 276
>   general, 258-62

stress management
>   mindfulness, 256-7
>   neuroscience case study, 44
>   tolerance for change, 108-9

success, building on, 264-5

Success Profile® methodology, 181

support networks, 282

Surviving Survival: The Art and Science of Resilience
(Gonzales, L.), 281

talent strategy
>   neuroscience case study, 43-4
>   within organisations, 189-90

telling
>   *see also* story-telling

comparison with coaching, 177-80
leadership style, 199-201

tenacity, *see* 'grit'

Theory of Moral Sentiments (Smith, A.), 203

Thinking Fast and Slow (Kahneman, D.), 79

thirst, effect on decision-making, 80

threat response
assessment as trigger, 185
change management triggers, 147, 162-3
feedback triggers, 126
general, 11-12, 15, 99
performance management triggers, 130
telling v. coaching, 178-79

threats
case studies using neuroscience, 39-40, 43-6
CORE model, 15-18
overcoming, 17-18
reduction using CORE model, 100-1
triggers, 45

tiredness, *see* sleep deprivation

training programmes
see also development centres; leaders
auditing, 132
creating behavioural change, 165
design, 164-5, 167, 169-71
importance of endings, 225
leaders, 168-72, 278
limiting content, 164
memory training, 223
motivation to attend, 161-3
training for particular roles, 166-7

trust, 198, 202-4

Tversky, Amos, 69, 79, 84

unconscious learning, 72-3
see also learning programmes

understanding others, 9-11

vagus nerve, 70-1
see also gut feelings

Vanzant, Iyanla, quote, 216

virtual learning, 173-8
see also learning programmes

well-being, neuroscience case study, 44

'what' questions, brain responses to, 52-4, 181-4

'why' questions, brain responses to, 52-4, 181-4

WIIFM (what's in it for me?), 170, 174
see also training programmes

willpower, 57-8, 88-89, 234
see also self-control

working memory, 221-3
see also memory

working patterns, 12